BUMIDOM (1963–1982) and its Afterlives

New Directions in Francophone Studies: Diversity, Decolonisation, Queerness

Published
BUMIDOM (1963–1982) and its Afterlives: Literature, Memory and Migration
Antonia Wimbush

Forthcoming
Dissident Universalisms and Postcolonial Citizenship in Contemporary French Literature
Mrinmoyee Bhattacharya

Graphic Narratives of Resistance: Advocating for Representation and Social Justice in French-language Bandes Dessinées
Edited by Jennifer Boum Make and Charly Verstraet

Sex Work in Southeast Asia: Scenes of Ambivalence in Literature and Film
Leslie Barnes

African Authors and the Politics of Literary Recognition
Madeline Bedecarré

BUMIDOM (1963–1982) and its Afterlives

Literature, Memory and Migration

Antonia Wimbush

EDINBURGH
University Press

Edinburgh University Press is one of the leading university presses in the UK. We publish academic books and journals in our selected subject areas across the humanities and social sciences, combining cutting-edge scholarship with high editorial and production values to produce academic works of lasting importance. For more information visit our website: edinburghuniversitypress.com

Edinburgh University Press Ltd
13 Infirmary Street
Edinburgh EH1 1LT

First published in hardback by Edinburgh University Press 2026

Typeset in 11/13 Adobe Sabon
by Manila Typesetting Company, and
printed and bound in the UK using 100% renewable electricity by CPI Group (UK) Ltd

A CIP record for this book is available from the British Library

ISBN 978 1 3995 2157 4 (hardback)
ISBN 978 1 3995 2158 1 (paperback)
ISBN 978 1 3995 2159 8 (webready PDF)
ISBN 978 1 3995 2160 4 (epub)

FSC www.fsc.org MIX Paper | Supporting responsible forestry FSC® C013604

This book is printed using paper from well-managed forests, recycling and other controlled sources

Contents

Acknowledgements

I am truly indebted to the many people who have supported me during the writing of this book. This book would not have been possible without the financial support of the Leverhulme Trust. The research was funded by a Leverhulme Early Career Fellowship, carried out at the University of Liverpool from 2020 to 2023. I am especially grateful to my mentor, Charles Forsdick, for all his tremendous support, guidance, feedback and encouragement. Thank you to colleagues and friends in the Department of Languages, Cultures and Film at Liverpool, and especially to Sarah Arens, Nicola Bermingham, Penny Ding, Rebecca Dixon, Abigail Loxham and Anna Saunders, for their valuable friendship and support. My students at Liverpool have also been a great source of inspiration, and I would like to thank in particular my postgraduate students Alison Clare and Jemima Hodgkinson for their interest in my work. Thank you to colleagues in the School of Languages and Linguistics at the University of Melbourne for encouraging me in the final stages of the project. I would especially like to thank Bertrand Bourgeois, Tess Do, Véronique Duché, Jacqueline Dutton, Andrew McGregor, Diane de Saint-Léger and Nicholas Strole.

At Edinburgh University Press, I would like to thank Susannah Butler and Elizabeth Fraser for their editorial assistance, as well as the commissioning editors and the anonymous reviewers of the proposal and manuscript for their extremely helpful feedback. Thank you to Loïc Bourdeau for his belief in the project. I am hugely grateful to a number of scholarly societies and associations for providing me with additional funding opportunities to develop public engagement activities about the BUMIDOM, including the Society for French Studies, the Association for the Study of Modern and Contemporary France, the Society for the Study of French History and the University Council for Languages.

Thank you, too, to the many librarians and archivists who assisted me in my work on the BUMIDOM at the Bibliothèque nationale de France, the Archives nationales, the Archives départementales de la Guadeloupe and the Archives territoriales de Martinique. Thank you to everyone who shared their stories with me during my fieldwork in the Caribbean, and to everyone who participated in interviews. A special thank you to Charlise Curier who so generously gave her time to welcome me in Guadeloupe.

Last but not least, this book would not have been possible without the support of my friends and family. A special thanks must go to Doreen Pastor and Laura Sefton for their fantastic friendship, and to Polly Galis and Maria Tomlinson for all their encouragement, advice and support. My family have always believed in me. They have lifted me up when times have been hard and celebrated my adventures and achievements. Thank you to my grandparents, my uncles, my sisters Felicity Wimbush and Heather Wimbush, and my parents Angela Wimbush and Timothy Wimbush, for their unfaltering love.

Sections of Chapter 1 draw on my chapter 'Colonialism, Race and Caribbean Migration: A History of the BUMIDOM', which was published in *Colonial Continuities and Decoloniality in the French-Speaking World* (2024), edited by Sarah Arens, Nicola Frith, Jonathan Lewis and Rebekah Vince. I would like to thank the editors for their permission to use this material.

Introduction: Memorialising Migration

During my fieldwork in Guadeloupe in October 2022, I was invited to participate in a radio phone-in show on Radio Horizon AP. The station, which broadcasts on radio and via Facebook, was established in 2020 to provide a platform for locals in Guadeloupe who are involved in sports, culture and politics to disseminate their work. I was asked by Jocelyn Obertan, one of the radio presenters, to talk about my research on the BUMIDOM alongside Charlise Curier, author of the autobiography *Mon aventure avec le BUMIDOM* (2019) [My Adventure with the BUMIDOM].[1] On 27 October 2022, we travelled to the small, brightly coloured, makeshift studio in Les Abymes on Grande-Terre island. During the programme, people from Martinique, Guadeloupe and mainland France rang in to ask us questions about the BUMIDOM and its operations. I was struck by Curier's comments about the lack of governmental recognition of the BUMIDOM and the absence of community events to restore the Bureau into the French and Caribbean cultural memory. However, she was also optimistic that the growing interest in the BUMIDOM among young people will encourage community-led memorialisation practices to emerge:

> je pense que le fait que les jeunes prennent cette chose en main maintenant, qu'ils commencent à s'intéresser à ce sujet [. . .] donc au fur et à mesure les jeunes vont s'intéresser et ça va nous encourager, ils pourront nous donner des idées pour nous organiser. (Curier 2022)
>
> [I think the fact that young people are taking this thing in hand now, that they are starting to become interested in the topic [. . .] so gradually young people will become interested, they'll be able to give us ideas for us to get organised.]

It is this lack of official, governmental practices of memorialisation of the Bureau (which is particularly striking when compared to migration from the anglophone Caribbean islands to the United Kingdom, where there is significant national memorialisation), and simultaneously an urgent need to recover this memory among Antilleans living in the Caribbean or in Europe, which is at the heart of this book. The BUMIDOM (Bureau pour le développement des migrations dans les départements d'outre-mer [Bureau for the Development of Migration in the Overseas Departments]) was the state-organised migration scheme in operation between 1963 and 1982. It was implemented in response to a set of overlapping economic, demographic and political circumstances in mainland France and the overseas departments in the Caribbean and Réunion. Rising birth rates and a growing unemployment rate put pressure on the islands' resources, which in turn led to an increasing sense of dissatisfaction with departmentalisation. Mainland France, meanwhile, was in urgent need of a workforce following World War II. Effectively, the BUMIDOM was a labour recruitment agency; following an application process, Guadeloupean, Martinican, Reunionese and Guianese workers were given a one-way boat or plane ticket and were found housing and employment in sectors such as transportation, health care and domestic service. Approximately 160,000 people migrated through this scheme, and a similar number migrated of their own accord, assisted by family members or friends who had already settled in continental France (Paris 2020, 96). These people were French citizens moving from one department to another; their emigration was an internal migration within the French nation. However, as I shall argue in Chapter 1 and throughout this book, they were often treated as migrants and subjected to racial discrimination, particularly when looking for work and housing.

BUMIDOM (1963–1982) and its Afterlives: Literature, Memory and Migration argues that the French state has been reluctant to memorialise the BUMIDOM through official, national commemorative practices because this would mean acknowledging that the Bureau operated on racial lines, and would thus contradict the ideology of republican universalism as it is conceived in France, according to which all citizens are equal, regardless of race, culture, religion or gender. However, by being subjected to state-sponsored racial discrimination, French citizens of colour from Guadeloupe and Martinique were being denied their Frenchness or their full rights. The BUMIDOM is thus an example of historical silencing as it has often been left out of historical narratives about twentieth-century

French history and has not appeared in history textbooks or school curricula about French immigration or emigration histories. Michel-Rolph Trouillot critiques the absences and lacunae in historical narratives in *Silencing the Past: Power and the Production of History* (1995). In his analysis of the power dynamics at work in the production of history, Trouillot argues that:

> silences enter the process of historical production at four crucial moments: the moment of fact creation (the making of *sources*); the moment of fact assembly (the making of *archives*); the moment of fact retrieval (the making of *narratives*); and the moment of retrospective significance (the making of *history* in the final instance) [original emphasis]. (1995, 26)

Trouillot locates his analysis in a very specific time and locale – the Haitian Revolution – but the broader arguments he makes about the inequalities of power in the production of sources, archives and narratives have relevance beyond Haiti in the nineteenth century. Indeed, they can be applied to gaps in the historiography of the recent past, in which the history produced in a variety of sites and by different actors is marginalised, overlooked or silenced, often for political motivations. The BUMIDOM is one such example. There are certainly sources about the BUMIDOM created by both governmental officials and people of the BUMIDOM generation who became actively involved in labour unions and civic associations in France. These sources have been preserved in archives in mainland France and in Martinique and Guadeloupe, and they are an important source of reference for this study. However, the BUMIDOM has been left out of the national process of historical production at the final two stages in Trouillot's model, in the making of narratives and history. It has not been included in France's national narrative of twentieth-century migration because of the colonial, institutionalised nature of the scheme – migration was used as a form of population control – but also because officials tapped into stereotypes about Black Antilleans and then organised work around these stereotypes, as I shall explore in the first chapter of this book.

I argue, then, that writers, artists, filmmakers and individuals with personal experience of migration are producing work about the BUMIDOM to fill the gaps of this collective political and social amnesia. Their creative work acts as strategies of recovery, restoring Frenchness to BUMIDOM participants and their descendants who have often not been able to engage in familial or community-led memorial practices. The French state set the tone for the repression of private and community memory, and so it is through cultural work that BUMIDOM participants are able to remember their past. Madeleine Dobie posits that little attention has been paid to migration from the Caribbean to mainland France in cultural work by writers and artists of Caribbean origin living on either side of the Atlantic, and this migration has not garnered significant interest in the French media or in scholarship either (2004, 150). While this may well have been the case, there has been a recent proliferation in cultural work about the Bureau since the 2010s. Indeed, the majority of the cultural outputs in my corpus were not produced during the BUMIDOM era itself but have been created very recently by second- or third-generation Caribbean migrants. One of the objectives of this study is to interrogate why there has been such a recent outpouring of cultural works about the BUMIDOM, and to investigate the extent to which these cultural practitioners can be considered as memory activists, bringing histories and memories of the BUMIDOM to light.

What is particularly striking about these cultural artefacts about the BUMIDOM is that they appear in a wide array of genres and media. The BUMIDOM is not only an important plot point in fictional novels, but it also appears as the central node in texts of life writing, fictional films, children's fiction, graphic novels and songs. In this book, I question how and why these different modes are employed to spotlight diverse perspectives, experiences and memories of post-war Caribbean migration to France. Much of the work I analyse is very personal in nature, produced by people with direct experience of the BUMIDOM. This is particularly the case with the texts of life writing. Curier, Françoise Ega, Lucienne Dangreville-Bellemare and Michèle Zabulon all employ the genre of life writing to come to terms with their migration, which, at times, was difficult and distressing. The personal nature of their writing is evident not only in the narrative style of their texts – such as through the use of the personal pronoun 'je' and in the biographical details they incorporate about their lives – but also through paratextual items they include in the books, such as photographs and epigraphs. The aims of their writing project seem not only individual but also familial and collective, as they seek to pass down their stories of migration to family members and to the wider community. Other items I examine in this book, such as the fictional novels *D'eaux douces* (2004) [Freshwater] by Fabienne Kanor and *Là où les chiens aboient par la queue* (2018) [*Where Dogs Bark with Their Tails: A Novel*] and the films *Le Gang des Antillais* (2016) [*Gang of the Caribbean*] and

Le Rêve français (2018) [*The French Dream*] draw on the experiences of the family members of their creators, but they also weave personal details with fictional stories to emphasise the diversity of experiences of migration. Some works, in contrast, are more concerned with relaying factual detail about the BUMIDOM. The graphic novel *Peyi an nou* (2017) [Our Country], written by Jessica Oublié and illustrated by Marie-Ange Rousseau, transmits historical information about the causes for the establishment of the BUMIDOM and its consequences on different populations living in the Caribbean and in mainland France. It also documents the research process involved in creating such a detailed, factual graphic novel and draws attention to the positionality of the two female protagonists as they undertake their research (and the positionality of the people they interview). In addition, the text has political undertones as it draws attention to the failings of the French state to provide meaningful training and work to BUMIDOM participants. The musical tracks I analyse often adopt a similarly critical stance towards the Bureau. Music is either a form of contestation which is used to protest about the BUMIDOM, or a vector of memories about Caribbean migration to draw public attention to the multiple and ongoing legacies of the Bureau. Finally, some items do not memorialise the BUMIDOM but use it as a contextual marker to explain the presence of a large Antillean population in the Hexagon. This is the case with Pascal Légitimus's *Antilles-sur-Seine* (2000) [Antilles-on-the-Seine], a comedy film which treats the Antillean community in a condescending and patronising manner. In this book I draw out the nuances, complexities and, at times, ambiguities in the cultural works which raise awareness (in different ways) of the racialised treatment of Caribbean citizens in France in the 1960s and beyond.

In order to do this, I bring the cultural items into dialogue with interviews with selected artistic practitioners and with archival material about the BUMIDOM through a contrapuntal reading which, to quote Edward Said, demonstrates 'awareness both of the metropolitan history that is narrated and of those other histories against which (and together with which) the dominating discourse acts' (1993, 51). The BUMIDOM files at the Archives nationales [National Archives] in Pierrefitte-sur-Seine, the Archives territoriales de Martinique [Territorial Archives of Martinique] in Fort-de-France and the Archives départementales de la Guadeloupe [Departmental Archives of Guadeloupe] in Gourbeyre will provide essential contextual information in Chapter 1 but will also be used to illuminate particular aspects of the cultural works. While the book focuses on cultural representations of the BUMIDOM, it situates these cultural items within the very specific historical time period of the BUMIDOM era, thereby providing a fresh perspective on the BUMIDOM and its legacies. Recent scholarship by Stephanie Condon (2020), Marine Haddad (2018) and Sylvain Pattieu (2016) has made significant contributions to our understanding of the BUMIDOM from a historical and sociological standpoint. These studies add to existing work about the BUMIDOM in French by scholars based at the Centre de recherche sur les pouvoirs locaux dans la Caraïbe [Centre for Research into Local Politics and Powers in the Caribbean] at the Université des Antilles et de la Guyane, such as Fred Constant (1987), Constant and Justin Daniel (1997) and Monique Milia-Marie-Luce (2007). Sociological and historical studies have also been produced in English, such as *Migration in Comparative Perspective: Caribbean Communities in Britain and France* (2008) by Margaret Byron and Condon and *Decolonizing the Republic: African and Caribbean Migrants in Postwar Paris, 1946–1974* (2015) by Félix Germain. These are important works which provide much-needed historical and demographic analyses of state-sponsored migration from the Caribbean to mainland France – and I draw on their insights in this book – but they do not explore the cultural impacts of emigration. In contrast to these previous studies, and drawing on H. Adlai Murdoch's comparative analysis of cultural representations of migration from the anglophone and francophone Caribbean, published in 2012, *BUMIDOM (1963–1982) and its Afterlives* seeks to explore how the BUMIDOM has had a long-lasting impact on the cultural landscape of the French Caribbean and mainland France.

The case studies I consider in this book are all produced by creators of Caribbean origin or heritage, whether currently living in Martinique, Guadeloupe or the Hexagon. I do not examine in detail cultural outputs from Réunion or French Guiana, for numerous reasons. Firstly, despite historical commonalities between the four overseas departments, given that they were all colonised by the French in the same time period (in the mid-seventeenth century), they are considerably divergent in linguistic, cultural and demographic terms. Examining cultural artefacts uniquely from the Caribbean makes for a more focused analysis of the migratory experiences of this particular community. Secondly, and more importantly, there has been considerably less cultural production about the Guianese and Reunionese contexts, even though more people actually migrated through the BUMIDOM from Réunion than from the other three departments.[2] In the case of Réunion, there has been increasing material in recent years, but much of this focuses on the specific case of the 'Enfants de la Creuse', the forced deportation of children from Réunion to repopulate rural mainland France in the 1960s and 70s.[3] While this alarming episode of French history requires urgent critical attention, and there are clear overlaps in the motivations behind both migration policies, my focus here is on the intersections between migration and labour histories, and therefore the Reunionese cultural output about children's experiences brings up a range of different issues which lie outside the scope of this project. However, recent examples of Reunionese cultural production will feature in individual chapters to demonstrate how specific media and genre engage with migration differently according to the cultural context. Likewise, the book does not deal with the case of French Guiana, but for different reasons. Relatively few Guianese people were recruited by the scheme, in comparison to the other overseas departments, because the territory did not suffer from the same issues of overpopulation. In fact, it was actually the receiver of a small number of migrants from Martinique and Guadeloupe through the BUMIDOM once the 'Plan Vert' [Green Plan] was implemented in 1975, meaning that the department was a channel for immigration rather than emigration.[4] Inevitably, then, the BUMIDOM does not carry as much cultural weight in French Guiana, and it is thus unsurprising that writers and artists from this department have not engaged with memories of the BUMIDOM to the same extent.

My approach in the book is informed by debates in memory studies, migration studies and francophone postcolonial studies. The analysis is underpinned by Pierre Nora's concept of *lieux de mémoire* [realms of memory], and by the subsequent work on postcolonial realms of memory initiated by Étienne Achille, Charles Forsdick and Lydie Moudileno in their 2020 volume, *Postcolonial Realms of Memory: Sites and Symbols in Modern France*. It asks how literature, film and other cultural items activate a collective postcolonial remembrance of the BUMIDOM, in the absence of state-sponsored commemorations and community-led and private memorial practices. In order to do this, it engages with recent theories and models of transcultural memory, such as Michael Rothberg, Max Silverman and Debarati Sanyal's notion of *nœuds de mémoire* [knots of memory], to investigate the connections between memories of the BUMIDOM and memories of enslavement and forced labour in the Caribbean imaginary. Debates around intergenerational memory are also useful for my analysis. Given that some of these cultural items were produced at the time of migration and some were created much later, Marianne Hirsch's notion of 'postmemory' allows me to understand how the 'generation after' remembers the BUMIDOM through the stories and images passed down to them. Furthermore, Alison Landsberg's concept of 'prosthetic memory' will be useful to think through how a collective memory of events which individuals did not live through can be created through film and television. The book also teases out issues surrounding racial identity and Blackness in France to reflect on why the BUMIDOM has not been a part of the national narrative. Finally, as the following section will demonstrate, I engage with debates about Caribbean migration, diaspora and citizenship to better understand the complex status of BUMIDOM participants living in mainland France, who were both French citizens and members of a Caribbean diasporic community.

Migration, Diaspora and Citizenship: The French Caribbean Context

Movement towards and away from the Caribbean, and within the region itself, is not a new phenomenon; rather, incoming and outgoing migration has been instrumental in shaping the region. European settlers arrived during the colonial era. The infectious diseases they brought with them, coupled with their systematic use of force and violence, almost entirely destroyed indigenous populations. Once the colonies had been established in the Caribbean, enslaved African peoples were forcibly transported there in appalling conditions during the transatlantic traffic in enslaved Africans. Following abolition, indentured Asian labourers were brought to the Caribbean as a substitute for the labour of the enslaved. In the twentieth century, the Caribbean was principally a space of outward migration, as people emigrated to Europe and the Americas to find work, and the BUMIDOM is an example, albeit an institutionalised, highly regulated one, of this outward labour migration. The twenty-first century has seen an increase in return migration to the Caribbean, particularly to anglophone islands; those who sought work in Britain in the 1950s and 60s, as part of the 'Windrush generation', increasingly desire to return to their place of birth in their later years. As Gert Oostindie and Inge Klinkers note, migration 'is still central to the lives and awareness of [Caribbean] inhabitants today', as they engage in what is often a series of transnational movements in the contemporary globalised world (2003, 177).

These displacements, whether enforced by the colonial power or undertaken voluntarily by people searching for political freedom and economic stability, inevitably involve a recalibration in attitudes towards both the homeland and the hostland. Interactions between individuals and their homeland and hostland are particularly complex when thinking about diasporic communities because people often maintain affective ties to both countries. This is all the more multifaceted in the French Caribbean. In this case, homeland and hostland are the same country in political terms (that is, they are both part of the nation-state of France), but the multiple historical, cultural and linguistic differences between the two mean that it can still be challenging for people born and raised in the French Caribbean to fully integrate into life in mainland France.

The transnational configuration of this community evokes the notion of diaspora, a term originating from ancient Greek meaning 'to sew' or 'to scatter'. Initially 'diaspora' referred to the 'forced expulsion and dispersal, persecution, a sense of loss and a vision of return' of the Israelites from the Kingdom of Israel in the eighth century BCE (Vertovec 2005, 1). Its use was later expanded to include the displacement of other religious minorities, and since the 1970s it has had a wide range of meanings and applications. Generally speaking, diasporic communities are scattered across different countries at different periods of time but are united in their collective remembering of the original homeland. Thomas Faist argues that, while the definition of diaspora has become more flexible over time, there are three principal criteria which determine a diaspora: the cause of dispersal or migration, which can be enforced or voluntary; the connections between the destination and the homeland, which can involve a desire to return or can mean a willingness to create further transnational connections; and a sense of integrating into the society of the hostland, which may or may not be possible, depending on how the term 'integration' is defined (Faist 2010, 12–13). A further characteristic of a diasporic group is the shared sentiment of belonging to a particular community. Diasporans are 'transnational community members or isolated individuals who, wherever they are, share a sense of a common belonging to a homeland where they are not', as Peggy Levitt explains in *The Transnational Villagers* (2001, 15).

Can the French Caribbean community living either in mainland France or in Martinique and Guadeloupe be considered as diasporic? If we consider the origins of the Caribbean community, the notion of diaspora does hold up, because this is a group which underwent a forced displacement from Africa during the transatlantic trafficking, and which, subconsciously or not, maintains connections to their original African homeland. For Édouard Glissant, the forced diasporisation of their African ancestors is at the heart of the French Caribbean collective imaginary. Indeed, many of his earlier sociological and philosophical works, including *Le Discours antillais* (1981) [*Caribbean Discourse*] and *La Poétique de la relation* (1990) [*Poetics of Relation*], examine the legacies of enslavement and forced displacement on diasporic Caribbean identity, even if, in his later work, he has moved away from the concept of diaspora to focus more on transnational connections across the globalised world. For Sam Coombes, Glissant's work is 'an important missing link in diaspora studies, an important plank which has thus far been largely overlooked because the now settled communities of the Caribbean do not invite reflection on immigration and migrancy' (2019, 774). While I agree with Coombes that Glissant's philosophy illuminates a great deal about the African origins of the Caribbean community, his comments on the settled nature of Caribbean communities should be nuanced. As I shall argue in this book, the Caribbean has been a locus of movement and exchange long before the BUMIDOM was established, and migration patterns between the Americas and Europe have continued to this day as people continue to cross the Atlantic on a regular basis for personal and professional commitments. Indeed, the very fact that it is difficult to define the migratory status of Caribbean peoples shows very clearly that this community is rooted in notions of migrancy.

While Glissant considers the French Caribbean community as diasporic because of their initial displacement from Africa, Mickaella Perina (2006) focuses on the second movement of this group, and the one I analyse in this book: their migration to live in the Hexagon in the 1960s and 70s. Perina acknowledges the fact that the term 'diaspora' may not be entirely appropriate for this group because their country of origin and their destination is 'the same administrative entity, the same state, and moreover a single destination' (2006, 5). However, she argues that there are two caveats to this. Firstly, she suggests that this displacement did not only occur between the Caribbean islands and mainland France, but also potentially to other overseas departments (such as French Guiana), meaning that the destinations to which these groups travelled were plural (Perina 2006, 5). Secondly, she posits that individuals living in Martinique and Guadeloupe were already diasporic because they were members of the African diaspora living in the Caribbean. They do not stop being a diasporic group simply because they relocate somewhere else, but on moving to the Hexagon, they continue to construct and transform their identity on the other side of the Atlantic. She thus defines this group as a form of 'modern diaspora' which emerges from 'new waves of immigration' as well as from international and transnational connections between different locations (Perina 2006, 5).

The situation of Martinicans and Guadeloupeans living in mainland France is complicated further by their French citizenship. Perina draws on Michel Laguerre's concept of diasporic citizenship to explain how Martinicans and Guadeloupeans can be both French citizens and members of a diasporic group. Diasporic citizenship challenges the assumption that there is a unilateral relationship between a particular group or ethnic identity and the territory in which this group has formed a community. It recognises that people often maintain multiple identities deriving from place and ethnicity, but also from the multiple migrations they undertake throughout their lives, and from other identity markers such as religion, class, gender and sexuality. In *Diasporic Citizenship: Haitian Americans in Transnational America* (1998), Laguerre defines diasporic citizenship as:

> the situation of the individual who lives outside the boundaries of the nation-state to which he or she had formally held primary allegiance and who experiences through transnational migration (or the redesign of the homeland boundaries) the subjective reality of belonging to two or more nation-states. (1998, 12)

For Laguerre, then, diasporic citizenship allows individuals to hold political, social, economic and cultural allegiances with more than one nation-state. Yet Laguerre here is examining the specific case of Haitian Americans who migrate to the United States, 'outside the boundaries of the nation-state' of Haiti, who maintain connections with Haiti, the United States and potentially with other nation-states with which they may become involved following further transnational migration. Is this concept appropriate for diasporic Caribbean communities from Guadeloupe and Martinique who migrate to the nation-state of France? If the Caribbean islands themselves are reconfigured as a form of nation-state, as Perina suggests (2006, 10), it seems that the concept does hold up for French overseas citizens who migrate to France. They seek to pledge allegiance to mainland France in order to assert their French citizenship, but they are also eager to retain connections to their native Caribbean islands.

Laguerre has developed his thinking on diasporas further, and his most recent theoretical contribution to this field is the notion of 'postdiaspora'. In *The Postdiaspora Condition: Crossborder Social Protection, Transnational Schooling and Extraterritorial Human Security* (2017), Laguerre argues that, unlike the category of diaspora, which for him denotes the marginalisation of minority communities, postdiaspora is an emancipatory condition because it allows individuals to reposition themselves as equal to people in the homeland and the hostland. He defines postdiaspora as:

> the situation of individuals who live in a polity other than that into which they or their parents were born – their hostland – but possess full citizenship rights in their ancestral country – their homeland – similar or identical to those enjoyed by its intramural population. (Laguerre 2017, 20)

He sees postdiasporisation as a continuous process of contestation which can occur at different times for different people. However, once again, Laguerre's notion raises issues when applied to people of Caribbean origin moving between the Caribbean and mainland France. They were French citizens even before moving to mainland France, a status held since abolition in 1848, as we shall see shortly. Does this mean, then, that they are already a postdiasporic community before this displacement occurs, and that their postdiasporic status does not depend on a form of displacement? After tracing how the status of postdiaspora is acquired and theorised in the existing literature – through continuity, rupture, return and dispersion (Laguerre 2017, 26–7), Laguerre proposes a final model: the cosmonational postdiaspora model. He argues that here 'postdiaspora is a legal disposition made possible by the constitution and the transnational organization of state agencies and institutions' (2017, 28). In this model, postdiaspora is dependent on a cosmonation – a multisite nation like France – rather than on a single nation-state. It is thus more applicable to the case of French Caribbean communities which have become postdiasporic through the granting of citizenship in 1848, in turn enabling them to engage in transnational movements, than the other models outlined by Laguerre.

Yet Laguerre's conceptualisation of postdiaspora is not without its problems. Pat Noxolo points out that Laguerre is:

> remarkably silent about the obvious postcolonial relations of power that underpin France's cosmonational status, the privileged historical

> conditions under which France's diasporic movements came about, and the forms of oppression and impoverishment that have brought about large diasporic movements to France from formerly colonised countries. (2020, 138)

In addition to the lack of discussion about colonial power dynamics in Laguerre's work, Noxolo displays hesitation towards the term 'postdiaspora' because it presupposes a departure away from the concept of diaspora, which is still valid in her opinion. She therefore proposes to unite the two concepts through the term '(post)diaspora' 'as a way of keeping both diaspora and postdiaspora in play' in recognition that 'both have valid claims' (Noxolo 2020, 134). She puts forward her own theorisation of (post)diaspora, drawing on concepts from quantum physics such as entanglement and materiality. Noxolo insists that (post)diaspora be understood as material entanglements between people and places in order to emphasise the shared histories of different communities and move away from neoliberal conceptualisations of diaspora which are always already gendered and class-based, privileging the white, rich male (2020, 144).

As *BUMIDOM (1963–1982) and its Afterlives* makes clear, the lives of (post)diasporic communities living in Martinique, Guadeloupe and mainland France are entangled and materially connected to each other – and they are also connected to transnational diasporas living in other countries and experiencing migration as 'an unending sojourn across different lands' (Lie 1995, 304). The constant displacement of people, languages, ideas and cultures across and beyond the Atlantic is evident not only in the cultural production analysed in this book, but also in the lived experiences of Antilleans whose lives are fertilised by multiple transoceanic encounters and entanglements.[5] These entanglements are made possible by the French citizenship they have held since 1848, and which should have rendered possible the integration of BUMIDOM participants in the mid-twentieth century.

The process of acquiring citizenship in Martinique and Guadeloupe was quite different from the laws implemented in France's new colonies. Natasha Pairaudeau explains that, as the empire expanded, the French government realised that it could not afford for everyone in each French colony to become citizens (2016, 18). It was particularly difficult to extend citizenship to everyone in the large new colonies such as Algeria. Being a French citizen meant demonstrating political loyalty to a nation in exchange for protection, the right to vote and the right to have civil matters such as marriage and inheritance regulated by the French Civil Code. While local populations in the old enclave colonies of French India and Senegal's Four Communes (Saint-Louis, Dakar, Gorée and Rufisque) accepted electoral franchise, they were less happy to embrace civil equalities, particularly in Senegal because the largely Muslim population was reluctant to abandon their indigenous religious practices. In the case of French India, it was the French colonial authorities who were unwilling to enforce allegiance to the French Civil Code. In these colonies, then, the local population held a 'colonial not-quite-citizenship' (Pairaudeau 2016, 5) as they had voting rights but did not have access to civil equalities. Before citizenship was granted to people in the colonies, either through a change in law (as in Guadeloupe and Martinique) or through an application for naturalisation (as in Indochina), people in the colonies were colonial subjects rather than French citizens. As Emmanuelle Saada explains, subjects enjoyed political power locally; however, they were not allowed to participate in national elections and the roles they could hold in the civil service were limited (2007, 109–11).

In Martinique and Guadeloupe, the right to be fully French citizens was acquired through the struggles of the enslaved and free people of colour, struggles which began long before abolition in 1848. The law of April 1831, following the uprising in the same year, extended civil rights to free people of colour. This was formalised in 1833 when full French citizenship was granted to this group, even though white Creoles maintained social and legal control (Semley 2017, 140).[6] A further uprising among free people of colour erupted in 1833 as people were becoming discontented with the lack of progress regarding emancipation. Revolts on the island in spring 1848 triggered the formal abolition of slavery, following which the status of Guadeloupeans and Martinicans was changed from subject to citizen. However, as Lorelle Semley argues, 'emancipation in 1848 no longer looks like an iconic moment at the end of a triumphal march towards freedom' because, even though they were legally French, Martinicans and Guadeloupeans were still considered second-class citizens (2017, 119). Even when they became members of French overseas departments through the departmentalisation law of 1946 – a law which represented 'the first French attempts to fully integrate racial "others" into the nation itself – not merely as colonial, subject peoples, or as guest workers, but as citizens with full rights' – they were still not treated as equal to metropolitan French citizens because the policies were designed in favour of the former colonial centre (Childers 2016, 9).[7] The BUMIDOM is a further example of the ways in which French citizens from the Caribbean departments were not treated as equals to their metropolitan counterparts, as they were offered jobs which white French citizens from mainland France refused to do. The following section draws on key concepts in memory studies to show how this example of state-sanctioned racial discrimination has been concealed from France's national narrative.

The BUMIDOM as a Postcolonial *Lieu de Mémoire*?

In this book I ask whether the BUMIDOM has recently become, or has the potential to become, a postcolonial *lieu de mémoire* (an argument proposed by Murdoch in his contribution to *Postcolonial Realms of Memory* (2020)), and how this may have happened. I also explore the extent to which texts, films and songs by individual artists can constitute vectors of collective memory about the BUMIDOM in their own right. In his 1925 book *Les Cadres sociaux de la mémoire* [*On Collective Memory*], Maurice Halbwachs distinguishes between personal and collective memory. Interrogating how society remembers the past, Halbwachs argues that memory is created by the social interactions between individuals and communities. Nora draws on this idea that memory creates a form of shared identity when coining *lieux de mémoire*, a concept he theorises and exemplifies with other scholars in a series of seven collective volumes published between 1984 and 1992. A *lieu de mémoire* can be a place, object or concept which is laden with historical significance in the popular collective imaginary, such as a museum (the Palace of Versailles), a monument (the Panthéon), an event (the French Revolution) or a symbol (the 'Marseillaise'), to give some examples. In 'Between Memory and History', Nora explains that these artificial sites of memory exist because 'there are no longer *milieux de mémoire*, real environments of memory' (1989, 12). Spontaneous sites of memory do not exist either, he argues, so we must create these sites and imbue objects and concepts with memory so that they do not fall into oblivion. *Lieux de mémoire* must be simultaneously material, functional and symbolic for them to work, and they must depend on both memory and history – there has to be a will to remember a particular event or symbol, but these sites must be connected to a historical period to convey historical meaning (Nora 1989, 19).

Nora's model of collective memory has been groundbreaking for scholars working in the field of memory studies, but it is not without its problems, as has often been pointed out. Firstly, *lieux de mémoire* tend to homogenise local memories and fail to capture the tensions and conflicts which exist within these memories, particularly when they become appropriated by governments to become part of official, national memories (Rothberg 2009, 270). Secondly, they overlook institutional sites of forgetting, or what Nancy Wood has termed '*lieux d'oubli*'; that is, 'sites that public memory has expressly avoided because of the disturbing effect that their invocation is still capable of arousing' (Wood 1999, 10). By focusing on the parts of history society has intentionally remembered, the model ignores those which society has intentionally forgotten. The most widespread criticism of all, however, is that Nora's project fails to acknowledge the memories of enslavement and colonialism, and that there is very little focus on the wider francophone world. For Achille, Forsdick and Moudileno, 'it is high time for Francophone postcolonial studies to address systematically the flaws that have been identified in Nora's *Les Lieux de mémoire* by numerous critics', and their volume *Postcolonial Realms of Memory: Sites and Symbols in Modern France* represents the first step in postcolonialising sites of memory across France (2020, 1). They conceptualise postcolonial realms of memory as 'spatial/functional or immaterial sites, potentially subject to abstraction and imbued with a symbolic aura that [. . .] refers to more or less tangible memory traces linked to the colonial' (Achille, Forsdick and Moudileno 2020, 9). They examine sites of colonial memory in constitutional modern France, transcending Nora's boundaries of the Hexagon to consider memory traces in the *Outre-mer* [overseas departments] as well as in mainland France. However, given the spatial constraints of the volume, they have not included realms of memory in France's former colonial empire. Other initiatives have taken up the editors' call to 'extend the geographical reach' of the project (Achille, Forsdick and Moudileno 2020, 14), and a special issue of *Francosphères* which I co-edited with Jonathan Lewis in 2021 seeks to explore how 'colonial and postcolonial memory is conceptualised across the far-reaching geographical space that has been shaped by France's colonial project' (2021, 4). In addition, a recent special issue of *Modern and Contemporary France*, edited by Hannah Grayson and Nina Parish, adopts a more explicitly interdisciplinary approach. The volume traces the memory practices at work across the French-speaking world in disciplines such as history, literary and cultural studies and anthropology to investigate how they 'interact with France's official narratives of its national and global past' (Grayson and Parish 2024, 1).

Has the BUMIDOM become a postcolonial realm of memory, then, or is it an example of 'repressive erasure', the most extreme form among Paul Connerton's seven types of forgetting? According to Connerton, 'repressive erasure' is when a state seeks to shape the memory of a nation and eliminate the past by openly or covertly erasing memories of troubling events (2008, 60–1). As will become clear throughout this book, the BUMIDOM has the potential to move away from being a 'lieu d'oubli', to quote Wood again, and become a postcolonial realm of memory (as Achille, Forsdick and Moudileno understand it), even if this process has not yet happened via national frameworks of remembrance. It is through cultural production – through novels and films, through life writing and children's fiction, and through music and *bande dessinée* – that the BUMIDOM is remembered, and that a different narrative of Caribbean migration is created than the one put forward by the French state, which either overlooks the BUMIDOM entirely or focuses solely on the benefits of migrating via the Bureau without mentioning the difficulties and hardships experienced by participants. The cultural works offer a more nuanced perspective, transforming history into memory through a process of 'shared knowledge and collective identification and participation', to quote Aleida Assmann (2006, 216). They use different strategies to transmit memories across generations, cultures, media and genres, enabling the BUMIDOM to become an important part of the collective memory of French and Caribbean communities.

Cultural practitioners thus tap into recent debates in memory studies about the mobility of memory. Lucy Bond, Stef Craps and Pieter Vermeulen argue that, while memory was once thought to be static and fixed, it is now widely acknowledged that memory moves across time and space: 'memory, then, is presently conceptualised as something that does not stay put but circulates, migrates, travels; it is more and more perceived as a process, as work that is continually in progress, rather than as a reified object' (Bond, Craps and Vermeulen 2016, 1). They trace the new key trends in memory studies, focusing on four elements of memory which spotlight its mobility: transcultural, transgenerational, transmedial and transdisciplinary perspectives. These new models alter our understanding of what memory is and how it operates. As I argue in this study, writers and artists engage with a selection of these different models in order to integrate the BUMIDOM and its colonial and postcolonial implications more actively into practices of collective memory.

Transcultural memory practices are those which involve 'the transmission, circulation, mediation, and reception of memory between and beyond ethnic, cultural, or national groups' (Bond, Craps and Vermeulen 2016, 3). This type of memory departs from the idea that memory belongs to particular geographic or cultural groups, a notion which is at the heart of theories conceptualised by Halbwachs and Nora, as explained above. The best-known model of transcultural memory is multidirectional memory, theorised by Rothberg, Senyal and Silverman in a 2010 special issue of *Yale French Studies*. The authors argue for 'new models and metaphors for the heterogeneity and circulation of histories in contemporary cultures of remembrance' (Rothberg, Senyal and Silverman 2010, 1). Positing that traumatic events, and particularly the Holocaust, have been presented as singular, unique and incomparable, they suggest that it is more productive to consider how histories and memories are connected and created across different cultures. In *Multidirectional Memory: Remembering the Holocaust in the Age of Decolonization* (2009), Rothberg proposes the need to move away from competitive frameworks of memory – 'a zero-sum struggle over scarce resources' – and embrace multidirectional understandings of memory which are 'subject to ongoing negotiation, cross-referencing, and borrowing' (2009, 3). Expanding on this work, Silverman puts forward the term 'palimpsestic memory'. In *Palimpsestic Memory: The Holocaust and Colonialism in French and Francophone Fiction and Film* (2013), Silverman proposes that memories of one particular event are superimposed onto the memories of another, so that traces of the past are always visible and always inform other events. Other models of transcultural memory include cosmopolitan memory, theorised by Daniel Levy and Natan Sznaider and which emphasise the role of globalisation in the creation and transformation of memories (2005), and travelling memory, a model which, according to Astrid Erll, foregrounds the 'incessant wandering of carriers, media, contents, forms, and practices of memory, their continual "travels" and ongoing transformations through time and space, across social, linguistic and political borders' (2011b, 11). These forms of transcultural memory foreground the fluidity and openness of memory which has the capacity to create connections across national and ethnic boundaries.

Transgenerational memory, which interrogates how memories are transmitted across generations, is the second category of memory identified by Bond, Craps and Vermeulen. These models are particularly useful for my analysis of cultural production about the BUMIDOM, given that much of the creative work examined in this book is produced by descendants of BUMIDOM participants rather than by participants themselves. Like transcultural memory, the point of departure of transgenerational memory is the memory of the Holocaust. This globalisation of memory through comparisons to the Holocaust has been critiqued by Jie-Hyun Lim and Eve Rosenhaft for its creation of 'a new frame for heightened competition among the parties to contending national memories' (2021, 4), as states have appropriated Holocaust remembrance to conceal their own war crimes and justify a resurgence in nationalist discourse. Yet memory does not only travel through space but also through time. From the 1980s, children of Holocaust survivors began to reflect on what it was like to grow up with memories of trauma that they did not experience first-hand. Hirsch's notion of postmemory is the most influential of transgenerational memory practices. Hirsch first used the term in relation to family photographs in Art Spiegelman's *Maus* before developing the concept in other cultural contexts in photography and in literature in her monographs *Family Frames: Photography, Narrative, and Postmemory* (1997) and *The Generation of Postmemory: Writing and Visual Culture after the Holocaust* (2012). Hirsch argues that postmemory is transmitted across generations through stories and images which contain an affective link to the past. These stories, images and behaviours are imbued with so much emotion and affect that the subsequent generations take on these memories as if they were their own. Hirsch argues that 'postmemory's connection to the past is thus actually mediated not by recall but by imaginative investment, projection, and creation' (2012, 5). The concept has been critiqued by scholars such as Ernst van Alphen (2006) and Samuel O'Donoghue (2018) for its conflation of suffering between the survivors of trauma and their descendants. Hirsch has responded to these criticisms by acknowledging the difference between memory and postmemory; postmemory is not memory, she claims, but it 'approximates memory in its affective force and its psychic effects' (2012, 31). Another controversial theory of transgenerational memory is Landsberg's notion of prosthetic memory. In *Prosthetic Memory: The Transformation of American Remembrance in the Age of Mass Culture* (2004), Landsberg argues that individuals can acquire memories of events they have never personally experienced through mass media such as films and television. In Chapter 4, we will examine the problems of this model further, interrogating how the use of the ableist language of 'prosthesis' to refer to the process of adopting someone else's traumatic memories is insulting both to disabled communities and to the survivors of trauma. Other models of transgenerational memory, such as Ellen Fine's absent memory (1988) and Henri Raczymow's *mémoire trouée* [memory shot through with holes] (1994), have gained less traction in academic work, but they raise interesting questions about the fragmented, incomplete nature of the memory transmitted to the next generation. In all of these theorisations of transgenerational memory, we are reminded of Amy Hungerford's pertinent question: should future generations remember traumatic events, or learn from them? (2003, 155). I shall take up this question in Chapter 5 to reflect on the intersections between memory and pedagogy, and how they are manifested in graphic novels and children's fiction.

While memory studies has long focused on the mediated nature of memory, the transmedial turn emphasises how memories are shaped by interactions across different media and foregrounds the role of recent technology in this process of memory storage and transmission. Ann Rigney argues that there has been a recent shift in thinking through how memory is carried across different media through literary works. Literary works act as monuments, providing fixed points of reference in relation to memory, but they also 'continuously morph into the many other cultural products that recall, adapt, and revise them in both overt and indirect ways' (2010, 349). She goes on to suggest that fictional narratives can play five different roles in relation to memory: they can be 'relay stations', 'stabilisers', 'catalysts', 'objects of recollection' or 'calibrators' (Rigney 2010, 350–1). Erll and Rigney argue that these memory carriers work together through networks of transmedial interaction in a process of remediation: 'all representations of the past draw on available media technologies, on existent media products, on patterns of representation, and medial aesthetics' (2009, 4). In a further example of transmedial memory, Anna Reading examines how memory is transmitted across the world through digital media. Coining the neologism 'the globital memory field' to refer to the 'synergetic combination of the social and political dynamic of globalization with digitization' (Reading 2011, 242), Reading argues that digital media allows memories which are personal and localised to travel to multiple places across the world at the same time. She then outlines six characteristics of this digital media transfer: transmediality, velocity, extensity, modality, valency and viscosity (Reading 2011, 248–50). These transmedial modes of memory transmission not only emphasise the dynamic nature of memory which is always in flux and not static, but also bring private memories into the public sphere, thus blurring boundaries between the public and the private.

The final development in memory studies is the transdisciplinary turn. Although memory studies has always been conceived of as a field which spans the humanities and the social sciences, there is increasing recognition, as Erll puts it, that the discipline is a 'genuinely transdisciplinary phenomenon whose functioning cannot really be understood through examination through one single perspective' (2011a, 38). Memory studies can only be enriched by increasing dialogue between disciplines, as scholars in the sciences, such as Richard Crownshaw (2016), look to the study of memory to explore the positionality of particular scientific phenomenon in the contemporary cultural imaginary.

The cultural outputs analysed in this book transmit memories of the BUMIDOM primarily through transcultural and transgenerational models. They complicate and contest oppositions between cultures, nationalities and generations, revealing that memories of the BUMIDOM do not only belong to a single group of people; that is, those from Martinique and Guadeloupe who migrated to mainland France through the BUMIDOM. Rather, they demonstrate that these memories are part of the heritage of French and Caribbean communities, regardless of their own migratory trajectory. In this way, the works deconstruct binaries between France and the Caribbean, migrant and citizen, and first and second generation. In the following section, I analyse racial identity, universalism and Blackness in France in order to interrogate why the BUMIDOM has been overlooked in the French national narrative, and why it has become the role of writers and artists to fill this mnemonic gap.

Racial Identity and Blackness in France

In response to the global resurgence of the Black Lives Matter Movement in June 2020, following the murder of George Floyd on 25 May 2020 at the hands of Minneapolis police officer Derek Chauvin, French President Emmanuel Macron blamed academics in the humanities and social sciences for encouraging debates about racial identity in France. In an article in *Le Monde* by Françoise Fressoz and Cédric Pietralunga, published on 11 June 2020, he was quoted as declaring that universities in France have encouraged 'l'ethnicisation de la question sociale' [the ethnicisation of social issues] which means 'casser la République en deux' [splitting the Republic in two]. Macron sees theoretical work about race and identity as a dangerous and 'woke' import from the United States which contradicts

French republicanism and stirs up revolt among the young French population seeking justice for inequalities and racial discrimination. While many French academics were scandalised by Macron's comments, others welcomed them, and in January 2021 the Observatoire des idéologies identitaires et du décolonialisme [Observatory of Identitarian Ideologies and Decolonialism] was established by a group of researchers under the umbrella of the Laboratoire d'analyse des idéologies contemporaines [Laboratory for the Analysis of Contemporary Ideologies]. According to their website, the observatory aims to offer 'un regard critique, tantôt profond et parfois humoristique, sur l'émergence d'une nouvelle tendance de l'Université et de la Recherche visant à "décoloniser" les sciences sociales' [a critical perspective, which is at times deep and at times humorous, on the emergence of a new trend in universities and in research which aims to 'decolonise' the social sciences]. This group of mostly white, established, male academics regards identity politics as suspicious for going against the notion of free speech, and they ridicule decolonialism, viewing it as a direct criticism of the knowledge production in which they are engaged. Stéphane Beaud and Gérard Noiriel have added to this debate with their controversial book *Race et sciences sociales. Essai sur les usages publics d'une catégorie* [Race and the Social Sciences: Essay on the Public Uses of Categories], published in 2021. They argue that the category of social class is the most important factor in the discrimination and oppression of French citizens, but that it is often overshadowed by discussions about race.

It is thus evident that, even in the twenty-first century, France is still struggling to accept that research on race is crucial if we are to fully comprehend what it means to be French today. This research is even more important if we consider that 'today France probably has the largest Black population in Europe', even if the exact figures are unknown because of France's refusal to collect statistics about racial difference (Sibeud, Pattieu and Stovall 2022, 2). In other words, race continues to be a taboo topic in the French academy, and in society more broadly. This is not to say, however, that the discipline of Black French studies is not thriving and does not have a long history behind it, but rather to show how research on race in France has been marginalised by the mainstream academy. Researchers such as Mame-Fatou Niang, Pap Ndiaye, Audrey Célestine, Françoise Vergès, Maboula Soumahoro, Pascal Blanchard, Dominic Thomas and Trica Keaton have paved the way for the creation of Black studies 'à la française'. This field of study unites scholars from history, sociology, political science and cultural studies to interrogate the Black experience in

France, a country which purports to be colourblind but in which systemic racism occurs as a legacy of its colonial past. It is telling that many of these scholars have conducted their work on race in France from beyond France, and primarily from the United States, demonstrating further that French institutions do not often support this work. This scholarship builds on foundational texts on Blackness and anti-colonialism by French thinkers in the mid-twentieth century, such as Aimé Césaire and Frantz Fanon. In *Peau noire, masques blancs* (1952) [*Black Skin, White Masks*], Fanon argues that colonialism and racism are intertwined because the colonial education system forced Black people to eradicate other aspects of their identity, and that they only became aware of their Blackness when confronted with the white metropolitan gaze (1952, 89). Fanon's call to understand how Black people were conditioned to consider themselves as inferior to white people through the colonial order has been taken up not only by scholars, but also by activists and journalists. In 2018, for instance, journalists and activists Rokhaya Diallo and Grace Ly launched their podcast *Kiffe ta race* [Love Your Race], in which they invite guests to reflect on contemporary manifestations of prejudice and racism from historical and sociological perspectives.[8] Meanwhile, activist Assa Traoré, who campaigns for justice for her brother Adama Traoré who died in police custody in 2016, continues to demand the end of police violence which has roots in France's colonial ideology.[9] More recently, in July 2023 an open letter by a collective of activists, writers and academics circulated online to protest the fatal shooting of Nahel Merzouk (a French young man of Moroccan and Algerian descent) in a traffic stop in Nanterre (Red Pepper 2023). Debates about race and Blackness are thus becoming increasingly visible in the public sphere.

Efforts to theorise the contemporary Black French experience have been led by Ndiaye, a historian who, from May 2022 to July 2023, was France's education minister following his role as director of the Musée national de l'histoire de l'immigration [National Museum of the History of Immigration].[10] In *La Condition noire* (2008) [The Black Condition], an anthropological study of the lived experiences of Black communities in Paris and Lille, Ndiaye defines being Black in France as being a minority, and this minority status transcends social class or other identity markers. This is a point Niang has also made forcefully when she argues that race and class are two different categories, and that race needs to be considered 'comme facteur discriminant, indépendamment de la réussite sociale des individus' (2020, 163) [as a discriminating factor, separately from the social success of individuals]. Ndiaye terms this minority status 'la condition noire' [the Black condition] because it emphasises the fact that Blackness is a social condition of inferiority affecting people over the long term; he is aware, however, of the problems associated with the term which presupposes erroneously that Black people constitute a homogeneous category (2008, 29). Indeed, in their introduction to a special issue of *African and Black Diaspora* in 2017, Célestine and Sarah Fila-Bakabadio argue that 'acknowledging the diversity of these populations is an important and primary step to any research on Blackness', and that the colonial history, migratory trajectory and citizenship status of different Black groups in France shapes the relationship of these communities with the French state apparatus (Célestine and Fila-Bakabadio 2017, 3). This has certainly been the case with many BUMIDOM participants and their descendants who have often been eager to distance themselves from African migrant communities. Even though they share a common Black ancestry, there has been little solidarity between these groups as BUMIDOM participants were eager to emphasise their Frenchness.

Ndiaye traces the development of the concept of race throughout the twentieth century. Until the mid-twentieth century, race was deemed a biological concept used to justify hierarchies between groups; indeed, biological racism was the principal intellectual pillar of Nazism. Following World War II, social scientists have sought to move away from conceiving of race as a biological concept, but of course race still exists as a form of social representation, and racism and racial discrimination are still rife in society (Ndiaye 2008, 30–1). For Ndiaye, race is a useful analytical tool, like other concepts such as gender and sexuality, but as an object in itself it does not exist; it is a socially constructed category. He warns of the problems of talking about race in a theoretical manner, namely that it could be adopted once again as an essentialising biological tool. His solution is to adopt a pragmatic approach and use terms such as 'racial' and 'racialised' rather than 'race' *tout court* in order to 'réfléchir sur les processus historiques par lesquels les "Noirs" sont devenus "noirs"' (Ndiaye 2008, 36) [reflect on the historical processes through which 'Black people' became 'Black'].

For Soumahoro, the question of race in France is a more personal affair. In *Le Triangle et l'Hexagone: réflexions sur une identité noire* (2020) [*Black is the Journey, Africana is the Name*], she offers an autobiographical account of her own research trajectory and explains how she has reached her understanding of what it means to be a Black French female citizen. The 'triangle' in the title evokes the geographical and historical connections between Europe, the Caribbean and Africa during the transatlantic trafficking of enslaved Africans in the sixteenth to eighteenth centuries, but this geographical space also has a personal resonance for Soumahoro because she has lived between Côte d'Ivoire, the United States and France. In fact, it is her mobility between these spaces which has enabled her to reclaim her Blackness. She explains that it was only when studying Black history and culture in the United States that she felt able to be proud of her Black identity and define her Blackness on her own terms: 'j'étais enfin devenue noire. De mon plein gré' (Soumahoro 2020, 84) [I had finally become Black. Of my own volition] (2021, 48). In France, in contrast, she was constantly asked to justify her existence and was subjected to racism. She is optimistic, however, about the recent work carried out by anti-racist organisations which will allow more people to choose their own definition of Blackness, like her (Soumahoro 2020, 146).

Soumahoro questions France's blindness towards race and racism, arguing that not considering racism to be a problem in France is to be entrenched within a system of privilege. This is an argument also taken up by Keaton in *#You Know You're Black in France When. . . The Fact of Everyday Antiblackness* (2023), a study of the daily microaggressions experienced by Black people in contemporary France. Keaton argues that it is the people who are 'racialized and politicized' as Black who are the 'targets of antiblack discrimination and racism that French raceblindness officially conceals in terms of race', while white French people have no reason to think about racism on a daily basis (2023, 2). In their 2022 manifesto *Universalisme* [Universalism], Julien Suaudeau and Niang take a more overtly political stance. They offer a critique of France's political model of republican universalism, in which the collective transcends individual differences like gender, nationality, religion or race to create a French nation which is one and indivisible. Created in 1789 at the time of the French Revolution, this was a system which was supposed to guarantee equality for all, but it was born out of colonisation, exploitation and enslavement, and so equality was not actually at its heart. The identity category of race is particularly contested. In fact, in 2018 the word 'race' was removed from the French Constitution, and so it is no longer illegal to discriminate on the basis of race; according to France's republican system, race does not exist and therefore should not be mentioned in any legal text (Le Monde and AFP 2018). For many people in France, this system is exclusionary and actually exacerbates the problems it is supposed to prevent.

Declaring that everyone is equal regardless of race is intended to avoid racial inequalities, but really it means denying that racism exists in France at all. Yet, as Sarah Mazouz explains, avoiding the term 'race' does not prevent racial discrimination from occurring, as other terms such as 'ethnie' [ethnicity] are used with the same intentions of racialising particular groups (2020, 57). Moreover, this racial discrimination has a long history in France which is tied to its colonial past, as Omar Slaouti and Olivier Le Cour Grandmaison observe (2020, 10). For Suaudeau and Niang, anti-racism and universalism are not mutually exclusive, and they advocate for a new form of universalism which is explicitly anti-racist in order to counter the ideology that to be French is to be white. They define current practices as 'pseudo-universalist' which do not defend the values of liberty, equality and fraternity, but rather seek to 'refouler l'histoire du colonialisme français, maîtriser le roman national et présenter le racisme comme un objet lointain, étranger, obsolète, sans aucune réalité ni actualité dans la France d'aujourd'hui' (2022, 38) [suppress the history of French colonialism, control the national narrative and present racism as a remote, foreign and obsolete object which is neither the reality nor the current situation of France today]. They advocate for what they term 'l'universalisme postcolonial et antiraciste' [postcolonial and anti-racist universalism] which 'appartient à tout le monde et à personne' [belongs to everyone and no one] so that all French people can feel included in France's political project and can make France a more just society (Suaudeau and Niang 2022, 62).

The cultural items I analyse throughout this book reveal very clearly the intersectional racialised and classist oppression of BUMIDOM participants and their descendants challenged by Ndiaye, Soumahoro, Suaudeau and Niang and others. They shine a spotlight on this particular instance of institutional racism, in which French citizens from Martinique and Guadeloupe were treated very differently from their metropolitan counterparts because of their class and race. These writers and artists are redefining what it means to be *both* Black *and* French.

Chapter Overview

BUMIDOM (1963–1982) and its Afterlives questions the extent to which cultural production, created both during the time of migration and today, is able to transmit memories of a shared past of migration between the Caribbean and Europe, in the absence of official, state-sanctioned projects of commemoration. Following an opening chapter which historicises the BUMIDOM and explains how the scheme worked in practice, the book then adopts a case-study approach to the cultural works. Items have been selected either for their explicit focus on the institutional nature of the BUMIDOM, or for their emphasis on how the Bureau impacted on their lives and those of their families. Each chapter offers a close reading of three or four works by different writers or filmmakers; this large corpus allows me to identify key trends about how items trigger personal and collective memories of migration. Of course, this corpus is not exhaustive and other items could well have been incorporated into the analysis. The works I have chosen seem to me to reveal the most about how the social and economic consequences of this migration policy play out on an individual and collective level. The items are grouped by genre to facilitate discussion of the ways in which memory is transmitted through and across genres and media. The genres speak to each other in different ways – the novels turn memoirs into fiction, which are then visualised through film, and text and image are brought together through *bande dessinée* and children's fiction, while music brings a sonic element to these memories. Bringing these different media and genres together enables me to trace a poetics of erasure of these difficult memories.

Chapter 1, 'A History of the BUMIDOM', draws on extensive archival research and existing historical analyses to expose the gendered and racialised nature of this migration scheme. The chapter asks why the Bureau was created, how recruitment operated and what the consequences of this organised migration policy were, both for populations living in mainland France and for those in the overseas departments. I argue that the gendered and racialised nature of migration organised by the BUMIDOM contradicted the French ideology of universalism. Moreover, I posit that the French government did not halt its use of migration as a form of population control when the BUMIDOM was closed down in 1982. In fact, the outward migration of young people to mainland France to work and study continues to be encouraged today, and the French government thus persists in positioning the Caribbean islands as 'peripheral' spaces in relation to the 'central' mainland of France.

Chapter 2, 'Gender, Work and Race in Caribbean Life Writing', examines the personal memories of those who emigrated to France through the Bureau. I argue that life writing is a means for BUMIDOM participants to share their own life story and use their personal memories to activate collective memories of emigration which have often been suppressed by participants for fear of stigmatisation. At the same time, they create an alternative history of the BUMIDOM which foregrounds the gendered and racialised lines on which the scheme operated. My corpus consists of Françoise Ega's *Lettres à une noire* (1978) [Letters to a Black Woman], Lucienne Dangreville-Bellemare's *Paroles de ma vie: de Fort-de-France Martinique à Saint-Denis (Seine Saint-Denis)* (2014) [The Story of My Life: From Fort-de-France Martinique to Saint-Denis, (Seine Saint-Denis)], Michèle Zabulon's *Parcours de vie d'une puéricultrice antillaise* (2017) [The Trajectory of an Antillean Childcare Worker] and Charlise Curier's *Mon aventure avec le BUMIDOM* (2019). Ega's text was written at the time of her migration from Martinique to mainland France, while the others were written much later; it is also the only one to have attracted any kind of critical attention. These texts offer different temporal and stylistic perspectives as the other three authors look back on their lives and write about their migration from a factual, almost sociological standpoint. My analysis is sensitive to these differences in time period and approach.

Chapter 3, 'National Identity, Diasporic Citizenship and Postdiaspora: The BUMIDOM in Fiction', investigates how novels transmit memories of non-belonging. It argues that the novels interrogate what a national French identity really means, how it intersects with regional Caribbean identity and how these identitarian models are complicated by (internal) migration. Engaging with Laguerre's concepts of diasporic citizenship and postdiaspora, I explore how the novels demonstrate the disparities between a Caribbean diasporic identity as desired by BUMIDOM participants and their descendants, and the migrant identity with which they were forced to negotiate on their arrival in France. In line with the overarching aims of this study, the chapter brings together well-known writers and texts with those yet to enter the French Caribbean literary canon in order to raise awareness of important but neglected manifestations of French Caribbean culture. The four texts I analyse are: Jacqueline Manicom's *Mon examen de blanc* (1972) [My Examination of Whiteness]; Maryse Condé's *Desirada* (1997) [*Desirada: A Novel*]; Fabienne Kanor's *D'eaux douces* (2004) [Freshwater]; and Estelle-Sarah Bulle's *Là où les chiens aboient par la queue* (2018) [*Where Dogs Bark with Their Tails: A Novel*]. Manicom's novel is the only one in the corpus to have been written during the BUMIDOM period itself; I thus consider how representations which were contemporaneous with large-scale Caribbean migration might differ to retrospective fictional accounts which operate in the realm of postmemory rather than history.

Chapter 4, 'Racism and Classism in Film and Television', analyses *Antilles-sur-Seine* (2000) [Antilles-on-the-Seine], directed by Pascal Légitimus; *Le Gang des Antillais* (2016) [*Gang of the Caribbean*], directed by Jean-Claude Barny; and *Le Rêve français* (2018) [*The French Dream*], directed by Christian Faure. These films differ in tone and genre, but they all reveal how BUMIDOM participants were promised a better life in mainland France and were sold an idealised version of the metropole, but were ultimately subjected to racial discrimination on an almost daily basis. The chapter interrogates the cinematic techniques adopted by the directors which enable the films to become vectors of memory about the racism and classism experienced by those who migrated through the BUMIDOM – whether that is through the use of documentary footage, voiceovers or flashbacks experienced by different characters. Chapter 4 thus approaches intersectionality – a term coined by Kimberlé Crenshaw in 1989 to refer to the study of multiple intersecting forms of discrimination – in a different way to Chapter 2. While Chapter 2 examines how the gendered oppression of female BUMIDOM participants is compounded by their race, Chapter 4 investigates how the intersections between race and class in the Caribbean context exacerbate inequalities faced by both men and women.

Chapter 5, 'Migration, Memory and Pedagogy in Graphic Novels and Children's Fiction', adopts a different approach to previous chapters and reflects on issues of education as well as commemoration. It explores the opportunities offered by graphic novels and children's fiction to teach young people about the BUMIDOM, and to facilitate reflection on how Caribbean communities interact with memories of migration in the present. I analyse the graphic novel *Peyi an nou* (2017) [Our Country] by Jessica Oublié and Marie-Ange Rousseau alongside the children's books *Maman-Dlo* (2014) [Maman Dlo] by Alex Godard and *Emil'Patt à Paris* (2018) [Emil'Patt in Paris] by Marie-Louise Danchet. I show how these works combine visual and textual material in innovative ways to offer factual detail about the BUMIDOM but also to allow young (and older) readers to reflect on overlaps and differences between history and memory.

The final chapter, 'Music as Memory: The Legacy of the BUMIDOM', interrogates the role of music in shaping the collective memory of the Antillean community. I argue that songs and music create a shared understanding of what the BUMIDOM was, how it was received at the time, and how it has impacted on Caribbean communities today on both sides of the Atlantic. The chapter takes both an ethnomusicological and a chronological approach, investigating how music has been used in different ways since the BUMIDOM was implemented in 1962. It considers how important musicians producing music during the BUMIDOM era, such as Guy Konket and Éric Cosaque, played with traditional gwoka music to critique the Bureau, while later bands such as Kassav' endeavoured to reconceptualise Antillean identity through the style of zouk. Finally, the chapter demonstrates how recent artists of Caribbean origin, including Soft, Delgres and Kalme La Fournaise, have memorialised Caribbean emigration through their music.

Overall, this study is about the state refusal to consider as French those Black Caribbean citizens who wish to be recognised as such, both in the 1960s and today. For the French state, the Blackness of this community obstructs their Frenchness. Cultural practitioners have had to engage with these issues because the state apparatus has been reluctant to do so, instead creating an environment in which individuals and communities have felt ashamed to discuss their experiences of emigration. The cultural works explored in this book are vanguard in the ways in which they offer a nuanced portrayal of emigration through the BUMIDOM and portray the intersectional forms of discrimination experienced by BUMIDOM participants. Above all, as this book will show, these cultural artefacts create a space in which key issues relating to memory formation and memory transmission can emerge.

Notes

1. All translations are my own unless otherwise noted. I have quoted from published English translations where available.
2. As H. Adlai Murdoch explains, Réunion 'provided over half the total' of arrivals (2020, 247).
3. During this period, 2015 children were forcibly removed from Réunion, which was deemed to be overpopulated. Some of these children were orphans but most were not; parents were forced to sign a document which gave responsibility of their child to the state, but illiteracy rates were high, and many did not understand what they were signing. The children were sent to different rural, underpopulated regions, but La Creuse received the largest number, hence the name 'Enfants de la Creuse'. Some children were adopted immediately; others were

housed in care homes; and others still found work on farms as unpaid labourers. In 2002, one of these children, Jean-Jacques Martial, took the French government to court and demanded one million euros in reparations for kidnapping and deportation. These claims were denied, however, because the action was judged to be legal at the time. In 2014, the French state acknowledged its moral responsibility in the deportation of Reunionese minors and a task force was set up to investigate the matter further, led by the sociologist Philippe Vitale. The final report, published in 2018, promised financial and psychological reparations to help people return to Réunion and find their families. Yet activists are still campaigning for France to apologise for its actions. Memorial work to commemorate this tragic case includes a bronze statue at Réunion's Roland-Garros Airport, inaugurated on 22 November 2013, and a small plaque at Paris-Orly Airport, unveiled on 17 February 2022, following campaigns by the Fédération des enfants déracinés des DROM (FEDD). These plaques, however, are placed in peripheral spaces, thus further marginalising this invisible population (Vergès 2017, 164). A conference was organised on this issue in November 2023 at Université Paris Nanterre. The FEDD held its own commemorative event in August 2023 in an agricultural college in Saint-Herblain, Loire Atlantique.

4. As Sarah Wood argues, from 1975 the French government attempted 'to reorientate these migrations back to and amongst the DOM' by sending people to French Guiana, in response to worsening social and economic conditions in mainland France (2015, 108). Only a handful of people from Martinique and Guadeloupe actually migrated to French Guiana through the BUMIDOM. The year 1977 saw the arrival of Hmong refugees, who were received in French Guiana with hostility.
5. Nicolas Rey offers an important anthropological study of Antilleans currently living in Paris and their entanglements with Antillean communities living in the Caribbean (2015).
6. Women from mainland France and the French Antilles were denied voting rights until 1944, meaning that full citizenship was withheld from women on both sides of the Atlantic.
7. Kristen Stromberg Childers explains that, in December 1947, when all metropolitan laws were supposed to be implemented in the new departments, the government passed a law allowing higher salaries for metropolitan civil servants than indigenous civil servants in Guadeloupe and Martinique. This triggered a wave of protests in the Caribbean departments (Childers 2016, 88).
8. They have also published a book with the same title. See Rokhaya Diallo and Grace Ly, *Kiffe ta race: explorer les questions raciales sans tabou* (2021).
9. Adama Traoré died on 19 July 2016 in police custody after being apprehended by the police. While the cause of his death has been contested, his sister claims that he died from excessive force used by police

officers to restrain him. Internal investigations have exonerated the officers involved, but Assa Traoré continues to fight for justice for her brother, organising large-scale protests through the organisation 'La Vérité pour Adama' [Truth for Adama].

10. There was considerable backlash against Ndiaye's appointment because of his stance towards race and republicanism, particularly among far-right politicians. Marine Le Pen is quoted in an article in *Le Monde*, published on 20 May 2022, as deploring his appointment as 'la dernière pierre de la déconstruction de notre pays, de ses valeurs et de son avenir' (Service politique 2022) [the last straw in the deconstruction of our country, its values and its culture].

Chapter 1

A History of the BUMIDOM

In the post-war economic boom, France was in urgent need of a strong workforce to rebuild its infrastructure. First employing labourers from the neighbouring European countries of Italy, Spain and Portugal, France was unable to compete with more attractive working conditions in Germany and Switzerland. It was thus forced to turn to its former colonies in the Maghreb, Sub-Saharan Africa and the Caribbean. These workers provided cheaper labour than European workers and enabled France to become a modern, industrialised nation. At the same time, migration was seen as a solution to the demographic and economic issues that afflicted the four overseas departments in the 1950s and 60s, which were suffering from overpopulation and economic decline. What is particularly striking about the BUMIDOM programme, which was in operation between April 1963 and June 1982, is its institutional nature. Through this scheme the French government was able to select participants and orient them towards training programmes or jobs in specific sectors, according to their gender or race. Migration through the Bureau was thus a form of population control for the French government. Of course, though, not everyone who emigrated to mainland France during this period did so via the BUMIDOM. Approximately the same number migrated on their own, although they often sought the services of the Bureau for financial and administrative assistance on their arrival, even if they had not left through the auspices of the BUMIDOM (Condon 2020, 125).

This transatlantic migration was made possible thanks to the departmentalisation law which was passed in March 1946, a law which converted these former colonies into French overseas departments. Remarkably, as H. Adlai Murdoch observes, this 'was the only occasion in European colonial history where former colonies were integrated into the political structure of the colonial power that had dominated and literally possessed them for over three hundred years' (2008, 16). In theory, departmentalisation meant that citizens in these locations had the same rights and responsibilities as those living in mainland France, including being able to move freely within the extended borders of France's global territory. Strictly speaking, then, people arriving from Guadeloupe, Martinique and Réunion were not immigrants, because they were undergoing an internal movement from one French department to another, rather than crossing national borders. However, as this chapter will argue, many BUMIDOM participants were treated as migrants; they were subjected to racial discrimination and were given low-paid jobs that the metropolitan, white population refused to do. Their treatment thus mirrors that of other migrant groups arriving in France during this period, such as Algerian workers, who were often employed in low-skilled jobs despite their qualification level and lived in precarious housing in shanty towns on the edge of the city (Cohen 2017). Murdoch argues that there lies a stark contradiction between the republican discourse of equality and the realities of departmentalisation, which in fact reinforced the centre–periphery relationship between France and its former colonies. It was 'the persistent, pervasive and pellucid ineluctability of such social inequities that led to departmentalisation's greatest demographic and cultural influence on the metropole': that is, the large-scale arrival of people from France's overseas departments (Murdoch 2008, 18–19).

The institutional aspect of these transoceanic migration flows means that migration patterns from the French Caribbean differ somewhat from migration from the anglophone, hispanophone and Dutch Caribbean to Europe during the same period. While migration from former British, Spanish and Dutch colonies to their European centres of power did take the form of labour migration, people from these locations often made an individual decision to migrate to find work, and did not participate in an organised migration scheme, as was the case in the French context. Examining the migration of the Windrush generation to Britain in the 1950s and 60s, Kennetta Hammond Perry defines this flow as 'an unprecedented movement of choice by self-selected individuals' (2015, 59). People migrating from the former Spanish territories of Cuba and the Dominican Republic to Spain also made a personal choice to leave for better employment opportunities. Meanwhile, migration from the Dutch Caribbean colonies of Aruba, Curaçao and Suriname to the Netherlands was more strongly tied to political factors, and emigration peaked in the late 1970s, in anticipation of the independence of Suriname (Peach 1991).

Yet the BUMIDOM does find an echo in another organised migration scheme from the Caribbean, not to Europe but to the United States, in the case of Puerto Rico. In fact, as Ramón Grosfoguel, Margarita Cervantes-Rodríguez and Eric Mielants explain, 'Puerto Ricans were among the first colonial groups to be massively recruited to work in the manufacturing and agrarian enterprises of the US Northeast' immediately after World War II, and recruitment was organised by the Migration Division, an apparatus within the colonial administration on Puerto Rico (2009, 5). In addition, a number of other, large-scale international migration schemes were implemented during the 1980s and 90s, after the BUMIDOM had ceased operating, such as the mass recruitment of African and Asian workers to the Gulf countries to work in the oil industry (Castles 2000, 274). In order to better understand the causes and consequences of post-war labour migration from the Caribbean, the BUMIDOM should not be analysed in isolation but within this global context of transnational migration and labour histories in the twentieth and twenty-first centuries. Yet this chapter also reveals the specificity of the BUMIDOM scheme, in which the French government actively intervened in the lives of its own citizens who were still part of the French nation but living beyond the Hexagon in the overseas departments.

In this chapter I analyse the causes and consequences of this organised migration policy on communities living on both sides of the Atlantic. I argue that this labour migration was highly racialised and gendered, and thus suggest that the BUMIDOM should be considered as part of a longer history of migration to France from the former colonies, in which the ethnic origins, racial groupings and gender categorisation of people arriving in France determined the ways in which they were received by the white French community. In addition, I argue that migration continued to be used as a form of population control even when the BUMIDOM was closed down in 1982. In fact, the government is still encouraging young people to leave the islands today through the office of L'Agence de l'Outre-mer pour la mobilité (LADOM) [Overseas Agency for Mobility], created in 2006. This scheme reinforces inequalities between the 'peripheral' Caribbean islands and the 'central' mainland of France and creates complex demographic issues on the islands, such as an ageing population. These demographic problems are a direct legacy of governmental migratory and developmental policies in place in the mid-twentieth century, and thus evidence of the pervasive nature of colonial narratives and attitudes at the heart of contemporary French political structures.

The chapter draws on original archival research as well as historical analysis from secondary sources. Most of the BUMIDOM files are now housed in the Archives nationales de France in Pierrefitte-sur-Seine, although specific files relating to individual departments can be found in their departmental or territorial archives. This means that it is relatively difficult to trace the contents of the files because the collection is spread over a large geographical area. Added to this, it must be remembered that the files have been deposited by different governmental bodies – the Ministère de l'Equipement [the Ministry for Infrastructure], the Ministère d'Outre-mer [the Overseas Ministry], the Ministère de l'Intérieur [the Ministry for Home Affairs], the Ministère des Affaires sociales [the Ministry for Social Affairs], the Ministère des Transports [the Ministry for Transport] and the Ministère de Postes et Télécommunication [the Ministry of Postal and Telecommunication Services] all held files relating to different aspects of the BUMIDOM's operations – and these institutions followed different procedures regarding the ways in which they stored and recorded information.[1] These files mostly contain reports and policy documents written by BUMIDOM officials, but they also contain newspaper articles and letters written to administrators asking for financial and administrative assistance. I also consulted a selection of the personal files of BUMIDOM participants, for which special permission was necessary because these files contain the personal details and medical records of people from less than fifty years ago.[2] These collections are part of French governmental archives, and so they have been selected and preserved by the French state. Achille Mbembe reminds us that the archive is 'not a piece of data, but a status', a site of power which reflects the interests of those who have created it (2002, 20). The records pertaining to the BUMIDOM must therefore be understood as a repository of state authority and power, as these records have shaped our understanding of the BUMIDOM today.[3]

Before the BUMIDOM: Early Migration to Mainland France

There is a long history of migration from the French Caribbean to mainland France which began much earlier than the creation of the BUMIDOM in 1963. While the numbers of people migrating increased rapidly from the turn of the twentieth century, even from the early 1800s there was a growing Black community living in the Hexagon, formed through emigration from the Caribbean and Sub-Saharan African colonies. This migration cannot be separated from France's 'coloniality of power', a concept coined by Aníbal Quijano which reveals how national and global structures of power remain embedded within colonial networks spanning centuries (2000). People arriving in France, like those migrating to any colonial metropolis, did not arrive 'in an empty or geopolitically neutral space' because the metropole is 'always "polluted" by colonial history – that is, a colonial imaginary, colonial knowledges, a racial/ethnic hierarchy linked to a history of dominance and subordination in the interstate system that can be traced directly to empire building and colonial relations' (Grosfoguel, Cervantes-Rodríguez and Mielants 2009, 8). Regardless of the period in which they arrived in France, whether in the colonial era or once France had formally dismantled its colonial structures following decolonisation, migrants arrived in a 'space of power relations that [was] always already informed and constituted by coloniality' (Grosfoguel, Cervantes-Rodríguez and Mielants 2009, 8).

As we have seen, early important dates in the history of Caribbean migration include 1833, when full French citizenship was granted to free people of colour, and 1848, when slavery was abolished for the second and final time in the French colonies. Abolition gave a new legal and social status to the formerly enslaved who, from then on, acquired the status of freemen and freewomen. This meant that, in theory, they could travel freely across the French empire, just like metropolitan French citizens could do, provided they had sufficient means to do so and a place of residency. However, as Marion Pluskota argues, in reality this new status changed very little for the formerly enslaved who often lacked the financial means to emigrate (2020, 105). Another crucial moment in the development of a Caribbean diaspora in France was the outbreak of World War I. Soldiers were conscripted from France's four 'vieilles colonies' [old colonies] of Martinique, Guadeloupe, Réunion and French Guiana to fight for France, after the 1905 conscription law was extended to the colonies on 7 August 1913. Many soldiers remained on the mainland following their conscription. David Murphy views World War I as a turning point in the emergence of a Black France, in which people from the Caribbean and West African colonies were eager to demonstrate their loyalty towards the French 'motherland', but at the same time, 'the conflict also sowed the seeds of a radical anti-colonialism that would eventually gain momentum in the aftermath of the second world conflict' (Murphy 2015, 240). For instance, it was after World War I that popular Black political movements were created in working-class communities across France, such as the Comité de défense de la race nègre [Committee for the Defence of the Black Race] in 1926, which sought to dismantle the French Empire.

Emigration from Martinique and Guadeloupe continued during the interwar years, yet what sets early migration during this period apart from later mass migration in the 1960s and 70s, in addition to the numbers, is the demographics of those migrating to France. The interwar years saw the arrival of middle-class students, intellectuals, writers and artists who, for the most part, settled in Paris. The best known of these migrants were Martinican Aimé Césaire, Senegalese Léopold Sédar Senghor and Guianese Léon-Gontran Damas. Black African Americans were also attracted to Paris because, as Tyler Stovall explains, they perceived 'the French as a people without colour prejudice, in stark contrast to white Americans', and given 'the interwar taste for exoticism and black culture, plus the popularity of jazz', Paris became the heart of the European Black artistic and musical community (Stovall 2009, 185). It was mostly men from the middle classes who emigrated during this period, although some women did make the journey across the Atlantic, too, and in fact, in recent years, there has been an increasing amount of academic scholarship which seeks to foreground the voices of pioneering Black women who made important artistic, cultural, political and social contributions to metropolitan life in the interwar years.[4] Black feminist figures were crucial in creating a space of resistance against patriarchal, capitalist, colonial and racist frameworks of power, and the Nardal sisters from Martinique were at the forefront of this movement. Jane and Paulette Nardal gathered together African Americans, Sub-Saharan Africans and Antilleans in their salon in the Parisian suburbs of Clamart. There they laid the theoretical and philosophical groundings of Négritude, the anticolonial cultural and political movement which sought to create a universal notion of Black experience, and which was later taken up by Césaire, Senghor, Damas and others. The contributions made by the Nardal sisters in the creation of a race consciousness are beginning to be officially recognised in France, through a variety of memorialisation practices. For example, on 31 August 2019, the Promenade Jean-et-Paulette-Nardal was inaugurated in the 14th arrondissement of Paris, and since then, the Mayor of Paris Anne Hidalgo has been campaigning for Paulette Nardal to be buried in the Panthéon (Marchal 2021).[5] Through these official practices of commemoration, the Nardal sisters are finally becoming part of the built environment of the city into which they breathed so much life.

This spontaneous migration from the overseas departments continued in the post-war period, but, unlike in previous years, this movement was mainly a form of labour immigration. The islands were experiencing high levels of unemployment, and therefore blue-collar workers looked to mainland France to find jobs in industry. While, during the 1950s, an increasing number of (male) students emigrated from the overseas departments to further their studies – higher-education institutions did not really exist on the islands until the mid-1960s, and both the Université des Antilles et de la Guyane and the Université de la Réunion were not created until 1982 – it was mostly people from the lower social classes who arrived in the Hexagon during this time. Stephanie Condon explains that during the 1950s, before migration from the overseas departments was institutionalised through formal schemes, individual administrative bodies such as the police force and customs targeted workers from the overseas departments; they had few formal qualifications and therefore would be a cheaper workforce (Condon 2020, 122). In addition, Caribbean and Reunionese workers were recruited directly by private companies in the automobile industry, such as Michelin and Renault. In 1960, military service was re-established in the Caribbean, after being abandoned since its initial implementation in 1913 because of budget cuts, and approximately half the contingent of conscripts were sent to mainland France. Condon sees military service as 'une nouvelle voie d'émigration durable' [a new route of sustainable emigration] which was motivated by political factors – it would remove young men from the islands where they were at risk of participating in anticolonial and independentist movements such as the Organisation de la jeunesse anticolonialiste de la Martinique (OJAM) [Anticolonial Youth Organisation of Martinique] and the Groupe d'organisation nationale de la Guadeloupe (GONG) [National Organisation Group of Guadeloupe] (Condon 2020, 122).

By the time the BUMIDOM was created in 1963, then, there had already been state-organised channels of migration in the form of military emigration, although the numbers emigrating through this conduit were nothing like those that would migrate through the BUMIDOM. In fact, France had been involved in labour networks since the early twentieth century and had signed agreements with Italy in 1904 and 1906, Belgium in 1906, Poland in 1919 and Czechoslovakia in 1920 to allow immigrant workers to come to France (Célestine 2011, 133). However, there are clear ideological and racial differences between these early immigration projects and the BUMIDOM. These early migration schemes were composed of white European immigrant workers, who were seen to assimilate much more easily into French society because they shared a common racial and cultural heritage with white citizens from metropolitan France.

In contrast, state-controlled migration from the Caribbean and Réunion involved people of colour who were not deemed to integrate well into metropolitan society. In fact, Caribbean and Reunionese people were initially kept in the periphery, away from the mainland, to discourage racial mixing. From as early as the 1950s, the French government was acutely aware of the economic and demographic issues afflicting the overseas departments, and therefore, by a decree passed on 29 April 1950, the Bureau pour le développement de la production agricole (BDPA) [Bureau for the Development of Agricultural Production] was created. The Bureau specifically targeted Reunionese farming families and sought to create a new agricultural settlement in a location in need of development while simultaneously reducing the population of Réunion. The government thus considered migration an effective tool of population control, having already implemented other methods to try to lower the birth rate, which, by 1959, was as high as 42 per cent (BDPA 1961, 1). Françoise Vergès deplores earlier methods, such as the compulsory use of contraception and forced abortions, as forms of racial violence stemming from slavery and colonisation (2017). Following an initial scoping expedition in 1951, Madagascar was selected to host these new arrivals since it had already been a site of emigration for Reunionese people in previous decades, and a new settlement was created in Sakay in the central region of Madagascar. It was named Babetville in tribute to Raphaël Babet, the Reunionese *député* who conceived of the scheme. Work on the settlement began in July 1952, and by August fifteen Reunionese families had been given a plot of land. By 1955, the numbers increased to a hundred families. The authorities envisaged this agricultural programme as 'un premier pas vers la recherche de l'émigration' [a first step towards the search for emigration] (BDPA 1961, 9), but they were also fully aware that 'l'installation à Madagascar de 100 familles d'agriculteurs par an [. . .] ne pouvait pas résoudre les graves problèmes par la surpopulation de l'Île Bourbon' [the settlement of 100 farming families in Madagascar per year [. . .] could not solve the serious problems regarding the overpopulation of Île Bourbon] (BDPA 1961, 10). Archival records show the type of migrant targeted by the scheme: migrants had to be younger than thirty-five and married, with experience in the agricultural sector and 'être reconnnu de bonne moralité et travailleur' [be known to be of good character and hardworking] (BDPA 1952, 1). The scheme was highly institutionalised and regulated, and migrants had to sign a contract before they were allowed to leave. Their travel to Madagascar was financed by the Bureau, and on their arrival in Babetville they had to undergo a year-long training on the settlement; if this training were successful, they could apply for a loan from Crédit Agricole in order to buy the farm themselves (BDPA 1961, 4). Social infrastructure was created to facilitate their integration, such as schools and health care facilities, and sports teams were also set up. While the men received training in agricultural matters, women were taught how to run a household and raise their children. The paternalistic, colonial attitude of the French bureaucrats is highly visible from the BDPA reports, as they treated the Reunionese women as helpless individuals who needed to be rescued by the French state and be taught domestic and family values:

> le BDPA s'efforce actuellement de donner aux mères, et surtout aux futures mères de famille, des connaissances ménagères indispensables. Des religieuses Trinitaires établies à Babetville s'efforcent de leur inculquer quelques notions importantes sur l'entretien d'une maison, la préparation d'un repas, la couture et la façon d'élever un enfant. (BDPA 1961, 30)
>
> [the BDPA currently strives to provide mothers, and especially future mothers, with essential domestic knowledge. The Trinitarian Sisters established in Babetville strive to instill in them some basic knowledge about maintaining a house, preparing meals, sewing and raising a child.]

This agricultural migration scheme continued concurrently with the BUMIDOM once the latter was established in 1963, but far fewer people were sent to Madagascar than mainland France. The settlement at Sakay continued to expand until 1977, when Madagascan President Didier Ratsiraka demanded that it be shut down because it contradicted the nationalist programme he was promoting. The Reunionese migrants were thus violently expelled by the Madagascan government. The older generations returned to Réunion while younger families settled in France. A small number, however, created a new farming settlement on the banks of the Guianese river Carapa, fifteen miles north-west of Cayenne. In this instance, it was the Reunionese migrants themselves who created these transcolonial connections between the 'peripheral' spaces of the French territory. Meanwhile, Antillean families were encouraged to migrate to French Guiana, which was sparsely populated at the time, through the Bureau intéressant les personnes immigrées en Guyane (BIPIG) [Bureau for People Immigrating to Guiana], also established in 1950. Initially created to provide jobs for refugees from Western Europe after the war, the BIPIG actively encouraged Martinicans and Guadeloupeans to settle in the village of Saint-Jean-du-Maroni, and gradually the village became a small commercial centre (Milia-Marie-Luce 1997, 148). Yet a lack of infrastructure in French Guiana soon made this scheme unfeasible. In August 1960, a branch was created within the BDPA to investigate the possibility of sending Antilleans either to mainland France or to New Caledonia (BDPA 1961, 11). Although these two labour migration projects operated on a very small scale, they were France's first institutional attempts at organising the emigration of its Antillean and Reunionese citizens, and therefore instrumental in laying the foundations for large-scale migration to France during the 1960s and 70s. The migratory experiment of the Sakay has attracted increasing attention in the Reunionese cultural imaginary in recent years, as writers and filmmakers have sought to bring this hidden history of transcolonial migration to light. For instance, in 2012, the French actor and film director Luc Bongrand produced a series of two documentaries about the Sakay under the collective title *Les Larmes de la Rivière Piment* [Tears of the Piment River], while, in 2017, Olivette Taombé created the documentary *De la Sakay à la Carapa* [From Sakay to Carapa], which combines interviews with Reunionese settlers in French Guiana with archival footage to explain how this migration programme worked. In addition, the French writer and playwright Emmanuel Genvrin published *Rock Sakay* [Sakay Rock] in 2016, a novel which centres on the love story of two characters who met at the settlement in Sakay. These films and texts denounce the colonial framework within which this institutionalised labour migration scheme operated, a framework which, as the following section will show, also undergirded the BUMIDOM.

The BUMIDOM: A Colonial Project

Why did the French government actively facilitate mass migration from Guadeloupe, Martinique and Réunion, and why was mainland France chosen as the receiving location, when previous iterations of this scheme had privileged sending migrants to the overseas departments? There are numerous intersecting political, economic and demographic reasons. The post-war period saw the overseas departments face considerable economic hardship, caused by rising birth rates and unemployment rates which put pressure on resources on the islands. Although Alain Anselin refutes the claim that population growth in the French Caribbean was becoming uncontrollable – he notes that in Martinique, the birth rate actually declined by 8 per cent between 1954 and 1968 (1979, 77) – the population was certainly growing at a much faster rate than in mainland France, and the economy was unable to support this demographic shift. The collapse of the sugar cane industry, on which the islands were almost exclusively dependent, further accentuated economic decline. An improvement in production methods and a greater reliance on modern and efficient machinery on the sugar plantations meant that fewer workers needed to be employed in this sector. Yet the islands had not sufficiently diversified their economy, and so people soon found themselves out of work. They lacked the training and qualifications to create professional opportunities for themselves, and so were left without prospects or any possibility for social advancement.

Meanwhile, mainland France needed a strong workforce to rebuild infrastructure which had been damaged or destroyed during World War II, and recruiting workers from former colonies which were now overseas departments provided them with cheap labour. It was also much easier for France to recruit Martinican, Guadeloupean and Reunionese citizens than foreign workers because they were French, and therefore they did not require administrative assistance or legal permission to work in France. The economic growth of France during the 'trente glorieuses' – the post-war boom of 1945–75 – could only take place because of its colonial frameworks which were beginning to be dismantled during this period. It was, in fact, thanks to the violent, 'dirty' business of decolonisation and the subsequent arrival of postcolonial migrants in France that the country was able to modernise and industrialise, as Kristin Ross points out in *Fast Cars, Clean Bodies* (1995). Ross connects narratives of modernisation to discourses surrounding Americanisation and argues that France could never have become a modern nation without support from its (former) colonies:

> without the labour of its ex-colonial immigrants, France could not have successfully 'Americanised', nor competed in the post-war industrial contest. In the economic boom years, in other words,

> France made use of the colonies 'one last time' in order to resurrect and maintain its national superiority over them – a superiority made all the more urgent by the ex-colonies' own newly acquired nationhood. (Ross 1995, 9)

The BUMIDOM project is thus not only an important example of institutionalised migration, but also a crucial marker of France's failed decoloniality. It demonstrates 'the various ways in which the practice of colonialism outlived its history', as Ross explains (1995, 7). By the 1960s, France no longer had a formal empire through which it could assert its authority and superiority, but it continued to dominate and control its former territories in less overt but similarly nefarious ways. In this instance, the government actively intervened in the lives of Caribbean and Reunionese peoples, organising large-scale migration from the islands for France's economic benefit. Interestingly, debates surrounding economic growth and decolonisation resurfaced among academics in France following the death of former president Valéry Giscard d'Estaing in December 2020, as France's role in the decolonisation of its former imperial territories became eclipsed by a public nostalgia for the 'good old times' of economic growth that occurred during Giscard d'Estaing's presidency. Julien Suaudeau reminds us that this narrative of France as an economic powerhouse and a contented, united nation is 'eurocentrique et ethno-centré' [Eurocentric and ethnocentric] which 'ne fixe que la version présentable de l'histoire de la France' [only emphasises the presentable version of France's history] and ignores France's role in the brutal wars of decolonisation which were waged during this period (Suaudeau 2020). Suaudeau warns against this dangerous discourse which 'devient une chanson de geste à la gloire du Centre' [becomes an epic poem about the glory of the Centre] and completely disregards the contributions of France's postcolonial citizens, who arrived in France precisely because of the French project of colonisation, exploitation and domination which had begun centuries earlier (Suaudeau 2020).

Governmental officials thus saw the BUMIDOM as a solution to the serious demographic and economic problems that were afflicting both the islands and mainland France. However, many people living on the islands believed that the BUMIDOM was actually created for political motives: it would remove young, politically active people from the islands, thus avoiding the threat of demands for independence. Guadeloupeans and Martinicans were become increasingly disillusioned with departmentalisation which had not granted them the equality it had promised, and so political activism was increasing, particularly among the youth. Kristen Stromberg Childers explains that frustration against departmentalisation was felt even as early as March 1946, when it became clear that policies concerning salary scales and personnel were always designed to favour metropolitan white French citizens (Childers 2016, 86–8). This disillusionment resulted in a series of important strikes in 1948, 1950 and 1953, which were, at times, violently put down. In March 1948, for instance, a policeman fired on workers at Le Carbet in Guadeloupe who were striking against a law passed in December 1947 guaranteeing higher salaries for metropolitan civil servants, and three people were killed; these protests 'signalled the resentment over lingering inequalities' which the Antilleans felt were based on their racial difference (Childers 2016, 89). Although metropolitan administrators were aware of the spiralling economic costs that governing these islands entailed, at the same time they were eager to retain control of them. France had already lost many of its colonies in Africa and Asia by 1960, and it was waging a long and bloody war to maintain control over Algeria. Losing possession of its Caribbean colonies would cause even greater damage to French prestige.

Of course, the official BUMIDOM records do not emphasise the underlying political reasons for the creation of the Bureau. In fact, officials took great pains to focus instead on the economic and demographic advantages that mass migration would bring to inhabitants of the islands. In a report evaluating French migratory policies dated 28 November 1978, officials described the project as one which would contribute 'à la solution des problèmes démographiques intéressant les DOM [. . .] en favorisant l'implantation en métropole de travailleurs volontaires et de leurs familles, dans une perspective de promotion sociale' (BUMIDOM 1978, 1) [to solving the demographic problems faced by the overseas departments [. . .] by promoting the settlement of voluntary workers and their families in mainland France, with a view to social advancement]. This notion of migration as a means for social advancement was far from the case for many migrants who often found themselves in more precarious employment and worse living conditions than they had done on the islands, and the following section of this chapter explores further the slippage between the official rhetoric of the BUMIDOM and the harsh reality faced by many migrants. The lived experience of Antillean and Reunionese migrants reveals that political factors were at the heart of the government's decision to create this migration scheme. These political motives were denounced by Antillean and Reunionese trade unions and organisations, such as the Union générale des travailleurs réunionnais en France [General Union of Reunionese Workers in France]. Taken to court by the BUMIDOM in March 1974 for defamation, following the highly critical newspaper article 'Frapper plus fort le BUMIDOM' [Hit Out Harder against the BUMIDOM] in its newspaper *Combat Réunionnais* [Reunionese Struggle], the union produced an information booklet in the weeks leading up to the court case to explain its position on the Bureau. In this booklet, the authors outline what they consider to be the 'vrais mobiles' [true motives] of this migratory policy, drawing on a speech made by the Prefect of Réunion on 17 May 1961: 'il s'agit de désamorcer les situations révolutionnaires que les conditions socio-économiques imposées rendent plus que probables' (Union générale des travailleurs réunionnais en France 1974, 2) [the purpose is to diffuse the revolutionary situation which the imposed socio-economic conditions make all the more likely]. They trace the high levels of unemployment and economic precarity on the islands directly back to French colonisation, criticising the fact that the government refused to diversify the economy which made economic decline inevitable following the demise of the sugar industry, and in fact made low-paid workers buy back the goods they produced at exorbitant prices. The report condemns this exploitative system designed to maintain the hierarchy between former coloniser and colonised, claiming that 'l'impérialisme français est gagnant sur toute la ligne' (Union générale des travailleurs réunionnais en France 1974, 5) [French imperialism wins in every way]. Very much aware of the colonial structures at play in the BUMIDOM operations, these resistance groups protested against the Bureau and called for a dismantling of these hierarchical networks of power (to which I shall return at the end of this chapter). They had to wait until a change of government in 1982, however, for the BUMIDOM to be closed down.

The Operations of the BUMIDOM

As we have seen, the BUMIDOM was implemented in an endeavour to solve the economic, social and demographic issues afflicting France's overseas departments in the Caribbean and the Indian Ocean in the 1950s and 60s. Yet France was not the only European country to be faced with problems regarding its migrant population; Great Britain was too, although it reacted quite differently at this time. Given that the large-scale migration from the anglophone Caribbean had begun earlier than in the French context (in the late 1940s), by the beginning of the 1960s the number of non-white British and Commonwealth citizens migrating to Britain was rapidly increasing. By June 1960, the non-white population was 250,000 people (Patel 2021, 75). Afraid that racial riots would break out, Britain chose to restrict immigration at the same time as France encouraged it in order to defuse its own 'latent social crisis' (Pattieu 2017, 12). In 1962, as the French government was preparing to formalise migration from the overseas departments and increase the numbers of people arriving in France, Britain passed the Commonwealth Immigrants Act which curtailed the free movement of citizens of Commonwealth countries and British colonies by limiting migration to specific categories of workers or dependants.[6] Of course, the constitutional situations of the anglophone and francophone Caribbean islands are not entirely comparable. France was encouraging migration from its overseas departments which, constitutionally, were and remain an integral part of the French Republic. In contrast, Britain was limiting immigration from the Caribbean at a time when these islands were becoming independent nations, which meant that they could enact their own citizenship laws. However, despite these constitutional differences, it is helpful to analyse the BUMIDOM alongside other large-scale movements from the Caribbean to Europe because it demonstrates differing attitudes towards citizens of colour. Faced with the growing resistance of its Black Caribbean citizens, the French government decided to move them to the mainland to curb resistance from within, whereas the British government preferred to send those deemed to be problematic citizens back to the Caribbean. In both cases, what becomes clear is a desire on the part of European governments to regulate and control its Black citizens.

In the French context, this migration control was legalised on 23 April 1963 when Michel Debré (former French prime minister and *député* of Réunion at the time) passed the decree to formally establish the BUMIDOM. However, organised emigration from Martinique, Guadeloupe and Réunion to mainland France had begun from as early as 1961. In fact, archival records from the BDPA reveal that the French government was seriously considering the possibility of sending Reunionese workers to France from the late 1950s. During this early iteration of the BUMIDOM scheme, unqualified labourers in the agricultural and domestic service sectors were targeted so that the Bureau would not have to invest too heavily in local training. A report produced by the BDPA office on 27 March 1961 reads: 'le programme suggéré pour 1961–1962 se bornera donc à amorcer le mouvement de migration vers la métropole, en proposant le placement d'une main-d'œuvre non qualifiée ou de personnel (domestique, par exemple) pouvant recevoir localement un minimum de formation' (BDPA 1961, 14) [the program suggested for 1961–1962 will therefore be limited to initiating the movement of migration to the metropole, by proposing the placement of unskilled labour or personnel (domestic workers, for example) who can receive minimal local training]. As this report makes clear, this early migration to mainland France was certainly not about offering social advancement or better professional opportunities and training to French citizens from the overseas departments. Rather, it was a means to provide an unskilled, under-qualified and low-paid workforce to sectors which needed bolstering, such as domestic service and the transportation sector. Throughout its eighteen-year period of operation, however, there was a development in its policies, as administrators began to realise the need to provide some level of training for migrants to enable them to carry out the required work as efficiently as possible. For instance, a report written in 1978 by the director of the Comité d'action sociale en faveur des originaires des Outre-mer en Métropole (CASODOM) [Committee of Social Action in Favour of People from the Overseas Departments in the Metropole], a sister organisation to the BUMIDOM created in 1956 to help migrants settled in mainland France, stated that the BUMIDOM needed to 'faire en sorte que tous les candidats au départ reçoivent une formation professionnelle en rapport avec la demande métropolitaine' (CASODOM 1978, 15) [make sure that all candidates for emigration receive professional training which is in line with metropolitan demand]. The following year the organisation noted an improvement in the training received by migrants before their arrival.

There were three principal routes through which people could migrate to mainland France under the auspices of the BUMIDOM. They could either be recruited directly to a particular company, be admitted to a training programme or join their family through the family reunification scheme. This final route has not been given much attention in academic scholarship even though, as Jennifer Bidet explains, family reunification was conceived as a cornerstone of the BUMIDOM project from its very inception, because officials believed that it would be easier for migrants to integrate into metropolitan life if they had their families with them (2023). In order to apply for financial and administrative assistance to migrate through the three channels, prospective migrants had to visit the BUMIDOM offices which were set up in Fort-de-France, Pointe-à-Pitre, Basse-Terre and

Saint-Denis. As part of their application, they had to sit maths and dictation tests and were then investigated by a social worker who would evaluate their employment history, their qualifications, their level of French, their family life and their moral values to verify that they would integrate relatively easily into life in mainland France. For example, M., who left for France from Guadeloupe on 9 July 1967, was applying to work as a mechanic; his skillset and employment history were deemed to be suitable for this job, and given that he was from a 'famille de gens honnêtes' [family of respectable people] and was of 'bonne conduite' [good behaviour], his migration was approved (BUMIDOM 1967).[7] This was not always the case, however. Some applications were rejected because young women, who were planning to travel on their own, had nobody to look after their children. In July 1967, for instance, J. was told to find a more suitable guardian for her children than a young woman who already had five of her own (BUMIDOM 1967). Other applicants failed the medical examination, often because they were underweight or suffered from a serious medical condition. A letter sent to the Martinican O. from Jean-Émile Vié (president of the BUMIDOM at the time) explained that his dossier was rejected because he suffered from 'une insuffisance pondérale importante' (BUMIDOM 1974) [being considerably underweight]. The selection process employed by the BUMIDOM administrators is problematic, given that the people it was turning down for assistance were French citizens who did not need to prove that they were good, 'moral' citizens in order to be able to move to the mainland. Their French citizenship failed to guarantee them with the rights to fully belong to France.

These personal dossiers also show that, in theory, prospective migrants knew to which sectors they were applying to work and the conditions of their journey to mainland France. Once their applications had been approved, they had to sign a form of contract with the BUMIDOM that specified that only their single journey would be paid for; this contract also gave the BUMIDOM the right to be reimbursed if the applicant refused or lost the job offered to them, or if they rejected a professional offer on three subsequent occasions (BUMIDOM 1967). This evidence contrasts with contemporary accounts of experiences of migration through the Bureau among people I interviewed in Guadeloupe and Martinique in October 2022.[8] Charlise left Guadeloupe for Marseille in 1971 hoping for a better life; she returned to Guadeloupe with her two teenage children in 1985 following the breakdown of her second marriage.[9] She explicitly denounces the BUMIDOM for the lack of information it provided about the jobs they would be doing and for offering them false promises: 'nous étions naïves. On nous faisait croire des choses' (Charlise 2022) [we were naive. They made us believe things]. It must be remembered that the interviewees were drawing on their memories of events which occurred over fifty or sixty years ago, and so their recollections of specific events may not be entirely accurate. This is not to say that interviewees such as Charlise were lying about their experiences, however. Such comments make us question how much the BUMIDOM officials explained to prospective migrants the legal consequences of signing this contract, and even whether it was actually signed by the migrants themselves. Illiteracy rates were high on the islands at the time – 25 per cent in Martinique and 33 per cent in Guadeloupe for people over fifteen years old in 1954 (Malignac 1967, 114) – and one can thus wonder whether prospective migrants really understood the document, especially as it was written in complex, bureaucratic language.

Once participants' cases were approved, they were given a 'bon de transport' [transport voucher] to travel to mainland France by boat or plane. In the early days of the BUMIDOM, participants arrived in Le Havre by boat, but as travel by plane became cheaper and more accessible, migrants arrived at Orly Airport in Paris. Again, this was a highly regulated affair, and in the BUMIDOM files held at the Archives départmentales de la Guadeloupe, lists have been kept of the names of people who left on particular days along with the details of their transport voucher. Participants were not free to choose when they would leave for France but had to follow the instructions of the authorities. On their arrival they were met at the airport or port and taken to the principal BUMIDOM headquarters at 7, rue Crillon in the eleventh arrondissement of Paris. There they would be given some financial assistance before being directed towards their training centre or place of work, although, as we will see from Charlise Curier's memoirs in Chapter 2, the financial assistance provided to them was often insufficient for their needs, especially in an expensive city such as Paris. They could ask the BUMIDOM for further financial assistance to buy the furniture and equipment they would need for their new life, but this eventually had to be paid back in monthly instalments, or it could be offset against their monthly salary. The BUMIDOM threatened legal proceedings against those who were unable to pay, although in practice it is unlikely that the Bureau was able to fully recuperate these debts, given the high volume of people asking for financial assistance.

One of the most striking aspects of the BUMIDOM project was its gendered nature. While initially ten times as many men arrived through the scheme as women, by the end of the 1960s, men and women were arriving in almost equal numbers. In fact, if we only consider those migrants who were placed directly into work through the BUMIDOM, between 1964 and 1968, more women arrived through the BUMIDOM than men. In 1964, 1,217 women arrived from the four overseas departments to work in France while only 924 men were recruited, and this trend continued until 1969, when the numbers of men emigrating overtook the numbers of women (BUMIDOM 1981, 6). These statistics are significant, because they demonstrate that, at this point, women were emigrating in their own right, and not only to accompany their husbands and families. In fact, female migration was actively encouraged for both demographic and moral reasons: it would not only lower the birth rate on the islands, but it was also hoped that women would transmit more 'modern' family values that they had learned in the metropole once they returned to the Caribbean. Yet, as Childers explains, encouraging young women to migrate meant splitting up families, which 'undermined the French insistence on family as the cornerstone for social and economic development in the Antilles' (2016, 177).

Furthermore, the work offered to BUMIDOM participants was also highly racialised and gendered. Despite being eligible (as French citizens) for administrative jobs in the public sector, they were not considered suitable for such roles. Women in particular were stereotyped as being natural domestics and mothers, rather than being ambitious and career-driven, as Félix Germain points out (2010, 482). Administrators tapped into these stereotypes, and in the first few years of the BUMIDOM operations, women were employed directly by rich families as domestic cleaners and live-in maids, while men were offered work as physical labourers and transportation workers. In March 1965, a centre to train women to carry out domestic tasks was set up in Crouy-sur-Ourcq, a small town north-east of Paris. The gender divisions in the distribution of labour are stark and are reminiscent of the ways in which enslaved men and women were separated during the Middle Passage. As Sowande Mustakeem observes, slave ships were often divided into separate compartments for men and women to keep them apart, 'reinforc[ing] constant divisions between men and women' (Mustakeem 2016, 65). Men were shackled together in pairs while women were kept below deck, confined but unchained so that they were more easily accessible for their captives to assault and rape them. While in the BUMIDOM era men and women were not subjected to such violent treatment, they were kept apart, not to strengthen divisions between genders but to maintain their traditional gendered roles. The patriarchal organisation of French Caribbean society which began during the transatlantic trafficking of enslaved Africans thus continued in the twentieth century, even though it was manifested in different ways. The gendered dynamics of the scheme reveal the colonial underpinnings of the BUMIDOM administration which endeavoured to assert control over Caribbean citizens of colour.

One way of maintaining control over BUMIDOM participants was for officials to give the impression that they were offering meaningful professional training to the participants. However, the instruction the women received did not better prepare them to work as *fonctionnaires* in mainland France, as they had been promised, but rather taught them how to work as maids, thus reinforcing their role as wives and mothers. The women were forced to work long hours from 8.30 am to 7.00 pm, attending cooking and cleaning classes to teach them how to run a household for middle-class French families (Germain 2017, 81). In Chapter 2 I shall explore life in this centre in more detail in Curier's autobiographical text, showing how beneath this supposed training lay a rhetoric of assimilation. Moreover, they were subjected to strict rules and infantilising rhetoric: they were not allowed to leave the centre during the week and had to request permission to go away at the weekend (Germain 2017, 81). The women were then placed either in domestic service roles or were given jobs as health-care workers in local hospitals. Condon argues that migrating through the BUMIDOM was emancipatory for women, who were making the most of the opportunities that were already available to men: namely, being able to leave the islands (2020, 131). The BUMIDOM did perhaps give independence and some financial stability to women who previously had not had the opportunity to earn a living, but the gendered limitations of this employment should not be overlooked, as this work replicated the caring and domestic jobs the women were already carrying out back home.

Men's experiences of state-controlled work were also determined by their race and gender. A trade school was opened in February 1968 in Simandres, approximately ten miles from Lyon. This centre offered training exclusively to male migrants in professions deemed more 'suitable' to men, such as metalwork, carpentry and plumbing. The instruction given to men was centred around gendered stereotypes of men being fit and strong and therefore capable of physical work. Germain notes that the rules for men at the centre in Simandres were not as strict as those at the women's centre in Crouy-sur-Ourcq: Caribbean men were allowed to socialise with each other at the bar or play ping-pong together, and they did not have to ask permission to leave the centre, as the women did (Germain 2016, 108). The gendered roles men were expected to assume were therefore to their advantage, which was often not the case for the women. However, even though they enjoyed these 'privileges of masculinity' and learned how to become the head of the household (Germain 2016, 108), they were still subjected to the paternalistic and neocolonial attitudes of the instructors. According to the information booklet produced by BUMIDOM officials about the centre, the training programme lasted between seven and fourteen weeks. For eight hours a day, five days a week, the men were taught 'législation concernant le citoyen et le travailler, approches du syndicat et de la politique, exigences de la vie courante: hygiène, circulation, papiers nécessaires, assurances, droits et devoirs personnels, sécurité, santé' (BUMIDOM 1968a, 2) [legislation regarding citizenship and employment, information about trade unions and politics, demands of daily life: hygiene, traffic, important documentation, insurance, personal rights and responsibilities, security, health care]. The fact that the French officials thought Guadeloupean, Martinican and Reunionese men needed to be taught how to look after their personal hygiene and complete simple administrative tasks (which they would also have had to do as French citizens living in the overseas departments) reveals very openly their derogatory attitudes towards people of colour. While their gender did not necessarily oppress them, then, male Caribbean migrants were often denigrated on grounds of race and ethnicity.

What is also noticeable about men's experiences of migration is the fact that, following their training, they were dispersed across the country and placed away from the Parisian centre, in order to avoid contestatory behaviour and to facilitate integration (Condon 2020, 132). Condon notes that, in 1962–3, the thirty-nine men who arrived were sent to twenty-four different training centres (Condon 2020, 132). This was another instance of gendered behaviour towards the BUMIDOM participants: officials had no qualms in finding work for women in the capital city and placing them among large groups of their compatriots, presumably because they did not consider women to be political agents advocating for their rights in the same way as men. This gendered treatment of migrants has a long history in France. The arrival of Black male soldiers during World War I provoked anxiety among French officials due to stereotypes about hypersexualised Black males having relationships with white women, while the creation of communities of male Algerian workers in the urban *banlieues* was also a cause for concern for the French government, and family reunification was encouraged to make the Algerian population seem less 'socially threatening' (Stovall 2015, 448). The racialised and gendered treatment encountered by Antillean and Reunionese men was therefore not new, but it is all the more shocking given their status as French citizens, which should have offered them some protection from institutional forms of discrimination.

In short, migration was considered by the French government as a solution to the demographic issues in the Caribbean and Réunion – and it was even proposed to remedy the situation of other territories struggling with overpopulation and overcrowding, such as Tahiti which was suffering from high levels of poverty and unemployment due to migration from neighbouring islands (BUMIDOM 1978, 7). However, governmental officials did not fully consider the impact migration would have on those emigrating to the metropole. Besides the problems with training and work examined above, Antillean and Reunionese people encountered considerable difficulties when finding housing. Many homeowners refused to let houses to Antillean tenants because they did not want to deal with people of colour, meaning that Caribbean people were forced to apply to housing agencies which dealt specifically with migrants. In addition, as the numbers using the services of the BUMIDOM increased, the office was unable to provide sufficient housing, and had to resort to temporarily housing Caribbean and Reunionese people in hotels or community centres. The accommodation offered to them was of very poor quality. In a letter sent on 15 May 1974 from the president of the BUMIDOM to the director of CASODOM, Vié writes that he went to visit the apartments that the BUMIDOM had acquired in Roissy-en-Brie and was shocked to find that 'les vitres sont cassées [. . .], les papiers peints sont décollés et déchirés, les revêtements du sol sont lacérés, les lavabos fendus et les portes défoncées' (Vié 1974) [the windows are broken, the wallpaper is peeling and torn, the floor coverings are ripped, the sinks are cracked and the doors are smashed in]. These struggles to find decent housing are another example of how Antillean and Reunionese people were denied the rights and opportunities that their French citizenship should have granted them. As Pattieu explains, '"citizen" migrants of the BUMIDOM were then categorised as non-French and therefore lost the benefit of citizenship in the housing market' (2017, 17). Emigration to mainland France was not the utopian solution to the social and economic precarity experienced on the islands, as the participants had been led to believe, and they therefore began to revolt against the BUMIDOM in a variety of ways.

Resistance to the BUMIDOM

The BUMIDOM was denounced as an exploitative policy from the top down. Caribbean and Reunionese politicians drew attention to the colonial framework of the Bureau through their speeches and political rallies, while workers employed direct action in protest against their appalling living and working conditions. Martinican *député* Césaire was particularly vocal in the Assemblée nationale [National Assembly] against migration between French Guiana, mainland France, and Martinique and Guadeloupe, which he regarded as an extractive and abusive form of population transfer. He is often quoted as referring to the BUMIDOM as 'génocide par substitution' [genocide by substitution]. Césaire employed this term in the Assemblée nationale on 13 November 1975, but rather than critiquing the organised migration of Martinicans and Guadeloupeans to mainland France, he was in fact criticising the plans of the French government to implement the 'Plan Vert' (which never really happened). France intended to develop French Guiana, creating ten thousand jobs and investing fifteen billion francs (Piantoni 2009, 206). White French administrators would be sent to run the department while the native Guianese population would be moved to France to undertake more physically demanding but low-paid tasks. The language Césaire used in this speech – 'nous redoutons le génocide par substitution, même s'il s'agit d'un génocide par persuasion' [we fear genocide by substitution, even if it is a genocide by persuasion] (1975) – is problematic, particularly in the context of the Caribbean's traumatic past of slavery, extreme violence and forced deportation. The two situations are not comparable – this population transfer was not a form of genocide, even if it was extremely exploitative and predicated on race. The phrase 'génocide par substitution' has been used in recent years by different community groups to condemn the BUMIDOM, and more broadly it has been adopted to criticise what are considered to be the neocolonial relations which still exist between the French Caribbean islands and mainland France.

For instance, in 2004, the term was employed by Martinican politicians and trade union representatives to denounce problems in the education sector; the contracts of 257 Martinican teachers were not renewed because of budget cuts, but, instead, teachers from mainland France were appointed to these positions (Palmiste 2012, 154). The phrase appeared again in 2020, as evidence of a growing anti-white sentiment on the islands. In response to a video produced by *La1ère* about the end of lockdown for Guadeloupean schoolchildren during the COVID-19 pandemic, some internet users commented on Twitter about the lack of children of colour on the video. One internet user employed the term 'génocide par substitution', which was then picked up by the far-right news website *Valeurs actuelles* and used as a headline to aggravate racial tensions on the islands (Valeurs actuelles 2020). Césaire's comments have thus had an afterlife beyond the BUMIDOM era, and their use by a range of community groups with differing political affiliations demonstrates the ongoing racial tensions between the Caribbean islands and mainland France, which were not resolved by the cessation of the BUMIDOM in 1982.

Caribbean and Reunionese migrants themselves also rebelled against the government's migratory policies. These protests took many forms, and much of the action was targeted towards the training centre at Crouy-sur-Ourcq. In 1971, the Groupe d'action de la communauté antillo-guyanaise [Action Group for the Antillo-Guyanese Community], a community organisation of Antillean and Guianese people living in France, investigated the living conditions at the centre, having heard many rumours of the appalling treatment of migrants there. They first sent a member of the group to examine the situation discreetly before launching a formal investigation, during which they interviewed the director of the centre and several female residents. In March 1971, they published the results of their investigation, which included a list of their immediate demands, such as informing people of 'la véritable nature du gentil office' (Groupe d'action de la communauté antillo-guyanaise 1971, 34) [the true nature of this kind bureau]. This report is unlikely to have had a significant impact on governmental policy, given that it was undertaken by a small group with limited resources to make change, but it is evidence of an increasing sense of activism among migrants who were no longer willing to accept the racial discrimination to which they were subjected. This activism took a more radical turn in 1974 when a feminist section of the Union générale des travailleurs réunionnais en France occupied the building at Crouy-sur-Ourcq in protest (Paris 2020, 106). Again, it is unclear how successful this activism was at changing the direction of the BUMIDOM, given that the centre remained operational until the BUMIDOM was finally closed down, but it is testimony to the solidarity that existed among female migrants who used their networks to raise awareness of the problems faced by their compatriots. More successful perhaps were the small-scale actions of self-emancipation carried out by individual women who sought to defy the BUMIDOM in their own discreet ways. According to Nora Eguienta and Pattieu (2023), these actions involved using different public services to their advantage and even appealing to the president of France directly for assistance with employment and housing, as well as physically running away from exploitative situations in the training centre or in the private houses where they worked.

Resistance was not only a feminist action, as men and women came together to criticise the government's migratory policies. They wrote letters to BUMIDOM officials complaining about their individual cases, but they also engaged in collective practices of resistance and rebellion. On 4 November 1973, a petition was launched by a couple from Lyon who accused the BUMIDOM of deceiving them and not fulfilling their promises: 'nous accusons le BUMIDOM de nous avoir trompé et de continuer à tromper nos jeunes compatriotes en faisons à la Réunion des promesses à profusion sans toutefois jamais les tenir' [we accuse the BUMIDOM of having tricked us and continuing to trick our young compatriots by making promises aplenty in Réunion without ever keeping them]. This petition was signed by many others from the overseas departments living in Lyon who shared the sentiment of being tricked into migrating to France. Newspaper outlets in mainland France also contributed to holding the BUMIDOM to account. Headlines from newspapers such as *Le Progrès* [Progress], the daily newspaper circulated in Lyon, read 'L'Emigration des Antillais et Guyanais en France: trop d'illusions et pas d'informations honnêtes pour les émigrés' (Valence 1974) [The Emigration of Antilleans and Guianese people in France: too many illusions and no honest information for emigrants]. Moreover, there was increasing resistance to the BUMIDOM on the islands themselves as islanders became sceptical that the Bureau would provide the answer to their social and economic issues. For instance, October 1976 saw considerable strike action in Martinique against the Barre plan (a European fiscal policy implemented to reduce inflation), and the BUMIDOM was targeted as part of this militant action. A letter from the secretary general of the CFDT trade union in Martinique to the prefect of Martinique on 13 October 1976 shows that one of its members' demands was 'mettre fin au scandale de l'emmigration' (Beausoley 1976) [to put a stop to the scandal of emigration].

BUMIDOM officials were acutely aware of the growing disenchantment of the migrants with the Bureau, and of the interest that media outlets across the French territories took in this organised migration scheme. Officials were eager to preserve the reputation of the BUMIDOM – after all, it was a governmental policy designed to solve urgent demographic issues, and they needed to guarantee its success. Letters were sent from Albert Bros, the *administrateur délégué* [chief executive] of the BUMIDOM, to Jean Aribaud, director of Affaires sociales et culturelles de l'Outre-mer [Social and Cultural Affairs of the Overseas Departments], informing him of any negative reports about the BUMIDOM in newspapers or in radio broadcasts, so that officials were alert to the increasing dissatisfaction of the French public with the Bureau and could thus curb any resistance. By the late 1970s, officials realised that the services provided by the Bureau needed to be improved to avoid contestation. A report dated 17 December 1979 by Jacques Ferret, president of the BUMIDOM at the time, reveals that the administrators were aware of what was not functioning well, and were in the process of creating working groups to examine particular issues, such as the training provided to migrants (Ferret 1979). In addition, surveys were carried out among BUMIDOM participants to measure the success of this scheme. According to a report from 30 September 1975, 17,148 migrants were surveyed, and while 86 per cent claimed to be satisfied with the welcome they received in the French mainland, only 54.27 per cent were happy with their accommodation situation and 17.84 per cent were satisfied with the training they received (BUMIDOM 1975a, 31–5). What is unclear from the BUMIDOM files is whether the training the participants received actually changed and improved as a result of these evaluations. It seems that administrators were motivated more by a desire to salvage the reputation of the scheme than to give participants better opportunities for personal and professional emancipation.

One method developed by the BUMIDOM to try to appease migrants was to give them paid trips back to the Caribbean and Réunion every three years. Pattieu points out the political motivations behind this scheme, which was named 'voyages vacances' [holiday trips]: the government had to prove that 'l'institution traite les migrants de façon humaine et leur fournit divers avantages' (Pattieu 2018, 72) [the institution is treating migrants humanely and providing them with various benefits]. Before the 'voyages vacances' system was established in 1965, the BUMIDOM had already negotiated with Air France to provide cheaper fares to migrants wishing to return to the islands, but this new system made it much easier and cheaper (in theory) for migrants to visit their families still living in the overseas departments. In 1968, the CASODOM became associated with the 'voyages vacances' scheme and helped to organise the temporary return of migrants. By the height of the scheme in 1980, some 20,000 to 25,000 return trips were being made to Guadeloupe, Martinique and Réunion each year (Pattieu 2018, 77). In order to benefit from these lower tariffs, participants had to be originally from the overseas departments and had to have lived in mainland France for at least five years. Different tariffs were available, depending on family income and the season in which people wished to travel – in 1982, for instance, prices for adults to travel to the Antilles and back ranged between 3,410 francs in the low season and 3,915 francs in the high season (BUMIDOM 1982). Although many participants benefited from having a paid trip home, they were obliged to reimburse the BUMIDOM office for their journey, although many were unable to pay back the high cost of the plane ticket. Pattieu thus considers the 'voyages vacances' scheme as 'la volonté d'un contrôle, même limité, de populations issues de l'ancien monde colonial' [wanting to control, even in a limited manner, peoples from the former colonies] – the scheme ensured that participants eventually returned to mainland France, while remaining tied and indebted to the BUMIDOM (Pattieu 2018, 78). The economic crisis of the late 1970s meant that Air France was forced to increase its air fares, resulting in the BUMIDOM being unable to continue this scheme. In 1978, a new tariff was introduced – the 'voyages pour tous' [trips for all]. This fare was not accessible to everyone, however, as in high season it constituted a 30 per cent increase in fares to the Antilles and a 40 per cent increase in fares to Réunion (Pattieu 2018, 82). Antillean and Reunionese populations were hostile to these changes and turned to the trade unions for support. Ultimately, then, the 'voyages vacances' scheme was unable to quell the growing dissatisfaction of Antillean and Reunionese communities with life.

Conclusion

It is undeniable that migration to mainland France was experienced by some Antillean and Reunionese citizens as a means for social advancement. Men who had been out of work now had a purpose in life, while women who previously had enjoyed little independence were suddenly able to earn a living, and therefore 'live a life that was less dependent on men' (Childers 2016, 188). This is borne out by the experiences of some of the women I interviewed, who report feeling grateful to the BUMIDOM for being able to enjoy professional success and personal emancipation that they would have been unlikely to have had if they had remained on the islands (Wimbush 2023). Yet, as this chapter has shown, the positions they were given and the training they received often reinforced the gendered and racial stereotypes that were attributed to them by white French citizens. For the most part, migration to France did not improve their quality of life, and increasingly more people were choosing to return permanently to the islands by the end of the 1970s. The BUMIDOM files contain many examples of letters written by individuals to BUMIDOM officials requesting financial assistance with their return trip. The reasons given for their desire to return to the islands were mostly affective and emotional; one person admitted feeling 'trop dépaysé loin de [sa] famille' [too homesick away from [her] family], while another wanted to go home after the breakdown of her marriage (BUMIDOM 1975b). Although the BUMIDOM was unable to pay for these tickets outright, it did offer discounted fares to those who wished to return permanently to the islands.

Migration from Guadeloupe and Martinique did not stop with the termination of the BUMIDOM in 1982. The agency was replaced in that year by the Agence nationale pour l'insertion des travailleurs d'outre-mer (ANT) [National Agency for the Integration and Promotion of Workers from the Overseas Departments], during a climate of economic decline. Escalating levels of unemployment in France meant that the country no longer needed migrant workers. Furthermore, in 1981, the Socialist François Mitterrand was elected to the presidency, and his term of office saw a change in direction of France's migration strategy as some of the stricter immigration policies adopted by the previous administration were relaxed. The ANT favoured family reunification over the recruitment of new workers and placed more emphasis on mobility between the mainland and the overseas departments rather than one-way emigration. For Christine Chivallon, this administrative change was positive and reflected 'not only the new conditions of the labour market but also the emergence of the "Caribbean question" concerning the treatment of French Caribbean people in metropolitan France, and featuring a political "will" to integrate those who had already migrated' (Chivallon 2011, 61). In reality, though, there was little actual change between the BUMIDOM and the ANT, and the ANT even took over the BUMIDOM's office in 7 rue Crillon, suggestive of a continuity between the two administrations. Guadeloupeans and Martinicans did not see a great improvement in their quality of life, particularly towards the end of the 1980s and beginning of the 1990s when public funding for migration policies was reduced.

In 2006, this office was replaced by LADOM, which is still in operation today. This programme has three axes: it gives financial and administrative assistance for short-term emigration to the metropole for work, study or for personal reasons.[10] According to the LADOM report 2022, in 2022, 60,000 people benefited from this project (3). While this scheme enables the islanders, particularly young people, to benefit from professional opportunities on the mainland, it is problematic that the government is encouraging workers and students to migrate to France to improve their life chances, rather than developing professional opportunities on the islands themselves. This policy creates greater inequalities between mainland France and the overseas departments and reinforces neocolonial attitudes concerning the 'centre', European France and the 'periphery', the Caribbean islands. The LADOM is thus a continuation of the BUMIDOM but in a different guise – it is couched in positive language and supposedly promotes mobility and professional opportunities but in reality, it is yet another instance in which the state is intervening in the migration of its Caribbean citizens.

This scheme is also having a negative impact on the demographical composition of the Caribbean islands. Social scientists are concerned that, following the push to encourage outward migration, there are now too many young people leaving the islands. In 2017, 40 per cent of young people aged between nineteen and thirty-nine, born in the Antilles, were living in France (Marie 2021). Unlike the young people who migrated to continental France in the 1960s and 70s, these emigrants are well qualified and highly skilled, meaning that France is removing a skilled workforce from the islands and causing a 'brain drain'. This accelerated departure of young people, coupled with a rise in life expectancy, means that there is an ageing population in Guadeloupe and Martinique, but with fewer people of working age to support them, public services are placed under increasing strain. A parliamentary report about the issues caused by an ageing population was presented to the government on 6 February 2020, with possible solutions including encouraging young people to stay on the islands and work in services to support the older population (Atger and Bareigts 2020). While these measures are yet to be implemented, local politicians are trying to facilitate the return of young people (although they require considerable financial investment from the government). For example, Martinican senator Catherine Conconne launched the organisation 'Alé Viré' [Coming and Going] in 2018 which aims to help long-term settlement in Martinique by providing practical and financial support (Samyde 2023). The LADOM itself is aware of the demographic problems caused by encouraging emigration. In January 2024, preparatory discussions were held about the 'passeport pour le retour' [return mobility passport] programme which provides financial assistance for people returning to the overseas departments, but only people who have already benefitted from funding to travel to France can apply, thereby limiting its effectiveness (Druelle 2024). Local initiatives, meanwhile, are seeking to raise awareness of the demographic consequences of long-term migration away from the islands. The documentary film *La Martinique, l'île des aînés* (2020) [Martinique, Island of the Elderly], directed by Vianney Sotès and Barbara Olivier-Zandronis, demonstrates very clearly that the political decisions taken by the French government to encourage emigration in the 1960s and 70s are at the root of Martinique's ageing population, the consequences of which are disastrous for the elderly and for young workers trying to look after them with little resource. The impact of the BUMIDOM thus continues to be felt on the islands today, even forty years after it was closed down. The government's current emphasis on movement away from the Caribbean demonstrates how the islands continue to be locked in a colonial relationship of dependency and inferiority with mainland France. As the rest of this book will show, contemporary Caribbean cultural works challenge these colonial frameworks which were at the heart of the BUMIDOM project, and which still govern French–Antillean relations today.

Notes

1. According to Stephanie Condon (2020), many personal records of BUMIDOM participants were destroyed when the ANT moved its premises from central Paris to Pierrefitte-sur-Seine in 1994. While conducting research at the office, she succeeded in persuading officials to retain 10 per cent of the samples for future research, and so approximately 30,000 dossiers have been retained (Condon 2020, 125).

2. I examined a selection of dossiers from 1966 to 1967, 1977 to 1978, 1976 to 1977, 1977 to 1978, 1982 to 1983 and 1988 to 1999 in order to investigate whether the application process changed throughout the BUMIDOM operations and once it was closed down.
3. For more information about the ways in which the archival records of the BUMIDOM administration are reflective of state hegemony, see Antonia Wimbush (2024).
4. See, for instance, Jennifer Boittin, *Colonial Metropolis: The Urban Grounds of Anti-Imperialism and Feminism in Interwar Paris* (2010); Tracy Denean Sharpley-Whiting, *Bricktop's Paris: African American Women between the Two World Wars* (2015); Annette K. Joseph-Gabriel, *Reimagining Liberation: How Black Women Transformed Citizenship in the French Empire* (2020); and Tracy Denean Sharpley-Whiting, *Negritude Women* (2022).
5. There has also been transnational interest in the Nardal sisters in recent years. On 12 October 2021, the search engine Google paid tribute to Paulette Nardal on what would have been her 150th birthday with a 'doodle' illustrated by Jessica Coppet.
6. The 1962 Act declared that only those born in the UK or who held a British passport as well as being a British citizen were allowed entry. As Ian Patel explains, this was a way to 'control the migration of non-white Commonwealth and British citizens' because, if passports were produced in a colony or Commonwealth state, individuals would be subject to immigration control (2021, 78).
7. Only first-name initials are given here to preserve the anonymity of migrants.
8. I conducted interviews with six people (four women and two men), identified through a snowballing method. Four of the interviewees now live in the Caribbean, and two have remained in mainland France.
9. I have not anonymised Charlise's name in order to give her agency and claim ownership of her own life story, following the approach advocated by Mia Martin Hobbs (2021). However, I have used only her first name to preserve her anonymity to a certain extent.
10. The LADOM provides financial assistance for adults aged over eighteen who are looking to study or work in mainland France, provided that they are unable to find work or training opportunities in the overseas departments. Those looking for work have to follow a minimum of seven months of training organised by the LADOM office. Their plane ticket is funded in part or in full, and they are given some financial assistance when in France. Students also have to prove that they are unable to complete their studies in the overseas departments. Their return flight and train ticket are paid for by the LADOM office. See https://ladom.fr/ [accessed 27 April 2024].

Chapter 2

Gender, Work and Race in Caribbean Life Writing

On the Facebook page on which Michèle Zabulon promotes her memoir *Parcours de vie d'une puéricultrice antillaise*, she describes her motivations for writing the text in a short video. She explains that 'j'avais envie de faire revivre des souvenirs personnels et d'évoquer entre autres un point de la vie antillaise que les jeunes générations ne connaissent certainement pas' (Zabulon 2017) [I wanted to revive personal memories and to evoke, among other things, a part of Antillean life that young generations do not necessarily know about]. For Zabulon, and for the other authors whose works are analysed in this chapter, life writing is both a personal project of memory retrieval and a collective, political endeavour to educate young people about significant but neglected episodes in French and French Caribbean history. The authors therefore subscribe to Aleida Assmann's argument that individual and collective memories are not two discrete categories but, rather, constantly interact with each other (2006, 211). For Assmann, memories are not only gained through lived experience but also 'via interacting, communicating, learning, identifying, and appropriating' (2006, 211). This chapter shows how memory transmission operates on both an individual and a collective level through the genre of life writing.

Taking as a starting point the argument sustained in Chapter 1 that the BUMIDOM was colonial in its conception and application, this chapter investigates how participants experienced migration, and particularly the work that was offered to them, as depicted in their accounts of life writing. How did their racial and gender identity determine the work that they were permitted to undertake? How did they resist against these gendered and racialised stereotypes imposed on them by the Bureau? What was the role of feminist solidarity and activism in countering these stereotypes? I argue that life writing enables BUMIDOM participants to share elements of their life story while also creating a counter-narrative of the BUMIDOM which emphasises the gendered and racialised nature of the scheme. In this vein, the texts fit within the tradition of postcolonial Caribbean autobiography which is an inherently political genre of writing. Writing is both an act of solidarity in which BUMIDOM participants encourage other members of the Caribbean community to share their stories of migration through local media appearances and community events, and a form of work in itself. Unlike the cultural works I analyse in other chapters of this book, which are published and circulated through established publishing houses and literary networks, most of the writers whose works are examined in this chapter have engaged in alternative strategies such as self-publishing. By writing and publishing their life stories themselves, these women, who have been engaged in domestic and care work throughout their lives, become writers. In this way, they disrupt the gendered and racialised norms and stereotypes which dictated the work they were allowed to do. Throughout this chapter, I use the term 'life writing' rather than 'autobiography' to refer to texts written by and about the lives of BUMIDOM participants, as this term is inclusive of different types of non-traditional forms of writing about the self, and is therefore more applicable to my corpus. I thus follow the strategy advocated by Natalie Edwards and Chris Hogarth, who call for a more expansive approach to writing about the self: 'we conceive of autobiography in the loosest way; to us there are as many definitions of autobiography as there are autobiographers, so our texts belong to different categories of what could be defined "life writing"' (Edwards and Hogarth 2008, 9).

Focusing on life writing by women, the chapter investigates 'the ideological construction of jobs and tasks in terms of appropriate femininity, domesticity, (hetero)sexuality, and racial and cultural stereotypes', as called for by intersectional feminist Chandra Talpade Mohanty (1997, 6). My corpus consists of Françoise Ega's *Lettres à une noire*, Lucienne Dangreville-Bellemare's *Paroles de ma vie: de Fort-de-France Martinique à Saint-Denis (Seine Saint-Denis)*, Zabulon's *Parcours de vie d'une puéricultrice antillaise* and Charlise Curier's *Mon aventure avec le BUMIDOM*. Ega's text was published during the BUMIDOM era, while the other three have been published in the last decade. The latter thus offer a different temporal perspective as the authors employ the genre of life writing to record their memories of a more distant past than the past evoked by Ega. Yet the selected texts share commonalities in the ways in which they focus on the institutional nature of the BUMIDOM and shine a spotlight on how it worked as a labour recruitment agency. Firstly, though, it is necessary to situate the texts among other works of autobiographical writing from the Caribbean to explore whether the authors have taken inspiration from this literary tradition, or whether they offer a new model of life writing about migration.

Life Writing in the Caribbean

Autobiographical writing has not traditionally been a major trend in French Caribbean literature, as authors have gravitated towards collective methods of expression. Forms such as the 'roman de nous', made famous by Édouard Glissant,[1] have been privileged over more personal styles of writing for their emphasis on values of collectivity and community. Louise Hardwick notes the contrast between the lack of autobiographical tradition in the French Caribbean and the rich array of life writing from the British Caribbean colonies, from slave narratives by Olaudah Equiano to autobiographical texts by major African American authors, such as George Lamming and Derek Walcott (2013, 2). Maeve McCusker adds that autobiographical writing has also been prominent in Latin America through the literary form of *testimonio*, a first-person narrative in which the narrator bears witness to a traumatic event or a preoccupying social issue (2004, 438). The absence of a tradition of life writing in the French Caribbean is thus somewhat surprising, given its long-standing history in other parts of the region.

And yet, as Renée Larrier points out, even though autobiographical writing has not occupied a central position within French Caribbean literature, there are many first-person (semi)-fictional narratives in French Caribbean writing (2006, 6). For Larrier, this literary trend is a direct response to the colonial period, as Caribbean peoples have used personal forms of writing to challenge colonial authority. During the colonial period, the authorities published official documents and travelogues about colonised peoples that excluded them and made them the subject of investigation. In the postcolonial period, Caribbean communities have written themselves into their own stories by using the first-person pronoun 'je', thus moving away from being 'the previous object of discourse' and gaining subjectivity (Larrier 2006, 7). This literary strategy employed to make indigenous voices heard reflects key concerns of postcolonial autobiographical writing more broadly. As I have argued in *Autofiction: A Female Francophone Aesthetic of Exile* (2021), autobiography is a key writing strategy for postcolonial writers, both within and beyond the French-speaking world, because historically marginalised subjects have been able to activate historical memories through their personal accounts, while inflecting a predominantly Western discourse with their own hybrid language, syntax and narrative structure (Wimbush 2021, 25–6).

Despite the lack of autobiographical tradition within French Caribbean writing, there has been a noticeable boom of autobiographical narratives from the early 1990s, as male and female writers have turned to life writing to embark on a personal identity quest. Writers have focused predominantly on their childhood. Patrick Chamoiseau began this trend with *Antan d'enfance* (1990) [*Childhood*], a narration of his early childhood in Martinique.[2] Other important works which have since gained significant critical attention include Raphaël Confiant's *Ravines du devant-jour* (1993) [Ravines of Dawn] and the later text *Le Cahier de romances* (2000) [Notebook of Romances]; Gisèle Pineau's *L'Exil selon Julia* (1996) [*Exile according to Julia*]; Maryse Condé's *Le Cœur à rire et à pleurer* (1999) [*Tales from the Heart*]; and Daniel Maximin's *Tu, c'est l'enfance* (2004) [You Are Childhood]. These autobiographical texts have boosted the profile of many of these writers, who were not particularly well known when they engaged in practices of life writing, by making them familiar and relatable. McCusker points towards a change in reading habits and market forces to explain this surge in life writing by Caribbean authors. She explains that editors and publishing houses have played a role in promoting autobiographical work; for instance, many of the autobiographical texts by Caribbean writers have been published in Gallimard's 'Haute enfance' series, a collection which brings together life writing focusing on the formative period of childhood (McCusker 2004, 440). This editorial input has gone hand-in-hand with a general increase in interest in life writing by both readers and critics. This is not the only reason, however. The surge of scholarly interest about collective memory, and particularly the relationship between trauma and memory, during the 1990s has had a significant impact on the growth of the autobiographical genre. As McCusker argues, 'a touchstone of contemporary intellectual debate, memory has inevitably become a particular obsession for postcolonial writers' who use autobiographical writing as a means to recuperate their individual memories and to assert their identity while simultaneously bringing into focus the Caribbean's collective history of forced transportation and enslavement (2004, 440). The decade of the 1990s was particularly charged for Caribbean communities in terms of uncovering lost memories. For instance, 1992 was the 500th anniversary of Columbus's arrival in the Americas, while 1998 marked the 150th anniversary of the abolition of slavery in the French colonies. Against this backdrop of traumatic history which dispossessed Caribbean peoples of their collective past, the search for their personal origins has become all the more important.

This focus on the individual does not preclude concerns about collective identity formation, though, and therefore Caribbean autobiographical writing often contains both a personal and political agenda. Edgard Sankara likens postcolonial autobiographies written by Caribbean and African authors to *littérature engagée* [committed literature] because they are representations of a people burdened by the traumatic history of enslavement and colonisation, and thus an inherently political message is latent in their personal writing (Sankara 2011, 11). Larrier also points towards the political function of Caribbean autobiography, as she reads her corpus in terms of advocacy. She argues that Caribbean autobiography, and autofiction in particular, 'is invested in remembering and recording history and in challenging society's perception of Caribbean people' (Larrier 2006, 24). In this vein, the corpus of narratives written by Guadeloupeans and Martinicans about the BUMIDOM demonstrates how the personal is political. The authors explain clearly how their own personal and professional lives have been affected, for better or worse, by state migration policies which are rooted in French colonial practices. Remembering and recovering forgotten histories is arguably a more important project for these authors than engaging in debates around truth and authenticity, as advocated by metropolitan French theorists of autobiography such as Philippe Lejeune and Serge Doubvrosky.

The four authors studied in this chapter are not the first to employ the genre of life writing through which to discuss migration between the Caribbean and the Hexagon. Indeed, the first (semi)-autobiographical narratives about migration appeared in the 1950s. Joseph Zobel's *La Fête à Paris* (1953) (Adventures in Paris) and Glissant's *Le Soleil de la conscience* (1956) [*Sun of Consciousness*] both discuss the authors' experiences of post-war migration. These early examples of life writing about migration – Glissant's work is not necessarily autobiographical per se, but combines personal recollections of his own life with critical reflections and sociologically inspired studies of Martinican life – were produced by writers who had already begun their literary career in the Caribbean. They came to mainland France, alongside other writers and intellectuals, in search of a more established cultural landscape. *La Fête à Paris*, rewritten by Zobel and republished as *Quand la neige aura fondu* [Once the Snow Has Melted] in 1979, is a first-person narrative which recounts the Parisian adventures of José Hassam, whom we first met in *La Rue Cases-Nègres* (1950) [*Black Shack Alley*].[3] Migration to Paris brings disappointment to José because the reality of his experiences do not live up to his expectations, and the racial prejudice he encounters is shared by many who arrived in the aftermath of World War II, and also during the BUMIDOM period. In contrast, migration opens up possibilities to the unnamed narrator of Glissant's *Le Soleil de la conscience*, presumed to be Glissant himself given the biographical connections between author and narrator. Written in poetic and philosophical prose, the text reveals how the identity of the narrator is formed in the in-between space, between Martinique and Paris. Glissant calls attention to the alienation experienced by Martinicans who must grapple with the convergence of their own Antillean identity with their inherited European culture, and to the dislocation experienced through continuous migration between the two continents. Yet overall, migration appears to be a more positive experience for Glissant's narrative persona than for Zobel's because it expands horizons and enables new and dynamic exchanges and encounters.

A gap can be observed in Caribbean life writing from the 1960s to the 1980s, when the BUMIDOM was in operation. This lack of autobiographical texts during this period is mirrored by a paucity of French Caribbean literature more generally to discuss the theme of migration. Perhaps a degree of critical distance was required for writers to be able to process and write about such a traumatic period, in which they were often separated from their families and experienced racism and rejection. From the 1990s, however, there has been a surge of autobiographical texts by Caribbean writers of which the main theme is migration to mainland France. Their publication date maps onto the period in which life writing was becoming an important tradition in French Caribbean literature. Some of these texts focus on migration during the pre-BUMIDOM era, and so concerns surrounding labour exploitation and financial precarity are not necessarily emphasised in these texts. For instance, Maryse Condé's *La Vie sans fards* (2012) [Life without Embellishment] tells of her migration to Paris in the mid-1950s before she left for the African continent. Condé was a student in Paris during this time, and although she did experience difficulties in the French capital, particularly during her first pregnancy, she was not exploited in the same way as BUMIDOM participants. Given that Condé came from a middle-class, bourgeois background, she was not forced to rely on the BUMIDOM to find work, unlike people from more modest, working-class backgrounds, and therefore was not subjected to the same level of exploitation and hostility. Thérèse Parise Bernis's *Parise: souvenirs encombrants de la Guadeloupe* (1997) [Unwanted Memories of Guadeloupe: A Tale], written in collaboration with Catherine Vigor, disrupts this trend somewhat. Bernis discusses her economic migration to Paris where she fled to escape from poverty, meaning that financial precarity is very much at the heart of her story. Furthermore, like Condé, her migration took place during the mid-1950s, thereby challenging the notion that migration prior to the establishment of the BUMIDOM was mostly undertaken by men. Other examples of life writing produced during this period are narrated by child narrator-protagonists, who migrated during the BUMIDOM period but who did not choose to leave the Caribbean themselves. They were too young to make this choice, and simply followed their parents on their journey to search for work. Their narrative focus is therefore different, and they discuss schooling, family and friendships rather than issues related to labour. Examples include Daniel Radford's *Le Maître-pièce* (1993) [The Masterpiece], Pineau's *L'Exil selon Julia* and Alain Foix's *Ta mémoire, petit monde* (2005) [Your Memory, Little World]. In contrast, the works to which I now turn were all written by people who migrated through the BUMIDOM as adults in search of work, and this motivation for their migration is a core theme in their life writing.

Writing, Work and Female Solidarity in Françoise Ega's *Lettres à une noire*

Ega was born in Case-Pilote, on the western coast of Martinique, in 1920. She grew up in a modest family; her father was a gamekeeper and her mother a seamstress. She lived in Martinique until she got married, when she followed her husband, a soldier in the French army, on his military engagements in Benin and Madagascar. They then moved to Paris before settling in Marseille with their four young children in 1956 (Faner 1988, 3). Ega was above all a social activist. She helped Antillean migrant families who had recently arrived in France with administrative tasks and literacy skills. Moreover, she set up sports and cultural associations, such as the Association culturelle et sportive antillo-guyanaise (ACSAG) [Antillo-Guianese Cultural and Sports Association], to support the integration of Antillean and Guianese communities. An association was set up in Ega's name, following her death in 1976, to continue her work for social justice. In 1988, the Comité Mam'Ega Vivre ensemble [Madame Ega Living Together Committee] was established in La Busserine, a northern district of Marseille, 'qui a pour objectif la lutte contre l'illettrisme et toute forme d'exclusion' [which aims to fight against illiteracy and all forms of exclusion].[4]

Her desire to cultivate solidarity among other Antilleans living in mainland France, and particularly among women, is also evident in her writing, and not only in *Lettres à une noire*. Indeed, Ega stands apart from the other author whose works I analyse in this chapter, given that she is the only one to have written other works as a professional writer, even though only one text, *Le Temps des madras* (1966) [The Era of the Madras Headscarf], was published when she was alive. Her writing evokes gendered experiences of Martinican life in different periods of the twentieth century. The autobiographical *Le Temps des madras*, for instance, recounts the poverty she experienced as a child growing up in the 1920s and 30s, while the novel *L'Alizé ne soufflait plus (Antan Robè)* (2000) [The Trade Winds No Longer Blow (in the Time of Robè)] is set during World War II and passes comment on how women who remained on the islands suffered their own hardships and restrictions during the Vichy regime.

Writing, gender issues and social activism intersect the most visibly, however, in *Lettres à une noire*, published posthumously in 1978 with support from the Comité Mam'Ega Vivre ensemble. In fact, the very reason Ega wrote the text was to raise awareness of the racial discrimination faced by Antillean women of working-class backgrounds migrating through the BUMIDOM. Ega worked voluntarily as a domestic maid between 1962 and 1964, and during this period she took detailed notes of the derogatory treatment she received. These notes would later become *Lettres à une noire*. The text plays with genre and form in interesting ways. It is a first-person narrative, and the narrative persona is named Maméga, an abbreviation of 'Madame Ega'. In this way, *Lettres à une noire* conforms to traditional notions of autobiography and fulfils Lejeune's autobiographical pact, as the author, narrator and protagonist are one and the same person (1975). However, the autobiographical nature of the text is complicated somewhat by its epistolary form. At the beginning of the text, Maméga reads a piece in *Paris Match* about Carolina Maria de Jésus, a Brazilian maid living in the slums of São Paolo. Carolina had worked as a domestic maid but was soon fired after becoming pregnant. She ended up in the shanty towns and began to write about her experiences; she was discovered by journalist Audálio Dantas and eventually published her diaries in 1960. The text was translated from Brazilian Portuguese into thirteen languages, including French; *Le Dépotoir: le journal d'une favelada* [*Child of the Dark: The Diary of Carolina Maria de Jesus*] was translated by Violante do Canto in 1961, and it was the global dissemination of the text that provoked debate in international publications (Fernandez 2013, 140). *Paris Match* also published extracts from the diary, which strikes a chord with Maméga, because she realises that they share similar experiences of racism and exclusion. She decides to write a series of letters to Carolina, even though she never sends them to her. Although they share many experiences, they do not speak the same language. For this reason, she is ridiculed by her family for writing to a stranger from whom she will never receive a response, but Maméga simply replies that 'nous n'avons pas le même langage parlé, c'est vrai, mais celui de notre cœur est le même et il fait bon se retrouver quelque part, là où nos âmes se rejoignent' (Ega 1978, 24) [we don't speak the same language, it's true, but the language of our hearts is the same, and it's good to meet somewhere, where our souls can come together]. Maméga reminds us here of Assmann's assertion that 'our personal memories include much more than what we, as individuals, have ourselves experienced' (2006, 211). Maméga feels the need to connect her own memories of traumatic events to those of an individual with whom, even though they have never met, she feels a sense of affinity, creating a network of collective memories which are transient, changing and volatile.

Yet Ega also plays with this intermingling of individual and collective memory and identity. The epistolary pact – 'the call for response from a specific reader within the correspondent's world' (Altman 1982, 89) – fails because the intended addressee (Caroline) never reads the letters. In fact, the contemporary reader of *Lettres à une noire* becomes the unintended addressee of these letters. Ultimately, Maméga writes to and for herself. The letters give her the textual space to analyse her own experiences of migration critically, enabling her to process her own memories and become an active agent in her own subjectivity. At the same time, the lack of communication between Maméga and Carolina operates on a deeper level as a powerful metaphor which 'symbolises the difficulty with which minority groups can engage in a dialogue without being overheard or interrupted by dominant voices' (Rosello 1996, 75). Interestingly, *Lettres à une noire* was translated into Brazilian Portuguese as *Cartas a uma negra* in 2021. Although Mamćga's letters never reached Carolina, they are finally able to be read by a wider Brazilian audience, thereby establishing dialogue between Brazilians and Martinicans about their shared history of marginalisation and precarity, despite significant differences between their pasts.

In *Lettres à une noire*, we are introduced to different forms of Caribbean migration and the varying motivations behind individuals' displacement, whether for professional or personal reasons. The lack of men in the text is striking, as Annabel Rea points out (1997, 300), and in this way Ega points to a gendered flow of migration from the Caribbean during this period. The narrative time is situated in the early 1960s: the text begins in May 1962, just before the BUMIDOM is formally established, and closes on 5 December 1963. Mamóga's own migration, therefore, does not occur through the BUMIDOM as she was already living in Marseille when this office was created. Yet critiques of the BUMIDOM scheme, as well as other forms of exploitative migration, are highly apparent within the text. Early in the narrative, we learn about the migration of young women whose passage across the Atlantic is paid for by their wealthy employers, who then expect reimbursement once the women are working for them as cleaners and maids. The Caribbean women are trapped in an impossible situation. Many have left their children in Martinique and Guadeloupe and send remittances back to their families to help with childcare costs, but given how little they earn and how much they owe their employers for their passage, they are left with almost nothing. Mamóga equates this exploitative situation to 'le trafic humain' (Ega 1978, 13) [human trafficking], and she pities the young women who think they are coming to France for a better life, only to be treated as modern-day slaves:

> en effet, il y a beaucoup de filles que l'"on fait venir" à Marseille. Elles laissent les îles pour une destinée meilleure. [. . .] Elles sont achetées presque pour un certain temps. [. . .] Il y en a quelques-unes qui tirent de bons billets à cette loterie, elles tombent sur des gens pleins de dignité et d'humanité. Il y en a d'autres, ce sont les plus nombreuses, qui ploient sous le joug. (Ega 1978, 13)

> [indeed, there are lots of girls who 'are brought' to Marseille. They leave the islands for a better life. [. . .] They are almost bought for a certain period of time. [. . .] Some draw good lottery tickets; they

> come across people full of dignity and humanity. Others, and these are the most numerous, bend under the yoke.]

Here, the lack of agency of these women is emphasised by the passive structure 'on fait venir'. The transactional nature of their migration is also salient, and the vocabulary Ega employs, such as 'ployer sous le joug' and 'trafic humain', provides an echo with the Caribbean's haunting past of the transatlantic trafficking of enslaved Africans. Through her writing, Ega criticises the treatment of Caribbean domestic maids who are brought to France in a practice which, in her eyes, is a continuation of enslavement and oppression. This quotation demonstrates how multidirectional memory operates. Michael Rothberg argues that different historical memories – which he defines as 'the past made present' (2009, 3) – do not compete with each other for attention, but rather interact with each other. Memories are not owned by one particular group; their borders are 'jagged', and a memory which appears to belong to a community might actually be 'a borrowing or adaptation from a history that might initially seem foreign or distant' (Rothberg 2009, 3). For Ega, memories of migration interact with memories of enslavement, a trauma which continues to haunt the Caribbean psyche. However, Rothberg's theorisation needs to be approached with caution when it is applied to such a distressing context. We must avoid trivialising the plight of enslaved women who were subjected to rape, violence and dehumanising treatment. The women working as maids in France were subjected to humiliating treatment and appalling working conditions, but they were not treated as chattel.

Later in the text, Mamméga talks explicitly about the BUMIDOM project with her Guadeloupean friend Solange. The BUMIDOM is first mentioned by Solange in the diary entry dated 3 July 1963, only a few months after the BUMIDOM was formally established. Solange has heard about an office in Paris which helps young women to find work, but she erroneously names this 'Zubidom', in an indication that the office is new and unfamiliar to her (Ega 1978, 135). On learning more about the BUMIDOM, Solange explains that she is not in favour of the project because she thinks it will become much easier for French women to manipulate young Antillean girls without even having to pay for them to come to France. Solange describes the BUMIDOM as 'un bureau qui, je crois, est créé pour faire venir les négresses' [a bureau which, I think, has been created to bring over negro women] and, as she explains to Mamméga, 'les dames n'auraient plus besoin de se "décarcasser" pour leur payer le voyage, elles n'auront qu'à téléphoner et elles auront ce qu'il leur faut sous la main' (Ega 1978, 214–15) [ladies would no longer need to "go out of their way" to pay for their trip; they will only have to phone and they will have what they need to hand]. The racial element of this migration is clear through the use of the pejorative noun 'négresses'. Solange is critical of the BUMIDOM project which will allow white French employers to 'order' a Black Antillean maid from the BUMIDOM office whom they will then have at their disposal. She perceives the BUMIDOM not as a solution to improve the standard of living of Caribbean communities, but rather as a means to tighten the yoke of servitude under which they are forced to live in mainland France. Mamèga gives numerous examples of women whose treatment borders on the sadistic; her friend Renée is forced to continue working even when she is suffering from appendicitis (Ega 1978, 127), and Solange catches her employer turning the clock back so she will work longer hours (Ega 1978, 63).

Mamèga experiences this humiliating treatment herself, which she calls out as racist in her letters to Carolina. For instance, she is turned down for a job as a typist because of the colour of her skin. On arriving at the office for an interview, she is simply told there is no longer a vacancy. In another letter to Carolina, Mamèga describes how her Blackness restricts the types of jobs she is able to do. She recalls how she is immediately hired to clean the floors in an apartment block, with the caretaker stating 'les négresses sont sérieuses et travailleuses; d'ailleurs, ce n'est pas pour rien qu'on dit "travailler comme un noir!"' (Ega 1978, 57) [Negro women are serious and hardworking; besides, it's not for nothing that we say 'working like a Black person!']. This episode illustrates the stereotypes that circulated about Black women at the time, who were hired for physically demanding tasks which the metropolitan French refused to do, but were never given the opportunity to take on positions of responsibility. The simile 'travailler comme un noir' demonstrates clearly how these very rigid and dismissive stereotypes were predicated on race. In a more extreme example of this racialised treatment, Mamèga is dispossessed of her own name when she replaces her friend as a maid, and the lady of the house simply calls her by her friend's name, 'Renée', because she thinks all Black Antillean maids are the same (Ega 1978, 128). She is 'depersonalised; that is to say, disembodied and desexualised, and is not considered to be a "woman"' (Flannigan-Saint-Aubin 1992, 53). Writing the letters to Carolina, even if they are never sent or read, is thus a way for Mamèga to take back control of her own body and identity.

Writing is also part of a collective endeavour for Maméga, given that she started writing in order to raise awareness of the appalling treatment of Antillean workers. She was triggered to undertake this project after learning of the terrible working conditions of a fellow Martinican woman: 'une fille de mon pays m'a raconté de telle choses sur sa vie chez son patron que j'ai juré d'en avoir le cœur net. Je gagne de l'argent et je fais le point: je suis femme de ménage depuis cinq jours' (Ega 1978, 9) [a girl from back home told me such things about life with her boss that I wanted to be sure. I'm earning money and taking stock: I've been a maid for five days]. She is also involved in active intervention. At numerous times in the narrative, she encourages the women to rebel against their employers, insisting that they must negotiate better working conditions such as sick pay and social benefits. In this regard, her project of feminist solidarity recalls bell hooks's call for action against patriarchal oppression. Hooks argues that 'solidarity strengthens resistance struggle. There can be no mass-based feminist movement to end sexist oppression without a united front – women must take the initiative and demonstrate the power of solidarity' (1986, 127). Maméga takes hook's appeal further by calling for a rejection of racial injustice as well as sexual oppression. However, it is problematic that Maméga feels she has to participate in this labour herself in order to denounce the treatment of Antillean maids. Rosello defines Maméga as an 'ironic version of the colonising ethnographer', who appropriates an identity which is not really hers, in order to show solidarity to her fellow compatriots (1996, 60). Despite her good intentions, Maméga ends up perpetuating negative stereotypes about Antillean maids who do not rebel against their appalling treatment and whose individual concerns become more important than the collective struggle. At one stage, Maméga is forced to take on cleaning and domestic work to support her family because of her own financial precarity, rather than to make a political statement about labour conditions. For instance, in the letter to Carolina dated 18 February 1963, she explains that she replied to an advert for a house cleaner not 'par amour du prochain, mais bien pour ramener [ses] six cents francs en deux heures' (Ega 1978, 76) [out of love for [her] neighbour, but rather to take home [her] six hundred francs in two hours]. She does try to publish her account about working as a maid, and she even makes a trip to Paris in an attempt to meet editors who might be interested in her work. Yet most of the publishing houses are closed for the summer, and the editors she does meet reject her writing. Ultimately, her project of sharing feminist solidarity breaks down because she is unable to get her own voice heard. She is forced to revert back to cleaning and domestic work while waiting to find a publisher, explaining 'pas de fric pour une pareille aventure' (Ega 1978, 184) [no money for such a risky venture]. Writing is not a successful strategy of feminist resistance, as Maméga had initially thought.

While Maméga initially takes on domestic work to write about it and raise awareness of Antilleans' appalling treatment, her writing is not allowed to be disseminated. Writing about her labour may well be a successful individual project for Maméga as it enables her to emancipate herself from her husband, gain financial independence and insert her individual voice into a history which has long overlooked the Black working class. Yet her collective endeavour is perhaps less fruitful, despite her attempts to help other women navigate the difficulties of life in the Hexagon. Do the other writers succeed in negotiating between the individual and the collective?

BUMIDOM: Exploitation or Emancipation? Charlise Curier's *Mon aventure avec le BUMIDOM*

Curier (like Dangreville-Bellemare and Zabulon) has a different profile from Ega. She is not a professional writer, and the only text she has written and published is *Mon aventure avec le BUMIDOM*. Curier was born in 1951 in Guadeloupe. She left for mainland France in 1971 and her migration was organised and financed through the BUMIDOM, as she explains in the narrative (2019, 9). She lived in the Parisian suburbs and enjoyed a successful career in administration before returning to Guadeloupe following an acrimonious divorce. In the same vein as Dangreville-Bellemare and Zabulon, she has turned to life writing later in her life. She is now retired and thus has more time to dedicate herself to other pursuits, including writing. In interviews she has given to publicise the text, Curier has explained her motivations for writing her life story: she wishes to pass down her family history to the next generation and leave a legacy behind, but she also sees writing as a form of catharsis. In an interview given on 6 June 2019 for the Club du troisième âge [Senior Citizens Club] in Vieux-Habitants, Guadeloupe, she explained: 'c'est une histoire qui est encore douloureuse, et j'ai voulu écrire cette histoire parce que c'est un peu une thérapie pour moi' (Curier 2019b) [it's a history which is still painful, and I wanted to write this history because it's a bit like a therapy for me]. In the text itself, this individual process of recovery through writing takes on an additional collective level. In the opening pages of the book, she recognises that many BUMIDOM participants struggle to discuss their experiences because of the trauma they faced, but she also realises the need to work through this trauma together through writing and shared communication: 'le BUMIDOM fait partie de notre histoire. N'ayons pas honte, parlons-en' (Curier 2019, 8) [the BUMIDOM is part of our history. Let's not be ashamed, let's talk about it]. As I shall demonstrate shortly, on an extratextual level, Curier has participated in events to encourage others to share their stories about the BUMIDOM, thus facilitating a collective remembering about this suppressed past.

The ways in which the BUMIDOM has shaped Curier's life are evident from the title of the narrative. The noun 'aventure' evokes excitement and pleasure, suggesting that her experiences in mainland France were largely positive, despite the difficulties she undoubtedly encountered. The text is a first-person narrative, written in the past tense as Curier looks back on her working life. Photographs of herself, her family and the belongings she took with her are dispersed throughout the text, rendering her story more poignant and relatable to the reader. The text is structured chronologically and thematically; chapters address her work history, her struggles to find housing in Paris, the activities she enjoyed in her spare time and the racial prejudice to which she was subjected at times. What is particularly noticeable is the fact that, within each chapter, Curier includes subheadings in bold font to divide the sections further. This means that sections are relatively short, which is perhaps reminiscent of the oral traditions of Caribbean culture. The text is written as though Curier is talking directly to her audience about her memories of the BUMIDOM. *Mon aventure avec le BUMIDOM* is published by Éditions Nestor, a Guadeloupean publishing house, which alongside the oral qualities of the text – short sections and paragraphs, the employment of the past tense and the use of exclamatory phrases – suggests that Curier is targeting a local Caribbean readership. However, Creole does not feature much in the narrative, and the rare phrases and expressions given in Creole are translated into French in footnotes (perhaps at the publisher's stipulation), thereby complicating the assumption that she is solely writing for Caribbean, creolophone readers. There is a certain flattening of literary style in Curier's text – and a similar observation can also be made about the life writing of Dangreville-Bellemare and Zabulon. It seems that the literariness of their narratives is not their main focus. Rather, the authenticity of the migratory experience is foregrounded over narrative choices of language, form and structure. This approach is reflective of their political agenda – they seek to share their stories of migration as clearly and succinctly as possible, in order to encourage discussion and debate about the BUMIDOM in local Caribbean circles.

Through Curier's memories, it becomes clear that her primary motivation for migrating through the BUMIDOM was to find work. Her family were very poor, and she stopped her studies at the Lycée Gerville-Réache de Basse-Terre in order to find work and help her family financially: 'j'avais besoin d'argent, car à la maison, c'était la pauvreté!' (Curier 2019, 11) [I needed money because at home, we lived in poverty!]. Initially she worked in temporary, part-time jobs as an office worker which, while granting her independence and financial freedom, did not fulfil her intellectually or professionally. Although work was emancipatory for her to a certain extent, she was also aware that by putting an end to her education, she was limiting her life choices. Her professional options were already restricted by her gender; as a woman her options were limited to working in public administration or working as a teacher, but neither option appealed to her. When she heard about the BUMIDOM office, then, she was eager to sign up for what she thought would be more fulfilling work. At the office she was assessed on her level of French and was then told she would be an 'ouvrière spécialisée' (Curier 2019, 21).[5] She did not know what this category meant, but was proud to be able to earn a living: 'j'allais enfin pouvoir travailler et aider mes parents' (Curier 2019, 21) [I was finally going to be able to work and help my parents]. This feeling of pride at being able to work and contribute financially to the family unit contrasts sharply with the sentiments of shame frequently associated with the BUMIDOM, evoked by Curier in the opening chapter of the narrative. Although the narrator was upset to leave her family, she was excited for the adventures that awaited her. She describes her journey by ship from Pointe-à-Pitre to Marseille through the metaphor of flight, reinforcing her eagerness for a new life of independence and opportunity: 'toutefois, ce jour-là j'étais heureuse car c'était la première fois que j'allais "voler" de mes propres ailes' (Curier 2019, 24) [however, I was happy on that day because it was the first time I would 'fly' with my own wings].

Yet the following chapter, which tells of her arrival in Marseille and the coach journey to Crouy-sur-Ourcq, is entitled 'fin du rêve' [end of the dream]. Curier's disillusionment here is stark. She had subscribed to the rhetoric promoted by the BUMIDOM office that her quality of life would be greatly improved in mainland France. Playing on the notion of the 'American Dream', officials promoted migration as a means for upward social mobility, yet in *Mon aventure avec le BUMIDOM*, Curier describes how, in reality, the BUMIDOM was an exploitative programme which offered her humiliating training and work. Besides *Mon aventure avec le BUMIDOM*, there are few texts, of life writing or literature in any other genre, to offer a detailed description of life in the training centre at Crouy-sur-Ourcq. Curier remembers how Guadeloupean and Martinican women were separated at the centre from the Reunionese women, and rumour had it that this separation was due to differences in their skin colour (2019, 31). She thus calls attention to the racialised and gendered treatment at this centre. The women were very much aware that they were being oriented towards roles deemed 'feminine', which is reflective of a wider gendering of work during this period. Although the BUMIDOM had initially promoted migration as a means for social emancipation, in practice the work they were given reinforced their domestic roles as mothers, caregivers and homemakers. Just like Ega, Curier sees this work as a continuation of the Caribbean tradition of servitude and enslavement. Thus, her individual memories of her own embodied experience are fused with the 'collective, social, and constructive side of our relations to the past', to quote Rothberg (2009, 4): 'dès le début de la formation, j'avais compris que le BUMIDOM nous destinait à être des futures femmes de ménage, voir des servantes' (Curier 2019, 31) [from the beginning of the training I had understood that the BUMIDOM planned for us to become housemaids, and even servants]. In her own way, Curier explores what Mohanty calls out; the ways in which 'gender identity (defined in domestic, heterosexual, familial terms) structures the nature of the work women are allowed to perform or precludes workers from being "workers" altogether' (Mohanty 1997, 6).

The training was all the more alienating because of the cultural differences between life in Guadeloupe and life in Paris. Curier offers a list of the domestic chores they were taught, including instructions for how to make a bed. Many of the women had never slept in a bed in Guadeloupe because their families could not afford one, so this was a completely new and difficult task for them. The work they were given was physical, demanding, 'épuisant et humiliant' (Curier 2019, 32) [exhausting and humiliating]. Moreover, the education they received about how to take the metro, how to speak in Hexagonal French and even how to wash themselves without wasting water, was insulting. Curier found the latter particularly rude because in Guadeloupe natural resources were plentiful: 'c'était insultant pour moi qui suis née dans la belle commune de vieux-habitants [*sic*], où l'eau coulait à profusion, et où nous nous baignions à notre guise' (Curier 2019, 32) [it was insulting for me who was born in the beautiful district of Vieux-Habitants, where water flowed abundantly, and where we bathed as much as we liked]. Here, Curier denounces the neocolonial attitude held by the managers of the centre, who considered the Caribbean islands as 'backward' and 'inferior' to the Hexagon; Curier reverses this idea to show that, in some instances, life was more advanced on the Caribbean islands. Yet at the centre the women were treated as though they were children in need of parental guidance, in a real-life illustration of the metaphorical parent–child relationship between the metropolitan 'centre' and the Caribbean 'periphery'. This infantilising and insulting treatment of Antillean women that Curier denounces is evident in the policies of the BUMIDOM found in the archives. As outlined in an official report in 1968, young girls could buy a trousseau for 250 francs containing clothes they would need in continental France. There were two options containing different clothes such as coats, shirts, skirts and underwear. While the BUMIDOM presented these packages as a means to ensure that 'le vestiaire soit à l'avenir mieux adapté au climat' [the clothing be in future better adapted to the climate], they could also be interpreted as patronising gestures; the clothes were akin to a uniform, meaning that all the young women looked the same and did not have the freedom to choose what to wear themselves (BUMIDOM 1968b, 2).

Curier denounces not only the training provided by the BUMIDOM but also the process the Bureau had implemented to find work for the women. After a month at the training centre, she was transferred to a hostel located near the Gare Montparnasse, run by nuns. She felt lonely, as she had been separated from her friends, although she was living with other women from the islands. Once a week she had to go to the BUMIDOM office in the fourth arrondissement, where she would be given some financial assistance, yet it was 'insuffisant pour prendre le métro et subvenir à nos besoins les plus indispensables' (Curier 2019, 37) [insufficient to take the metro and meet our most basic needs], particularly in an expensive city such as Paris. The BUMIDOM office was supposed to find the women work in professions such as health care and administration, but, as Curier remembers, most women were directed towards domestic work. They were taken to dormitories where they could be sexually abused by the master of the house, and some women turned to prostitution to earn more money (Curier 2019, 38–9). Curier's account is a strong indictment of how the BUMIDOM failed to protect the workers and provide them with meaningful training and employment.

Yet Curier's personal story is one of resilience and agency. On hearing these stories of exploitation, she was determined to find a job 'rapidement et sans l'aide du BUMIDOM' (Curier 2019, 40) [quickly and without the help of the BUMIDOM]. She first worked as an invoice clerk for a perfume factory in Paris, living in a hostel for workers nearby. She then moved to live with the family of her friend Alexis on the outskirts of the capital. Her experiences are very different from those of other BUMIDOM participants; she found work herself relatively easily and progressed in her administrative career. She recognises that her success was partly due to being employed in the private sector where salaries were higher, which enabled her to send back remittances to her family. Her parents were very proud that her migration had been a success: 'les parents étaient heureux et fiers car ils avaient besoin de cet argent et c'était aussi la preuve que j'avais réussi "là-bas"' (Curier 2019, 46) [my parents were happy and proud because they needed that money, and it was also proof that I had succeeded 'over there']. Here, the roles are reversed between parent and child, and it is now Curier who is providing for her family. This quotation also reinforces the fact that many Antillean families held up mainland France as the land of opportunity – Curier's parents were proud not only that their daughter was now working, but also that she had found professional success on the mainland. Yet she was successful there despite rather than because of the BUMIDOM, as she had negotiated more stable working conditions and a better quality of life in the private sector. It is somewhat ironic that, towards the end of her working life, Curier was once again connected to the BUMIDOM, as she worked for the ANT which replaced the BUMIDOM, helping her compatriots to find accommodation and more meaningful work (Curier 2019, 80). As Megha Amrith and Nina Sahraoui observe, agency within the context of work and migration 'goes beyond acts of resistance to exploitative power structures', but rather incorporates 'wider projects of individual and collective forms of gender and labour empowerment' (2018, 4). Curier's actions are demonstrative of the collective struggle to attribute more value to the work Antillean women were given. She paved a way for others to work outside the confinements of the BUMIDOM scheme, where in general they were treated with greater dignity and respect.

Curier thus uses the genre of life writing to work through her own difficult memories of the BUMIDOM but also to offer a critique of the scheme, particularly in relation to the work provided to participants and to facilitate a collective discussion about Caribbean post-war emigration. She has spoken about her book at local community events in Guadeloupe – in October 2022, for instance, she appeared on a radio phone-in show on Radio Horizon AP, while in June 2023 she participated in a literary discussion at Médiathèque Le Moule, Grande-Terre island. In personal correspondence with me in June 2023, Curier explained that, once she had presented her book at these events, other people then came forward to offer their own experiences and reflections of the Bureau. Curier's text has thus been catalytic in the sharing of stories and memories about the BUMIDOM at a local level. Moving away from a literary stance and favouring a more sociological approach, she succeeds in communicating memories of her lived expression to members of her own generation who also experienced these events. Moreover, she demonstrates in her writing how the jobs offered to women were informed by restrictive gender norms in circulation in France at the time. Despite these gendered stereotypes, she succeeded in breaking from the domestic roles encouraged by the authorities to establish her own career in administration. How do the other autobiographical narratives differ in terms of the ideals of domesticity and femininity they promote?

Caregiving, Domesticity and Femininity in Lucienne Dangreville-Bellemare's *Paroles de ma vie: de Fort-de-France Martinique à Saint-Denis (Seine Saint-Denis)* and Michèle Zabulon's *Parcours de vie d'une puéricultrice antillaise*

The life writing of Dangreville-Bellemare and Zabulon invite comparisons for their style and structure as well as for the themes they evoke. Both are first-person narratives which provide an insight into the gendered and racialised experiences of migration encountered by the two authors, and they are structured as a series of vignettes around different themes such as childhood, work, leisure activities and return. These vignettes are framed by photographs of important events in the narrators' lives, thus providing visual representations of their memories which complement the written text. The works engage in autobiographical tradition in different ways. While the name of the author/narrator/protagonist is never revealed textually in *Paroles de ma vie*, the autobiographical status of the text is clear in paratextual items such as the title and the blurb – thus confirming Gérard Genette's assertion that the paratext is 'a privileged place of pragmatics and a strategy, of an influence on the public, an influence that [. . .] is at the service of a better reception for the text and a more pertinent reading of it' (1997, 2). The use of the possessive adjective 'ma' in the title is a clear indication that these memoirs belong to Dangreville-Bellemare, while the blurb on the back cover positions the text as a 'récit autobiographique' (Dangreville-Bellemare 2014) [autobiographical narrative]. In contrast, Zabulon attaches the indefinite article 'une' to the noun phrase 'puéricultrice antillaise' in the title of the text, making its autobiographical status ambiguous from the title. However, the first chapter is entitled 'Michèle Zabulon', thus closing off any question about the identity of the narrator-protagonist from the outset.

A further comparison between the texts is the alternative publishing strategies the authors have adopted. *Paroles de ma vie* is published by Edilivre, a collaborative publishing platform based in Paris. *Parcours de vie d'une puéricultrice antillaise* is self-published through Publishroom Factory, a self-publishing platform which facilitates the promotion of authors and their books. These alternative publishing models have reduced the amount of editorial control over the texts and have given Dangreville-Bellemare and Zabulon a greater authorial voice. Having never published any writing before as they were engaged in care work throughout their careers, they have now become writers. Although, as we shall see shortly, notions of domesticity and femininity may be promoted on the diegetic level, on the extradiegetic level the authors disrupt these gendered ideas of work and open up possibilities for other Antillean women to engage in writing. However, although this approach gives the authors greater autonomy over their texts, it risks reducing the circulation and global reach of the narratives, because the authors have to create their own marketing strategies, meaning that their work is unlikely to be read by a large, global audience. Ultimately, the lack of editorial intervention reduces the cultural capital of these texts.

Paroles de ma vie provides a detailed account of how the BUMIDOM worked in practice. Although Dangreville-Bellemare received professional training in nursing at an institution in the north of France rather than domestic training at the centre in Crouy-sur-Ourcq (which had not actually been established when she made the journey to France in 1964), her journey was still organised through the BUMIDOM office. As a young woman, she subscribed to the rhetoric promoted by the BUMIDOM as the Hexagon as 'el dorado', the land of opportunity. She describes emigration as:

> la seule voie de l'espoir, du bonheur et probablement d'une autre façon de vivre [. . .]. Pour moi c'était le pays où je marcherais sans fuir le regard des autres, où la vie serait plus facile pour le travail. (Dangreville-Bellemare 2014, 225)
>
> [the only means of hope, happiness and probably another way of life [. . .]. For me it was the country where I would walk without running from the gaze of other people, where it would be easier to find work.]

Dangreville-Bellemare was optimistic that migration would elevate her socio-economic status because it would provide her with work, and thus would eliminate her sentiments of being judged by others in Martinique for being unemployed. She thus equated labour with financial stability and social acceptance. Having finished her education aged nineteen, she had few qualifications and even fewer job prospects. Her dream was to become a nurse and work with children but she realised that training opportunities were scarce in Martinique. Having applied to nursing schools in mainland France, she feared being unable to pay for her voyage. She thus wrote to Général de Gaulle asking for his advice after he had made a visit to Martinique, and was stunned to receive a reply, which told her to go to the BUMIDOM office. Dangreville-Bellemare does not provide much information about the selection procedure; she describes it as a relatively smooth and easy process, during which she talked to 'une employée fort sympathique' [a really nice employee] who collected information about her, gave her advice and '[l]'encourageait pour cette longue traversée' (2014, 228) [encouraged her for that long journey]. A few weeks later she was given a one-way boat ticket and a voucher with which to buy clothes. She left for France on 30 April 1964 and arrived two weeks later. The passengers dressed in their most elegant clothes on the day of their arrival, as they wanted to 's'habiller comme en France' (Dangreville-Bellemare 2014, 236) [dress as though they were in France]. This is yet another indication of the ways in which Caribbean peoples had internalised notions of cultural inferiority which were nurtured by a colonised mindset, because they had assumed the notion that people from mainland France were more sophisticated than Antilleans.

Dangreville-Bellemare demonstrates clearly how the BUMIDOM operated on gendered and racial lines, orienting Black Antillean women towards roles deemed appropriate for women, such as cleaners, housemaids or nurses working with children. The narrative persona believes she will have a better future as a nurse than as a domestic maid, and she considers herself lucky to escape this fate, commenting that 'j'étais destinée à un meilleur futur que celui de mes compatriotes' (Dangreville-Bellemare 2014, 239–40) [I was destined for a better future than that of my compatriots]. However, while she was not exploited to the same extent as those working as cleaners, and she did have better job prospects after her nursing training, life at the boarding school where she completed her training was still difficult. She had to follow her classes as well as help to look after young children suffering from tuberculosis. The tasks were physically difficult; she experienced this labour corporeally and her body was altered by the tasks had had to carry out. She describes the work as giving her 'des courbatures plein le dos' [aches all down her back] and making her operate 'comme un robot' (Dangreville-Bellemare 2014, 242) [like a robot]. Her earlier comments about nursing being a less exploitative profession are demonstrative of a certain naivety with which many Guadeloupean and Martinican women approached their migration and work.

In addition, this labour in the health-care profession was highly gendered because it tapped into the notion of women as caregivers. Through the BUMIDOM, the French state actively determined which jobs women, and specifically women of colour, were able to do to promote notions of domesticity, caregiving and femininity. These connections between labour and gender were not only a reflection of social norms at the time but were also the product of a policy promoted by the French government. As Félix Germain explains, Antillean women had the reputation of being natural domestics and mothers, and so the BUMIDOM took advantage of these stereotypes and offered the women work as nurses and cleaners, with the proviso that they would be given the opportunity to climb up the ranks (which almost never happened) (Germain 2010, 482). Germain also points out that the women were encouraged to be live-in domestics or to live in boarding schools, as Dangreville-Bellemare did, so that they would not have to find housing for them (2010, 482). Housing was already in short supply, partly because the *pieds-noirs* (people of French or European descent living in Algeria) had to be repatriated and housed following the Algerian War of Independence, and partly because the BUMIDOM encountered opposition when trying to negotiate rent agreements with private landlords and estate agents who did not want to deal with Antilleans. Dangreville-Bellemare was grateful to be housed and educated in the boarding school because it '[l]'avait éloigné des difficultés d'adaptation et de souffrance qu'avaient connues les Antillais arrivés par le BUMIDOM' (2014, 257) [had kept [her] away from the difficulties at adapting and the suffering experienced by Antilleans arriving through the BUMIDOM]. It had enabled her to make friends and integrate relatively easily into metropolitan French life. However, as Germain's observation makes clear, the integration of Guadeloupean and Martinican communities was not the sole concern of French officials who also had to think about the social cohesion of other migrant populations living in the Hexagon.

It appears that Zabulon had more agency in determining her professional career and chose herself to become a childcare worker. Nevertheless, to a certain extent her desire to work with children also played into the values of domesticity and care which were attributed to Caribbean women, even if she was not necessarily aware of this at the time. Zabulon was born in the mid-1950s and migrated to France later than the other women analysed in this chapter. There are few dates given in the text to position the narrative but she does reveal that the BUMIDOM paid for her plane ticket, thereby suggesting that her travel took place in the 1970s because the BUMIDOM first operated via boat travel until plane travel became more accessible and convenient (Pattieu 2017, 14).[6] Zabulon explains that she had always liked being surrounded by young children, and so 'le métier de puéricultrice paraissait tout à fait conforme à [ses] désirs' (2017, 29) [the profession of childcare worker seemed completely suited to [her] desires]. However, she seems to have had little choice in completing her training and exercising the profession in mainland France. She describes studying in France as 'un rite de passage naturel' (Zabulon 2017, 36) [a natural rite of passage]; it was expected that young people would travel to France to study and achieve success. She herself bought into this notion of France as the land of opportunity, which her mother also shared: 'ma mère avait une très haute idée de la France. Pour elle, c'était le summum' (Zabulon 2017, 36) [my mother also had a high opinion of France. For her, it was the pinnacle]. She thus used her mother's attachment to the 'motherland', and her mother's desire for her to have a stable career as a civil servant, to her advantage, allowing her to live on her own in France. This journey was positioned in terms of adventure and excitement. She sought to 'découvrir d'autres lieux, d'autres gens' [discover other places, other people] and 'élargir [son] espace vital' (Zabulon 2017, 36) [expand her living space], and she had been conditioned to think that emigrating to France was the way to do this.

Having applied directly to training schools in France, she received a positive response from a boarding school in Lagny, in the eastern suburbs of Paris. Although she did have a degree of agency because she chose what to study and where, the practicalities of the journey were organised and financed by the BUMIDOM. Her experience at the boarding school in Lagny were certainly gendered. The school was run by nuns, and only women were allowed to train there. However, she had a different experience from Dangreville-Bellemare in the sense that labour was not necessarily organised on racial lines in this instance. Zabulon recalls how she was 'la seule élève infirmière antillaise dans l'école' (2017, 58) [the only Antillean pupil at the school]. Although this centre promoted gendered notions of work, it did not explicitly advertise for people of colour. Zabulon does not describe any overt racial prejudice at the school, but she was treated with surprise and suspicion for the colour of her skin, particularly as there was nobody else who looked like her. For instance, during a placement at a local nursery school, a young child came up to her in the playground and asked her 'pourquoi tu ne t'est pas lavée? Tu es toute noire!' (Zabulon 2017, 57) [why haven't you had a wash? You're all black!]. The young white child had never seen a Black person before; the child was not necessarily acting with aggression, hostility or fear, like the child Fanon describes in *Peau noire, masques blancs* in the infamous phrase 'Tiens, un nègre!' (1952, 90) [Look, a Negro!] (1967, 111), but with innocence and ignorance. As Zabulon depicts in her life narrative, her subsequent experiences of work were mostly positive, and she worked in a range of hospitals and clinics in and around Paris without experiencing a huge amount of racial discrimination. In sum, then, her gendered identity did determine the work in which she was engaged (although she too played into these socially constructed norms by choosing this work in the first place), but her racial identity was less significant in this labour.

Conclusion

The life writing of Ega, Curier, Dangreville-Bellemare and Zabulon invite a comparative reading for the ways in which they use their personal memories to make a political statement about post-war migration from the Caribbean islands. Each text demonstrates how experiences of migration were inflected by race and gender, and reveals how these overlapping identity categories determined the types of work they were offered by the BUMIDOM office. In this way, the authors can be considered as social activists. Although Ega was more formally involved in activism than the other authors, in the organisations she established and assistance she gave to other Antillean women, the other authors, too, have sought to bring about social or political change. Through their personal writing, they consciously raise awareness of the racial and gendered lines on which the BUMIDOM operated while also engaging in techniques of narrative recovery to come to terms with their own memories of difficult events. In addition, they facilitate a collective remembering of the BUMIDOM by discussing their experiences on social media and at community events and encouraging other Guadeloupean and Martinican women to share their stories of emigration with pride rather than with shame.

These texts thus deserve inclusion in the emerging canon of personal writing about the BUMIDOM. The literary features of these narratives (with the exception of Ega's *Lettres à une noire*) are without doubt less pronounced than the literariness of earlier autobiographies of post-war Caribbean migration. Yet the clarity and accessibility of the prose, and the detail they provide about the Caribbean migratory experience from first-hand accounts, mean that these are important works which offer a unique insight into the mechanics of the BUMIDOM scheme. The texts are thus transformative: they enable a greater understanding of what it was like to migrate through the BUMIDOM, and act as a catalyst for the sharing and exchanging of stories of migration.

Notes

1. In *Le Discours antillais* (1981), Édouard Glissant explains that Martinican identity is always plural and is formed through connections between individuals. On a discursive level, this collectivity is constructed through the use of the first-person plural pronoun 'nous' (Fulton 2003).
2. Patrick Chamoiseau's second autobiographical narrative about his childhood, *Chemin d'école* [*School Days*], was published in 1994. The two texts were then published together by Gallimard and repackaged

as *Une enfance créole*. The third text, *À bout d'enfance* [At the End of Childhood], was not published until 2005, also by Gallimard.

3. Many of the references to race and sentiments of racial inferiority on the part of Martinicans which appeared in the original version were toned down (Hardwick 2018, 221–2).
4. https://vivreensemble.org/ [accessed 8 October 2023]. The association has created a radio programme, 'Les Echos du Grand Saint-Barthélémy', which is broadcast on Radio Galère, a local radio station in Marseille. The programme consists of debates about important social issues. The association is also engaged in literacy campaigns to promote reading and writing among disadvantaged children.
5. 'Ouvrier spécialisé' (OS) refers to semi-skilled/unskilled workers who do not require formal professional qualifications.
6. Sylvain Pattieu states that, by 1970, most Antilleans arrived at Orly Airport in Paris (2017, 14).

Chapter 3

National Identity, Diasporic Citizenship and Postdiaspora: The BUMIDOM in Fiction

Towards the end of Maryse Condé's novel *Desirada*, the third-person omniscient narrator offers a powerful reflection on the identity quest of the protagonist Marie-Noëlle. Inscribed in this quotation is a broader comment on the identity struggles of people of Caribbean origin living in France. Condé writes:

> pourtant, depuis quelque temps, elle se posait la question: est-ce qu'elle ne pouvait pas continuer de vivre comme elle le faisait? Sans identité, comme une personne à qui on a volé ses papiers et qui erre à travers le monde? Est-ce qu'ainsi elle n'était pas plus libre ? C'est une sale manie de vouloir savoir à tout prix d'où on sort et la goutte de sperme à laquelle on doit la vie. (1997, 243)
>
> [yet for some time now she had asked herself why not go on living as she was. Without an identity, like someone whose papers have been stolen and who drifts aimlessly through the world? Wasn't she freer like that? It's a terrible thing wanting to know at any cost where we come from and tracking down that drop of sperm that gave us life.] (2000, 223)

Marie-Noëlle is searching for her familial roots as she has grown up without a father, but alongside the absence of familial identity she also experiences a lack of national identity, having lived in Guadeloupe during her childhood, and in France and the United States (among other countries) as an adult. Her sentiments of rootlessness and statelessness are evoked through the verb 'errer', a verb which operates here in different ways to Édouard Glissant's empowering usage in *Poétique de la relation* as it denotes continuous displacement with no clear direction or objective.[1] Her situation is compared to someone whose official documents have been stolen, compounding her sense of nomadism. In addition, the troubling nature of her identity quest is encapsulated in the build-up of rhetorical questions in this passage, and in the negative description of her mission as 'une sale manie', a filthy habit or obsession which is detrimental to her well-being. Yet this passage also suggests a certain freedom in having no fixed or predetermined familial and national identity, as it enables Marie-Noëlle to define herself in her own terms.

This chapter investigates how novels by French Caribbean writers transmit memories of non-belonging. I argue that the novels raise key questions such as: What is national identity? How does it intersect with regional Caribbean identity and how is it complicated by (internal) migration? What does it mean to be French and at the same time to be denied a French identity because one's familial origins lie in the Caribbean? How does migration from Guadeloupe and Martinique to mainland France via the BUMIDOM impact on the national identity of BUMIDOM participants and their descendants? As I have made clear throughout this book, people arriving from the Caribbean islands during the 1960s and beyond were not immigrants but were French citizens. As Elena Barabantseva and Claire Sutherland remark, citizenship is a highly political notion which involves much more than simply giving someone the right to remain in a country: 'citizenship is a marker of identification dividing the society into those who belong there and those who belong somewhere else' (2011, 6). In theory, French citizenship guaranteed a sense of belonging to the French nation among people originating from the French Caribbean. Yet this chapter problematises this egalitarian notion of citizenship upon which the discourse of the French Republic is predicated. It engages with concepts of diasporic citizenship and postdiaspora as proposed by Michel Laguerre to investigate how communities endeavoured to maintain political, social and cultural ties to the Caribbean while also engaging in French life, but, for many, these attempts were thwarted by the treatment they received in France. I argue that the novels demonstrate in different ways the disparities between a Caribbean diasporic identity as desired by BUMIDOM participants and their descendants, and the migrant identity with which they were forced to negotiate on their arrival in France.

In line with the overarching aims of this study, the chapter brings together well-known writers and texts with those yet to enter the French Caribbean literary canon in order to raise awareness of important but neglected manifestations of French Caribbean culture. Analysing the novels chronologically, the chapter begins by examining Jacqueline Manicom's *Mon examen de blanc*, a novel which raises urgent questions about race, gender and Frenchness. This novel is the only one in the corpus to have been written during the BUMIDOM period itself; it is thus essential to consider, as in the previous chapter, how representations which were contemporaneous with large-scale Caribbean migration might differ from retrospective fictional accounts which operate in the realm of memory and postmemory rather than history. The chapter then discusses Condé's *Desirada* and Fabienne Kanor's *D'eaux douces* together because they approach transgenerational Caribbean identities and memories in complementary ways. These novels both show clearly how the BUMIDOM has influenced the identity politics of not only those who migrated during this period, but also their descendants and family members who were born and raised in France. Finally, I examine Estelle-Sarah Bulle's *Là où les chiens aboient par la queue* through the lens of diasporic citizenship. Authors such as Bulle, Condé and Kanor who are writing about the BUMIDOM today are recovering the voices of French Caribbean communities living in continental France, whose experiences have been neglected in state representations of migration. They interrogate what it means to belong to a nation which nevertheless excludes its citizens of colour.

Of course, these four texts are not the only novels to discuss the theme of the BUMIDOM, but they stand out for their emphasis on diasporic experience, belonging and identity. As I argued in the previous chapter, few texts about Caribbean migration of any genre, novel or otherwise, were actually written or published during the period in which the BUMIDOM was in operation. The novels which were published, including Michèle Lacrosil's *Sapotille et le serin d'argile* (1960) [Sapotille and the Clay Canary] and Roland Laouchez's *Confessions d'une prostituée antillaise à Paris* (1975) [Confessions of an Antillean Prostitute in Paris], focus primarily on the push factors for emigration and the difficult experiences of daily life in France. From the late 1980s and early 90s, prominent Caribbean literary figures, such as Raphaël Confiant, Gisèle Pineau and Patrick Chamoiseau, also wrote fiction about emigration to France. In some of their novels, the BUMIDOM is an important plot point – in Confiant's *Mamzelle libellule* (1994) [*Mamzelle Dragonfly*], the protagonist Adélise goes to the BUMIDOM office in Fort-de-France to find work but is turned away,[2] while in Pineau's *Morne Câpresse* (2008) [Câpresse Hill],[3] Pacôme returns to Guadeloupe and founds a congregation for women, following her negative experiences in France with the BUMIDOM. In other texts, such as Chamoiseau's *Chronique des sept misères* (1986) [*Chronicle of the Seven Sorrows*], the Bureau is given a fleeting reference in order for authors to make a political statement about the French government's unequal treatment of its Caribbean citizens. More recently, there has been an increase in Caribbean authors who are little known beyond Martinique and Guadeloupe writing about the BUMIDOM and migration trends between Europe and the Caribbean more generally. Novels such as *Une étoile en dérive* (2004) [A Falling Star] by Laure Moutoussamy, *Buisson joyeux* (2009) [Bright Bush] by Clarisse Bagoé-Dubosq, *Et ce fut l'opportunité d'un exil* (2020) [And It was the Opportunity for Exile] by Victor Gilbert Faraux and *Mary-Yvonne et les autres* (2024) [Mary-Yvonne and the Others] by Marlène Pidéri-Joncart are published by Caribbean publishing houses or included in series which collate works by Caribbean authors, suggesting that these texts are primarily aimed at local Caribbean audiences. These are important works which require detailed analysis, but they are not included in the corpus of this study because they do not focus to the same extent on issues of national identity and diasporic experience. In contrast, the key questions at the heart of the four novels under analysis here is whether it was possible to be Black, Caribbean and French in the BUMIDOM era, and whether such hyphenated identities are accepted in France today.

A Black, Caribbean and French Identity? Jacqueline Manicom's *Mon examen de blanc*

As Qiang Liu and David Turner posit, 'national identity is the product of the development of modern nationalism' and refers to the inherent connection of individuals with the country of origin and place of birth, as experienced through shared historical and cultural traditions, moral values, beliefs and ideals (2018, 1080). National identity has long been theorised, and different schools of thought approach the concept from differing perspectives: from primordialists and perinnealists who believe that nations are stable constructs which have existed over a long time span; to modernists who depict nations as modern concepts, created by elites in response to socio-economic and political changes during the nineteenth century; to postmodernists who see the nation as contemporary expressions of new patterns of identity; and to constructivists and instrumentalists who perceive the nation as social constructs created to emphasise the boundary between members of the group and outsiders (Smith 2010).

What many of these theorisations have in common, though, is the belief that a nation is a racially and ethnically homogeneous entity, and that an individual can belong to only one nation. What happens, then, in the case of migration? How is national identity reconfigured by the arrival of migrant communities, and how does this work in the case of the French Caribbean, where those migrating were French citizens?

Manicom's novel demonstrates clearly the impossibility of reconciling Black, Caribbean and French identities during the mid-twentieth century. Manicom was born in 1935 in Guadeloupe to a family of East Indian origin, who had migrated to the Caribbean as indentured labourers. She was highly trained, which was quite unusual for Guadeloupean women at the time; after studying law and medicine, she became a midwife in Paris. She was also a feminist activist, and thus comparisons can be drawn between her and Françoise Ega, whom we met in the previous chapter, in terms of their political commitment. While Ega's work focused on assisting those emigrating to France, Manicom was more interested in discussing the biopolitics of the female reproductive body and campaigning for women's rights. She created l'Association guadeloupéenne pour le planning familial [Guadeloupean Family Planning Association] with her husband in 1964 and co-founded Choisir [To Choose] in the 1970s, organisations which sought to provide information and advice for women about contraception and family planning, and she also participated in the movement to legalise abortion in France (Zancarini-Fournel 2019, 103–4). These issues are prominent in her writing too. Both *Mon examen de blanc* and *La Graine: journal d'une sage-femme* (1974) [The Seed: Diary of a Midwife], the only two texts she published, examine women's reproductive rights and explore how gender oppression is compounded by intersecting racial and class oppression.

The novel is a first-person narrative, told by the protagonist Madévie, a Guadeloupean anaesthetist who works in the gynaecological wing of a hospital in Pointe-à-Pitre with the white French surgeon Cyril Démian. Madévie has just returned from France following a failed affair with Xavier, a white Parisian member of the bourgeoisie. The narrative time of the text is situated in the early 1960s; Cyril evokes 'une accélération du plan de migration vers la France métropolitaine' (Manicom 1972, 35) [an acceleration in the migration plan towards mainland France], suggesting that the narrative action takes place just as the French government is stepping up its mass migration programme. In contrast to the other novels analysed in this chapter, Manicom's story is set in Guadeloupe rather than mainland France, thereby offering a different perspective on the BUMIDOM and demonstrating the effects of mass migration on Guadeloupean society rather than on continental France. However, through an analepsis recounting Madévie's earlier experiences with Xavier in Paris (differentiated from the principle narrative action through the use of italics), we also learn about what life was like in France for people of colour in this period. Moreover, these flashbacks are narrated in the third person, representing the fact that, through migration, the protagonist experienced a transformation in her identity as she attempted to become more 'French' to assist her assimilation. While the principal characters, then, have not participated in the BUMIDOM themselves, Madévie has undergone her own transatlantic migration prior to the implementation of this scheme. Furthermore, she remains marked by her time in Paris, damaged both physically and psychologically by her failed relationship with Xavier which ended in her aborting her own child. Her migratory patterns and the changes they provoke in her are reflected textually in what H. Adlai Murdoch calls a 'discursive doubling' (2002, 134). When talking to Cyril about her experiences in Paris, she refers to herself impersonally by her full professional title 'le docteur Ramimoutou' [Doctor Ramimoutou], and distances her professional subjectivity in the present narrative time from the naive young girl named Madévie who studied in Paris seven years ago: 'je lui parlerai d'une mulâtresse qui porte mon nom, dont j'ai peut-être gardé le regard [. . .], une jeune fille que j'avais appelée Madévie' (Manicom 1972, 37) [I will tell him about a mulatto woman who bears my name, whose look I've perhaps kept [. . .], a young girl I called Madévie]. This technique is repeated throughout the narrative, and, as Murdoch notes, this doubling of self and other connotes a character who 'remains split between past and present, Paris and Pointe-à-Pitre' (2002, 134–5).

The title of the novel evokes from the outset the impossibility of being Black, Caribbean and also French. Betty Wilson notes that Manicom herself offers an explanation of the title on the back cover of the book:

> the book-jacket explains that the phrase comes from a French West Indian expression 'passer son examen de blanc' which means 'imiter le blanc pour s'assimiler à lui et partager ses privilèges', suggesting the Antillais has successfully completed the process of assimilating, and/or being assimilated into, the system of white values of the European Colonizer. (Wilson 1987, 51)

Through the title, Manicom provides a commentary on Guadeloupeans who have successfully assimilated into French society and gained the same rights and privileges as citizens from mainland France, but the only way they have been able to do this is by imitating 'le blanc' [the white man] and thereby subconsciously eradicating their Blackness. Manicom's approach here is reminiscent of Frantz Fanon's argument in *Peau noire, masques blancs*, in which he denounced the typical Black Antillean obsession with white metropolitan language and culture. Manicom suggests that it is impossible to be Black *and* Caribbean *and* French, that these three identities are irreconcilable, and that one element of their identity always has to be abandoned in order to prioritise the others. This is certainly the case for Madévie. As Brinda Mehta points out, 'Madévie' is an Indian name and refers to 'the great goddess' (2009, 125), and Manicom thus provides a nod to her own East Indian heritage through the naming of her protagonist. Yet at no point in the novel does Madévie reflect on her Indian ancestry or locate her own identity as part of a fusion of Indian, Caribbean and French influences. She has been conditioned to overtly deny the Indian and Caribbean strands of her identity so that she can be perceived as French.

Madévie is very concerned by the ways in which she is perceived by others, and she enables them to impose an identity on her, rather than defining herself in her own terms. For instance, she admires the physical qualities of the young, white French nurse Marie-Dominique who works alongside her and Cyril, and she wishes she were 'belle, blonde, blanche et claire' like her (Manicom 1972, 14) [beautiful, blonde, white and fair]. The alliteration of the plosive 'b' sound connotes Madévie's frustration that she does not share the prized light-skinned complexion of her colleague, and the addition of the adjective 'claire' at the end of this alliterative list of adjectives reinforces the fact that she, like others in Guadeloupe, equate physical beauty with being white. She states that, in contrast to Marie-Dominique, 'je ne suis qu'une mulâtresse, avec une peau en chocolat, comme disent les petits enfants de France qui n'ont pas l'habitude des gens de couleur' (Manicom 1972, 14) [I am only a mulatto woman, with chocolate-coloured skin, as young children in France, who are not used to seeing people of colour, say]. The use of the restrictive 'ne . . . que' structure reduces her identity to her skin colour, and the illusion to the epithet 'peau en chocolat' once again demonstrates that her racialised identity is being imposed on her, this time by young French children. It was for this very reason that she left for France to study medicine, before the French government encouraged the mass migration of its Caribbean citizens. She thought that she would be able to escape from the racial politics imbedded in Guadeloupean society and 'to assume, instead, her "rightful" identity as a French citizen', as Sam Haigh puts it (2000, 29). Yet her relationship with Xavier was doomed to fail from the outset because of his aversion towards people of different ethnicities, and as a corollary, so was her acceptance into French society. Through free indirect speech, we learn of the engrained prejudice in France against Antillean women, as Xavier describes Madévie in stereotypical overtones as an exotic, sexual being, simply because she is of mixed race: 'une mulâtresse vierge, ça n'existe pas!' (Manicom 1972, 38) [virgin mulatto women don't exist!]. While he is initially excited at the news of her pregnancy and agrees to marry her in secret, he is eventually unable to stand up to his mother for whom such a union would be a 'déclassement' (Manicom 1972, 113) [social demotion]. He proposes to marry and then divorce her after the baby is born, but Madévie eventually refuses and aborts the baby herself. In her own eyes, she was 'doublement française' (Manicom 1972, 43) [doubly French]; the colonial status of Guadeloupe meant that it belonged to France, while the departmentalisation law of 1946 in theory guaranteed Antilleans the same rights as citizens of mainland France. Yet this was certainly not a sentiment shared by Xavier, who was not prepared to have a mixed-race child. Neither was it an opinion upheld by the white French bourgeoisie, who saw her as Black and Caribbean but not French. The abortion she undergoes is 'a bitter comment on the hypocrisy of French politics of cultural assimilation for colonial subjects, and she returns to Guadeloupe scarred by her encounter with metropolitan life', her body literally damaged from this detrimental encounter (Meehan 2006, 295).

While Madévie is denied a French identity because of her Blackness, Cyril is certainly not denied a Caribbean identity because of his Frenchness. In fact, Madévie explains that he has been the one to show her the beautiful landscapes of her own island: 'Cyril, lui, connaît tout cela presque mieux que moi puisqu'il s'est approprié mon île' (Manicom 1972, 29) [Cyril knows all that almost better than me since he has claimed my island for himself]. The fact that Cyril has appropriated Madévie's island demonstrates his superior position to her; he is able to be white and French, and yet simultaneously claim a Caribbean identity if he so desires. The novel thus explores the complexities of racial relations beyond the Hexagon and reflects on how whiteness remains the privileged condition for belonging in both France and Guadeloupe. Cyril's existence in

Guadeloupe is also important because it is illustrative of the reverse migration from mainland France to the Caribbean islands which also occurred, and was even encouraged, during the BUMIDOM era. The BUMIDOM files held at the Archives nationales contain letters written by people from mainland France wishing to emigrate to Guadeloupe, Martinique and French Guiana to work there between 1978 and 1979. Reference is made in one letter, sent on 18 July 1978, to an advert on La 1ère television channel on 15 July 1978 encouraging people to emigrate to French Guiana. The government, however, was looking for a particular type of skilled worker. A letter sent on 1 October 1979 by a governmental official from the Ministère des Affaires étrangères [Ministry of Foreign Affairs] to a man looking for work in the overseas departments explicitly stated that 'seuls peuvent avoir quelques chances d'y trouver une situation ceux qui bénéficient d'une formation universitaire ou technique très spécialisée' (Gérard 1979) [only those with university training or a specialist skill have a chance of finding a post]. Cyril fits this profile: he is a white, bourgeois, educated professional, and thus his migration is very much desired. His working conditions in Guadeloupe lie in sharp contrast to those of Caribbean people of colour living and working in mainland France in often very difficult conditions. In addition, Manicom's novel reveals that it was not just white French men who were able to benefit from this reverse migration, and the new, exciting experiences it proffered. The nurse Marie-Dominique is able to enjoy a carefree life in Guadeloupe, relaxing on the beach and meeting new people, but she will eventually return to 'le monde réel' [the real world] in Paris once her placement is over (Manicom 1972, 68). The allusion to France as the 'monde réel' suggests that she considers the Caribbean as an exotic location for pleasure and enjoyment, but that mainland France is her true home.

Cyril and Madévie talk a lot about the BUMIDOM during their interactions. Cyril considers it to be a beneficial policy which will assist Antilleans in integrating into life in continental France, and he describes it as 'un mode d'intégration qui me paraît très satisfaisant!' (Manicom 1972, 35) [a method of integration which seems very satisfactory to me!]. The use of the noun 'intégration' here suggests that, for him, people of Caribbean origin participating in the BUMIDOM are not French citizens but migrants in need of assistance to integrate into French society. While Cyril praises the French government for implementing a policy which will help Guadeloupeans and Martinicans to improve their social standing, Madévie criticises the exploitative nature of this scheme. Her reflections are heavily laden with irony. For instance, when helping a mother to give birth, she imagines that the baby will soon join the sugar cane workers to undertake back-breaking work to increase the profits of the *békés* (Caribbean descendants of white French settlers), 'à moins que sa génération ne soit celle qui prendra la relève des éboueurs parisiens ou des poinçonneurs de métro?' (Manicom 1972, 46–7) [unless his generation is not the one that will take over the jobs of Parisian binmen or ticket inspectors on the metro?]. For Madévie, emigrating via the BUMIDOM will only reinforce Black Caribbean people's position at the bottom of the social hierarchy, and they will not be offered the same professional opportunities as citizens from mainland France. She also denounces the fact that emigration is prioritised over the development of industry on the islands, retorting to Cyril that 'on peut très bien concevoir un nouveau plan d'industrialisation de l'île' (Manicom 1972, 35) [we can very well conceive of a new industrialisation plan for the island]. Yet later in the novel she becomes more despondent, admitting that, if the Bureau were to close, 'on ne trouvera pas comme par enchantement du travail pour les gens qui resteront ici' (Manicom 1972, 168) [we won't find jobs for people staying here by magic]. At times, this despondency becomes complicity when she disagrees with Cyril's views about the relationship between France and Guadeloupe but she dares not speak out for fear of angering him. Cyril believes that Guadeloupe should be grateful for France's financial support, because, without France, 'ce sera comme à Haïti, la misère, avec à la tête un quelconque papa-doc!' (Manicom 1972, 103) [it will be like Haiti, destitution with someone like Papa Doc at the head!]. Rather than challenging him on his views, Madévie chooses to remain silent. This parent–child relationship on which the affiliation between France and Guadeloupe is predicated is mirrored by the parental-like relationship between the two principal characters, in which Madévie remains in awe of Cyril and does not dare to contradict him. Although she is aware of the inequalities between France and Guadeloupe, of which the BUMIDOM is a salient example, she is not sufficiently emancipated in order to fully denounce these inequalities.

By the end of the novel, she does seem to have become more independent. She is no longer reliant on Cyril, and she has a more fulfilling relationship with Gilbert, a dark-skinned Guadeloupean man who treats her as his equal. Wilson notes that 'Madévie's relationship with Gilbert is the vehicle for her own liberation' because through this relationship she becomes more mature and independent (1987, 56), yet it is somewhat problematic from a feminist perspective to conclude that Madévie is only able to become emancipated through her relationship with another man. Wilson also views their union as a parallel in Guadeloupe's social and political development, and it thus symbolises 'hope for the future autonomy of Guadeloupe' (1987, 57). However, the ending of the novel is not entirely positive as Gilbert is killed during a demonstration in the cane fields, thereby implying that Guadeloupeans' ambitions for autonomy will never be realised. While the novel closes with Madévie promising to stay strong for her deceased lover, she continues to see planes flying overhead, carrying 'une cinquantaine d'Antillais [qui] s'envolent encore vers les hôpitaux, les usines et les trottoirs de Paris' (Manicom 1972, 185) [around fifty Antilleans [who] still fly out to Paris's hospitals, factories and streets], where they will be subjected to exploitation and racial discrimination.

Mon examen de blanc thus passes comment on the impossibility for Antilleans to be treated as equals to citizens from mainland France. While Madévie may well experience an individual sense of liberation by the end of the novel, this is not shared on a collective level because the large-scale migration of Antilleans continues beyond the space of the text, and with it their mistreatment. The novel was written and published during the BUMIDOM period itself, meaning that it is an imagined representation of what participants had to endure, rather than a space in which memories of migration are created and transmitted. Yet Manicom's objectives seem to be similar to those of Condé, Kanor and Bulle, in that she seeks to create a counter-narrative about the BUMIDOM and to reveal details about this migration scheme which were certainly not foregrounded in the rhetoric sustained by the French authorities. Specifically, she shines a spotlight on the impacts of the BUMIDOM for those remaining in Guadeloupe and emphasises the impossibility for Black Caribbean citizens to reconcile their local, regional and national identities.

Identity across Generations: Maryse Condé's *Desirada* and Fabienne Kanor's *D'eaux douces*

In a departure from Manicom's novel, *Desirada* and *D'eaux douces* both spotlight the identity quest of a younger generation. The principal protagonists of these texts did not experience migration through the BUMIDOM personally, but their parents did. They thus form part of what Michel Laguerre terms 'postdiaspora' – that is, they live in a different space from that where their parents were born, but also lay claim to the Caribbean through their French citizenship and their familial origins (indeed, all people of Caribbean origin living in mainland France possess citizenship in the Caribbean, in what Laguerre terms their 'ancestral country' (2017, 20) because the French Caribbean islands are French departments). Their memories of emigration are not their own but inherited from their parents in a process Marianne Hirsch terms 'postmemory'. For Hirsch, these transferred memories, passed down through one's parents' stories, are catalytic for one's own life, even to the extent of 'having one's own life stories displaced, even evacuated, by our ancestors' because of the affective force they contain (2012, 5). Indeed, for Kanor's narrator-protagonist Frida, her parents' memories of the past act as the origin of her present: 'je collecte les souvenirs et épluche mon histoire en commençant par le bout' (Kanor 2004, 7) [I collect memories and unravel my story starting from the end]. Frida was born in Tours, a city she describes in negative terms as a 'ville de rien, de chiens, qui avait vu stationner des centaines de familles antillaises' (Kanor 2004, 10) [a city of nothing, gone to the dogs, where hundreds of Antillean families had been parked]. Her daily life was impacted by the large-scale migration of Caribbean citizens to mainland France, as she became part of a larger community of Antilleans who had settled in Tours in previous years through the BUMIDOM. In contrast, Condé's narrator-protagonist Marie-Noëlle was born in Guadeloupe and emigrated to Paris as a child to join her mother, Reynalda. It thus becomes clear that the BUMIDOM has a significant impact on the families of those who emigrate, as well as on the participants themselves. Indeed, the novels reveal that it is the younger generation who often experience acute sentiments of rootlessness and alienation, as they struggle to make sense of who they are and where they have come from. This alienation is represented textually by the multiplicity of narrative voices in both novels. *Desirada* is mostly narrated in the third person and interspersed with chapters in the first person to represent the point of view of different characters. Dawn Fulton reads this interchanging of narrative perspective in *Desirada* as 'a constant refusal of any singular version of events', and thus the novel disrupts a 'single "straightened" version of the past' (Fulton 2005, 51). Yet it could also be interpreted as the failure of Marie-Noëlle to determine her own identity herself, because she is always confronted by overlapping voices and an overarching narrator who imposes an identity on her. Kanor's narrative strategy also implies Frida's lack of agency. *D'eaux douces* intertwines within the same chapter personal reflections by Frida, told in the first person, with a more impersonal narration by a third-person narrator, meaning that her thoughts are mediated by the omniscient narrator.

The diasporic identity of their principal characters is reflected in the subjectivity of both Condé and Kanor, who describe themselves as diasporic writers whose identity cannot be pinned down. This is also echoed in the themes they treat in their writing, and they address issues such as migration, displacement and rootlessness. The authors are of different generations and social standing – Condé was born in 1937 in Guadeloupe to parents who were part of the emerging Black bourgeoisie and died in 2024, while Kanor was born in Orléans in 1970 to working-class parents who arrived in France via the BUMIDOM. Kanor, therefore, like her protagonist Frida, is the recipient of transgenerational memories about the BUMIDOM. Despite these differences in their upbringing, their attitude to identity is remarkably similar, and in interviews they have both cited each other as literary influences, making the comparison between their novels all the more relevant. In an interview with Jason Herbeck in 2013, Kanor expressed her admiration for Condé who has united her gift for storytelling with her nomadic existence which 'lui a permis de marcher le monde tout en le racontant' (Herbeck and Kanor 2013, 974) [enabled her to travel across the world while narrating it]. Meanwhile, in an interview with Zineb Ali-Benali and Françoise Simasotchi-Bronès in 2009, Condé praised Kanor, alongside other postcolonial writers such as Nancy Huston, Dany Laferrière and Zadie Smith, for her interest in 'les notions d'origine, de lieu de résidence, d'identité collective, de langue maternelle' (Condé 2009, 23) [notions of origin, home, collective identity, native language]. A further connection between the two writers is the variety of their cultural output, albeit in different forms and guises. Condé wrote novels, plays, essay collections and short stories;[4] Kanor is a journalist, filmmaker and academic as well as a novelist and has produced documentaries about significant episodes in Caribbean history, including the BUMIDOM.[5] In addition, they have both received critical acclaim for their work. Condé won many international prizes and awards for her writing, including the New Academy Prize in Literature (the Alternative Nobel Prize for Literature) in 2018, while Kanor has mostly been celebrated by francophone literary establishments, winning the Prix Carbet de la Caraïbe et du Tout-Monde in 2014 for *Faire l'aventure* (2014) [Becoming an Adventurer]. The fact that such celebrated Caribbean literary figures have produced work about the BUMIDOM reveals the significance of the Bureau, and the mass migration it engendered, in the French Caribbean imaginary today.

Desirada tells the story of Marie-Noëlle's life and her search to discover her origins. Born in Guadeloupe, she is initially brought up by Ranélise, a cook at a local restaurant who saved Marie-Noëlle's mother Reynalda from drowning in the sea. Aged ten, she is taken to Paris to live with Reynalda (whom she barely knows), Reynalda's husband Ludovic and their son Garvey. Marie-Noëlle is desperate to know the identity of her father, and the novel centres around this crucial question. Indeed, this identity quest is apparent even from the title of the novel. Fulton explains that 'the "desired" narrative signalled by the novel's title [. . .] is that of Marie-Noëlle's mother', who knows who her father was (2005, 48). When Marie-Noëlle is an adult, her mother reveals that she was raped by Gian Carlo Coppini, an Italian jewellery maker who employed her mother Nina, but Marie-Noëlle later discovers that it was in fact her grandmother Nina who had been raped, by her cousin Gabin. The novel thus raises questions about the reliability and authenticity of information passed down by family members, and it also passes comment on the interplay between memory and imagination.

This is particularly salient in the discussion of the role the BUMIDOM played in Reynalda's emigration. Marie-Noëlle initially thought that her mother had relied on the services of the Bureau; she does not remember her mother's departure, so she has to trust the information her mother has given her. In the opening chapter, the narrator recounts that Reynalda announced she was leaving two weeks after her daughter's baptism. In an acknowledgement of the huge numbers of Antilleans who participated in the scheme, Condé writes: 'comme à tant de compatriotes à l'époque, le BUMIDOM lui avait procuré une place chez Jean-René Duparc qui habitait au boulevard Malesherbes, dix-septième arrondissement à Paris' (Condé 1997, 19) ['the BUMIDOM agency had found her a job, as they did for so many fellow islanders at that time – with Jean-René Duparc, who lived on the boulevard Malesherbes in the XVIIth Arrondissement in Paris'] (Condé 2000, 9). This information is confirmed by Claire-Alta, Ranélise's younger sister, when Marie-Noëlle returns to Guadeloupe to attend Ranélise's funeral. Claire-Alta tells her that she was upset when Reynalda left, particularly because she had not told anyone about her plans: 'elle avait constitué un dossier et avait été recrutée comme employée de maison' (Condé 1997, 152) ['she had filed an application and got hired as a domestic'] (Condé 2000, 138). However, later in the novel, when Marie-Noëlle is now living in the

United States, she visits Paris to find out more about her mother, in the hope that it will help her to discover the identity of her father. She pays a visit to her mother's old employer, Mme Duparc, who explains that she hired Reynalda directly because she did not trust the BUMIDOM to provide her with a sensible, hard-working maid: 'elle n'aurait jamais accepté d'introduire une personne chez elle sur la recommandation de fonctionnaires inconnus' (Condé 1997, 250) ['she would never have agreed to introduce someone into her home on the recommendation of some anonymous civil servant'] (Condé 2000, 229). The use of the negating adverb 'jamais' reinforces the social stigma attached to the BUMIDOM, both for those emigrating and for those employing people who had travelled via the Bureau. It is thus unclear whether Reynalda actually did participate in the BUMIDOM or whether she organised her migration herself, but this confusion demonstrates overtly the negative attitudes towards the BUMIDOM by both French and Caribbean citizens. This episode is also an example of the many occasions in the novel in which Marie-Noëlle is faced with conflicting narratives about her family's past. Fulton connects the impossibility that Marie-Noëlle encounters to reconstitute her mother's life with a more generalised inability to access a collective Caribbean memory. Fulton writes:

> just as Marie-Noëlle cannot be a lucid witness to her mother's experience, a collective Caribbean memory must acknowledge the necessary inaccessibility of the past. In essence, Conde's novel can be seen as a warning against the illusion of integrity in the formation of collective identity in the Antilles. (Fulton 2005, 57)

Kanor's *D'eaux douces* also explores these tensions between individual and collective histories, memories and identities in the Caribbean. The novel opens with the protagonist, Frida, admitting that she has killed her boyfriend Éric, and that she is about to shoot herself. The narrative time then changes and she explains how she has ended up in such a desperate situation. Frida struggles with her identity until she goes to university, where she learns about femininity, sexuality and political freedom. She joins the Mouvement de libération de la négresse [Negro Women's Liberation Movement], a Black feminist activist group, and she travels to Haiti with Éric to try to stir her revolutionary ideals into action. Yet, at the end of the novel, she is overcome with jealousy on discovering that Éric has had many sexual affairs with other white women, so she kills him and then prepares to commit suicide.

There are few textual details in *D'eaux douces* about the practicalities of the journey Frida's parents took from Martinique to Tours through the BUMIDOM. This could represent the humiliation her parents associated with requiring financial support from the state in order to emigrate, although they are described as 'heureux bénéficiaires du BUMIDOM' (Kanor 2004, 10) [happy beneficiaries of the BUMIDOM], suggesting that they perceived emigration as a socially advancing condition and were not ashamed to use the service. Frida's parents were among the early participants of this scheme – they had to travel by boat because plane tickets were 'hors de prix' (Kanor 2004, 12) [overpriced], and the crossing took approximately a month. The fact that her parents describe the Hexagon as 'la grande France' (Kanor 2004, 12) [great France] indicates that they subscribe to colonial rhetoric which created a hierarchy between the 'superior' metropole and the 'inferior' Caribbean islands. This idea is reinforced later in the novel, when we discover that Frida's mother travelled to Tours via Le Havre to marry a man she had met at a ball back in Martinique. According to the narrator, she was not really thinking about romance, but wanted to explore 'la France, illustre patrie des travailleurs, interdite aux mendiants, aux voyous et aux chômeurs' (Kanor 2004, 25) [France, that illustrious homeland of workers, forbidden to beggars, thugs and the unemployed]. The contrast between the celebrated and glorious image she has of France, as portrayed through the adjective 'illustre', and the negative depiction of the Caribbean, denoted by the list of three forbidden categories of people, reveals very clearly her differing attitudes towards France and Martinique.

While in Condé's text, then, it is unclear whether Reynalda ever did use the services of the BUMIDOM, Kanor's novel positions the Bureau clearly as organising and facilitating the passage of Frida's parents. Despite this difference, the novels illustrate in similar ways how emigration has impacted on the identity of those who emigrated and on their descendants. Indeed, both *Desirada* and *D'eaux douces* demonstrate generational differences in notions of belonging and identity. It appears that those who made the conscious decision to cross the Atlantic find it easier to identify as French, despite being victims of racism, whereas the second generation born in France continuously question where they belong. In *Desirada*, Reynalda claims a French identity relatively easily, despite the initial difficulties she has faced. She is certainly not immune to racial prejudice on her arrival – for instance, people refuse to sit next to her on the metro because she was 'la négresse à la mauvaise couleur' (Condé 1997, 166) ['the black woman of the wrong color'] (Condé 2000, 150). Yet she is treated well by the Duparc family, who were concerned about her well-being and education. They give her time to study and allow her to visit museums and exhibitions. This does not fully satisfy Reynalda, however, who dreams of being a student at the Sorbonne. Eventually, she leaves the family and enrols in a university course in social work, and she secures her first post at the town hall in Savigny-sur-Orge aged just twenty-three. Emigration thus enables her to experience social ascension relatively quickly and gain a professional identity which she is unlikely to have had if she had stayed in Guadeloupe. Her elevated social status in France is compounded by her activities as an academic and writer, a fact which angers Marie-Noëlle (a writer herself) who feels that her mother is trying to take over her own identity. When Marie-Noëlle is living in the United States, Ludovic sends her the book her mother has published, which she receives 'comme un coup de poing en pleine figure' (Condé 1997, 220) ['like a slap in the face'] (Condé 2000, 200).

Interestingly, the novel suggests that the generation previous to those who emigrate through the BUMIDOM are more eager to self-identify as Caribbean. For instance, Marie-Noëlle's grandmother Nina never travels to mainland France (possibly because she cannot afford the journey). She does leave her home on La Désirade to find work, but her migration is contained within the space of the Caribbean. Indeed, the farthest she travels is to Basse-Terre. Yet Lydie Moudileno argues that Nina disrupts the traditional image of the Antillean grandmother figure, suggesting a distancing from Caribbean identity markers. Rather than assisting family members to discover their origins and provide a stable notion of identity, Nina causes 'un brouillage inattendu des repères identitaires' [an unexpected blurring of identity markers] by challenging the account of her life which Reynalda gives Marie-Noëlle, and offering her an alternative narrative about her daughter's childhood (Moudileno 2003, 1151). Yet even if, as Moudileno asserts, Nina complicates the notion of identity for her daughter and granddaughter, she seems relatively sure of her own place in Guadeloupe, and her Caribbean identity takes prominence over her French one. Ranélise shares this conviction, too. She never leaves Guadeloupe either, and the fact that her speciality dish she cooks in the restaurant where she works is 'les lambis' ['conch'], cooked 'dans un bain de saumure et de feuille à bois d'Inde' (Condé 1997, 16) ['in a homemade mixture of brine and bay-rum leaves'] (Condé 2000, 6), emphasises her strong Caribbean identity, as this is a typical, traditional Guadeloupean dish.

The identity of Marie-Noëlle is more complex. She seems to reject the notion that her identity is bound to either France or Guadeloupe as she looks elsewhere to build her life, and this refusal to identify as either French or Guadeloupean mirrors her desire to cut herself off from her family and the models of identity they offer her.[6] Marie-Noëlle chooses to settle in the United States. She lives in different neighbourhoods of Boston, first with her musician husband, Stanley, and later on her own when she is working as an academic. Although she initially moves there because Stanley has been offered work at a club, she decides to stay, even though she cannot explain why she feels attached to the country 'qu'elle avait abordé par hasard comme ses illustres prédécesseurs, mais qui la retenait fermement' (Condé 1997, 162–3) ['which she had accosted by chance like her illustrious predecessors, but that nevertheless kept a firm hold on her'] (Condé 2000, 148). It seems that, even though she feels settled in the United States, she is unable to define it as home, but she does not feel attached to anywhere else either. Celia Britton argues that this rejection of identity models means that 'Condé thus moves away from the problematic of diaspora to that of decentered migration' (2008, 141). This statement rings true for Marie-Noëlle, who rejects the diasporic model of belonging offered to her by her mother and the Caribbean model proposed to her by her grandmother. Instead, she chooses to live in the United States, a neutral space which, unlike France and Guadeloupe, is not laden with historical baggage. However, Britton's statement cannot be applied to all characters; Reynalda and Nina, for instance, remain tied to a diasporic existence, and their sense of belonging is conditioned by their relationship to France and the Caribbean.

In a similar manner to Condé's novel, *D'eaux douces* implies that different generations within a family feel differing levels of attachment to France and the Caribbean islands. In Kanor's novel, we have access to the experiences and sentiments of only two generations – Frida and her parents, although Frida does briefly visit her great-grandmother on her return to Martinique, who tells her about their family's African roots and their connections to enslavement. Jennifer Jahn argues that Frida's parents feel so disillusioned with life in mainland France that they long to return to Martinique (2008, 148). The disillusionment of Frida's father begins on his arrival and he tries to convince his wife to demand a transfer back to Martinique. Yet Frida's mother refuses to return as 'la nostalgie ne paie pas' (Kanor 2004, 31) [nostalgia does not pay the bills]. This quotation refutes Jahn's assertion. It suggests an awareness on the mother's part that nostalgia for their former life in the Caribbean would not provide them with the economic stability and social status they currently enjoy in mainland France, and implies that, unlike her husband, she is not disappointed with her decision to emigrate. Frida's father never actually leaves – he packs a suitcase but following an argument with his wife it remains in the hall. Later in the novel, her mother does want to settle back in Martinique but she never commits to relocating. In a section narrated by Frida when she is in Martinique visiting family, we learn that 'elle rêve de revenir au pays, maman, jure qu'elle y sera plus heureuse, qu'ici l'attend une nouvelle existence faite de rires, de repas de famille, et de bains de mer' (Kanor 2004, 157) [Mum dreams of returning home, swears she will be happier there, that there a new life awaits her, full of laughter, family meals and swimming in the sea]. The image that Frida's mother portrays here of Martinique is an exoticising one which spotlights the beauty of the landscape, but which neglects the very real social, political and economic difficulties the islanders face on a daily basis. This suggests that she subscribes to French colonial discourse which positioned Martinique as an exoticised and eroticised space which served uniquely for the pleasure and entertainment of white metropolitan citizens.[7] Therefore, even though she considers returning to the Caribbean, it is implied that she has adopted a French colonial identity. This is also apparent in her reaction to the news that Frida's sister Brigitte, who has been living in Burkina Faso, is pregnant to a man from the country: 'non mais c'est vrai, est-ce qu'on a idée de partir au Broukina Façon, s'enticher d'un Africain en plus!' (Kanor 2004, 62) [no but it's true, are we thinking about going to Broukina Façon, becoming besotted with an African as well!]. The mother's mispronunciation of the name of the African country reveals her prejudice against African culture and society. She is and feels French, and she does not want her daughter to have anything to do with Africa, because she believes that that it would be a reversal of history and a return to the era of the transatlantic trafficking of enslaved peoples in the opposite direction: 'depuis quand une Antillaise refait le chemin à l'envers?' (Kanor 2004, 62) [since when does an Antillean woman make the reverse journey?]

Unlike her mother, Frida rebuffs the diasporic model she has been offered, just like Marie-Noëlle in *Desirada*. The family make many return visits to Martinique when she is a young girl. Early in the novel, Frida is transported back in time to one of these visits in July 1980, which is described using short sentences to illustrate her frustration at having to undertake the journey. Kanor once again provides a nod to the workings of the BUMIDOM through her explanation that they were given 'un voyage gratis aux Antilles tous les trois ans' (Kanor 2004, 15) [a free trip to the Antilles once every three years], referring to the 'voyages vacances' system established in 1965 which enabled Antilleans to visit their family on the islands, explored in Chapter 1 of this book. Yet when Frida is a student, she is keen to break from this French-Antillean mapping of identity which she considers to be oppressive and restrictive. In her small bedroom in the university residence, she discovers more about the history and geography of different locations through her reading so she can 'échappe à l'éternelle trajectoire Paris-Fort-de-France' (Kanor 2004, 34) [escape from the never-ending trajectory between Paris and Fort-de-France]. This is a sentiment shared by Kanor herself, who explained in an interview in 2020 that it was important to her to 'casser le circuit aller-retour des Antillais: Fort-de-France ou Pointe-à-Pitre/Paris (dans les deux sens)' (Arnaud and Kanor 2020) [break the return circuit of Antilleans: Fort-de-France or Pointe-à-Pitre/Paris (in both directions)]. However, while for Kanor this is a positive experience which enables her to 'envisager un monde Noir toujours plus large' (Arnaud and Kanor 2020) [envisage an ever-expanding Black world], for her protagonist it seems to be a reaction against an identity which has been imposed on her through her family history. Frida also rejects her Antillean identity in order to escape from the Caribbean's haunting past of enslavement. Even her most intimate experiences with Éric and other men are laden with these inherited memories of trauma and enslavement. During her sexual encounters she describes being dispossessed of her body, using vocabulary associated with the transatlantic trafficking of enslaved Africans: one man laughs when he '[lui] a retiré [ses] chaînes' (Kanor 2004, 66) [released [her] from [her] chains], while another imagines her being transported to the Caribbean 'par bateau' (Kanor 2004, 66) [by ship]. This inherited trauma of sexual violence and incarceration plays out in her own exploitation by Éric and other men, and explains why she seeks to shun her Antillean identity. The interconnectedness between her own individual memories and the collective memory of enslavement can be understood through Max Silverman's model of palimpsestic memory. Silverman uses the metaphor of the palimpsest because it 'captures most completely the superimposition and productive interaction of different inscriptions and the spatialization of time central to the work of memory' (Silverman 2013, 4). Just like a palimpsestic manuscript in which previous layers of writing are visible on the surface, Frida is haunted by layers of visible and non-visible memories of events she did not experience herself, but which have been passed down to her by the collective Caribbean psyche.

Her rejection of Caribbean identity also plays out in the trip she takes with Éric to Haiti. The fact that they choose Haiti, a country with a history of resistance and revolution, for this trip rather than Martinique is significant as it illustrates her desire to break the traditional bind between Paris and Fort-de-France. As Jahn posits, 'an association with Haiti therefore suggests their need to identify with a rebellious community rather than their own people who still rely entirely on the metropole for economic support and who are plagued by an identity crisis' (Jahn 2008, 150). Their trip is unsuccessful, though, and they feel disillusioned because they are confronted with a version of the island which is far removed from the idealised image of Haiti as a rebellious and culturally rich nation. This is evident in the following quotation, a rhetorical question evoking the absence of three important political and cultural figures of Haiti's past glory: 'où était donc passé l'Haïti chérie de Toto Bisainthe, l'île-désirs de Depestre, la terre-mystère d'Alexis?' (Kanor 2004, 116) [so where had Haiti gone, the beloved Haiti of Toto Bisainthe, the island of desires of Depestre, the mysterious land of Alexis?]. Frida's quest to adopt a nuanced version of a Caribbean identity is thus unsuccessful. The only way in which she is able to be true to herself and claim her own identity is by taking her own life.

Both *Desirada* and *D'eaux douces* reveal a need for the principal protagonists to renounce their fascination with inherited forms of French identity and to define themselves on their own terms. In *Desirada*, Marie-Noëlle achieves this through constant wandering, and eventually she learns the 'insignificance of nationality and nation state as determining concepts, as well as of family and family history, for her own sense of identity' (Schwerdtner 2005, 134). Frida learns this lesson too, but she only becomes aware of this at the end of the novel, when she is about to commit suicide. How does Bulle's novel expand on these discussions of diasporic identity?

A Migrant or Diasporic Identity? Estelle-Sarah Bulle's *Là où les chiens aboient par la queue*

The disparities between a Caribbean diasporic identity as desired by the BUMIDOM participants and the migrant identity with which they were forced to negotiate on their arrival in mainland France is particularly visible in *Là où les chiens aboient par la queue*. For Laguerre, diasporic citizenship allows individuals to hold political, social, economic and cultural allegiances with several nation-states (1998, 12). Yet the concept of diasporic citizenship is more complex in the case of the French Caribbean because, of course, people of Caribbean origin emigrating to mainland France were seeking to maintain ties with two locations which were part of the same nation-state. BUMIDOM participants were French citizens who were keen to form political, economic and cultural ties with mainland France in order to assert their rights as French citizens, but they were also simultaneously Caribbean communities who wished to retain their affiliation to Guadeloupe and Martinique. However, as Bulle's novel illustrates clearly, this diasporic citizenship was denied to many, as racism in France made them feel uprooted and alienated, and they were treated as though they were migrants and thus second-class citizens, rather than as French.

Là où les chiens aboient par la queue is not autobiographical – it is a fictional text which narrates the experiences of an imagined family whose lives are marked by continuous journeys between Europe and the Caribbean. Yet the novel is inspired by Bulle's own identity quest. In interviews, she has explained that the origins of the text lie in her own desire to discover more about her Guadeloupean heritage (her father is Guadeloupean and her mother is Franco-Belgian). In an interview for La 1ère, recorded on 17 March 2019, Bulle stated:

> je me suis inspirée quand même de ma propre vie parce que, à l'enfance, à l'adolescence, on se pose des questions d'identité, surtout quand on voit qu'on n'est pas tout à fait comme les autres jeunes de sa banlieue. (Boscher and Bulle, 2019)
>
> [I still took inspiration from my own life because, in childhood and adolescence, we question our identity, especially when we see that we're not quite like the other young people from our suburb.]

Comparisons can thus be drawn between Bulle, Condé and Kanor, who all use their creative writing to work through their own identitarian concerns, and who operate in the realm of postmemory because they are transmitting through writing the memories passed down to them from their parents. Like Condé and Kanor, Bulle has been celebrated for her work: *Là où les chiens aboient par la queue* won the Prix Carbet de la Caraïbe et du Tout-Monde and the Prix Stanislas du premier roman in 2018.

The title of the novel reinforces the importance of Caribbean identities for the principal characters, and also gives a nod to Bulle's own Caribbean origins. The phrase is a transliteration in French of a Creole idiom, which means 'a remote place', referring to the fictional Guadeloupean village of Morne-Galant where the principal characters were born, according to Bulle herself (2019). The novel is centred around the identity quest of a young woman living in the Parisian suburbs, who remains unnamed. Keen to reconnect with her Caribbean roots and understand her 'constant sentiment d'ambiguïté, de décalage' (Bulle 2018, 21) ['constant feeling of confusion, of being out of step'] (Bulle 2022, 15), she conducts interviews with her father, nicknamed Petit-Frère, and her aunts Lucinde and Antoine. She then writes her family history from the notes she made during these interviews, and the implication is that what follows is the story of her family members that she has written. The narrator collects and confronts their sometimes divergent narratives and memories which reveal the reasons that brought them to the Parisian suburbs in the mass exodus of the 1960s and 70s. Therefore, while each family member is given the narrative voice in turn, and chapters are narrated in the first person, their perspectives are inevitably mediated through the voice of the narrator. The text is structured chronologically and is divided into three sections: the first explores events in Guadeloupe between 1947 and 1948; the second addresses life from 1948 to 1960; and the third spans a longer time period between 1960 and 2006. The novel is bookended by poignant discussions between the narrator and Antoine as the latter is nearing the end of her life.

Each family member emigrates to France at different times and for different motives. Antoine is the last of the siblings to arrive – she emigrates in autumn 1968, following the deadly police crackdown of demonstrators in Pointe-à-Pitre in May 1967. She first hears about the BUMIDOM a few years earlier, when Martha, the young girl who assists her in her clothes shop, reveals her desires to participate in the scheme. Antoine uses Guadeloupean Creole to express her ignorance about the scheme's existence. She exclaims 'Bibidom, ka sa yé?' (Bulle 2018, 207) ['"Bibidom, ka sa yé?", I finally asked. What was that?'] (Bulle 2022, 207), thereby signalling her desire to retain her strong Caribbean identity through her linguistic affinity with Creole. It is somewhat ironic, then, that she eventually decides to leave Guadeloupe, too, particularly as she is aware that life was no easier in France. She states, for instance, that 'en France, ce n'était pas tout rose' (Bulle 2018, 208) ['things were not looking good in France'] (Bulle 2022, 208). She also learns from other young girls that the promises made to those who emigrated almost never came to fruition: the BUMIDOM offered them only 'quelques instructions pour apprendre à récurer convenablement les parquets, et un ticket de métro' (Bulle 2018, 208) ['a metro ticket and a few instructions about how to properly scrub floors'] (Bulle 2022, 208). It is particularly striking that she seems aware of the political motivations for the creation of the BUMIDOM, explaining that, according to the trade unionists, the BUMIDOM was created with the intention of moving young people away from the islands 'pour éviter les révoltes dans l'île' (Bulle 2018, 208) ['reducing the threat of revolts on the island'] (Bulle 2022, 209). Given her lack of knowledge about the scheme in the quotation analysed above, it seems more likely that this observation is made in hindsight as an older woman discussing her migration with her niece, rather than as a young woman about to depart for Paris. There is also little discussion in the text of the journey itself, or how it was organised through the BUMIDOM, except an indication that her flight was paid for by the office. She did, however, give her sister 'une bonne somme' (Bulle 2018, 253) ['a hefty sum'] (Bulle 2022, 258) to find her somewhere to live in Paris. The absence of explicit discussion here about the role of the BUMIDOM in her transatlantic journey could be interpreted as a representation of her shame at having to rely on state assistance to organise her passage. A parallel can be seen here between Bulle's and Kanor's novels: both imply that Caribbean emigrants were reluctant to admit that they had used the services of the Bureau.

On her arrival, Antoine finds herself housed on the outskirts of Paris, much to her dismay, and she is forced to live alongside other migrant communities in low-quality housing, thereby suggesting that she is required to adopt a migrant rather than a diasporic identity. Her brother-in-law Tatar meets her at the airport and drives her to the apartment he has found for her in the Parisian suburbs, but she does not realise that she will not be living in the centre of Paris, a much more glamorous location in her eyes. Her naivety is apparent in the short, simple sentence, 'je me demandais quand nous allions enfin entrer dans Paris' (Bulle 2018, 255) ['I wondered when we would finally get to Paris'] (Bulle 2022, 260). When Tatar suddenly pulls up outside a dull apartment block in the Parisian suburbs, she stammers incredulously, 'comment, mais . . . on n'est pas à Paris' (Bulle 2018, 255) ['"but how . . ." I said. "We're not in Paris."'] (Bulle 2022, 260). She exoticises the French capital and believes, like many Antilleans, that Paris will offer her excitement, adventure and professional success, so she is disappointed to be living so far away.

Bulle incorporates ellipses here into the quotation which, along with the interjection 'comment', signals particularly emphatically Antoine's astonishment and disappointment. Antoine exhibits the same obsession with white metropolitan culture that Fanon denounces in *Peau noire, masques blancs*, and which Manicom calls out in *Un examen de blanc*. She cannot imagine that poverty exists in France, as she exclaims 'pour moi, des bidonvilles, y en avait pas en France. Et puis je voulais Paris ou rien' (Bulle 2018, 258) ['I had yet to find out that slums existed in France. And I wanted Paris or nothing'] (Bulle 2022, 262). She had idolised continental France, and Paris in particular, to such an extent that she struggles to conceive of France as a country where people encounter problems in their daily lives.

Perhaps because of her initial disappointment with France on her arrival, Antoine seems more determined to maintain diasporic connections with Guadeloupe, and so she is able to negotiate some form of diasporic citizenship. She opens a clothes shop and maintains the independent lifestyle she had led in the Caribbean. She tends to associate with other Black women from Guadeloupe, Haiti and Senegal, and they become her clients, selling her the jewellery and leather shoes they make by hand for a relatively low price for her to then trade in her shop. In addition, she maintains direct links with the Caribbean through the fabrics she uses and the products she sells. She explains that, after earning some money, the first thing she does is 'envoyer une somme à man Pilote pour qu'elle me remplisse un container de tout ce que j'avais l'habitude d'acheter au marché Saint-Antoine' (Bulle 2018, 268) ['send a sum to Man Pilote so that she could fill a shipping container of all the things that I used to buy at the Saint-Antoine market'] (Bulle 2022, 273). These transnational connections are both economic and affective. She desires to keep in contact with Man Pilote, the woman who employed her and invested in her clothes business, and others who were dear to her back in Guadeloupe, but she also needs to maintain these links so that she can import products from the Caribbean to sell in France. She is thus able to maintain her sense of 'Caribbeanness' while at the same time benefiting from greater professional opportunities in mainland France.

Not every character succeeds in negotiating both a 'national and transnational outlook, attachment, and commitment', as Laguerre notes in his definition of diasporic citizenship (1998, 12). Antoine's sister Lucinde is the first of the siblings to migrate to France with her husband Tatar. Their voyage is not in fact organised by the BUMIDOM office because they leave for Paris at the end of 1961, shortly before the scheme has officially been established. There is also an indication in the text that the family have accumulated sufficient wealth from Lucinde's role sewing clothes for rich *béké* women, and even for Miss Guadeloupe contestants, that they can afford to pay for their own passage, and would not have needed to rely on state support had the BUMIDOM been in operation. Lucinde is initially elated to be in France because she considers herself to be superior to other Antilleans because of her middle-class status, if not because of her race: 'j'étais heureuse d'être en métropole, loin des jalousies et des yeux méchants. J'allais enfin pouvoir côtoyer des gens de mon niveau' (Bulle 2018, 239) ['I was happy to be on the mainland, far from the jealous people and glaring eyes. I was finally going to be able to rub shoulders with people of my calibre'] (Bulle 2022, 242). Adopting a neocolonial discourse, Lucinde chooses to reject her diasporic identity and embrace a uniquely French one. This self-imposed rupture from the Caribbean does bring her social benefits – she is able to afford a car and continues her clothes-making business – but it also causes the breakdown of her family unit. Tatar becomes increasingly homesick for Guadeloupe, and the couple eventually divorce because Lucinde becomes frustrated at his lack of ambition. Migration to mainland France, then, brings Lucinde professional success and enables her to become more independent, but it also breaks down the familial framework that held her life together in the Caribbean, suggesting that her project to maintain diasporic citizenship ultimately fails.

Petit-Frère, the narrator's father, does not emigrate through the BUMIDOM either, but his migration is organised by another patriarchal, hierarchical institution: the military. In Guadeloupe, he works as an electrician, but he feels stifled by the lack of prospects or employment opportunities that the island affords him. He describes the island's boundaries as 'les murs de [s]a prison' (Bulle 2018, 220) ['the walls of [his] prison'] (Bulle 2022, 221), such is his sentiment of confinement. He is first stationed in Germany with the 42nd regiment before arriving in Paris in June 1967. Unlike Antoine, he buys into the government's rhetoric which promotes emigration as a means of social advancement for Antillean citizens. He enjoys life in Paris and the cultural encounters that the capital city provides him: 'à Paris, des salles à profusion, des théâtres, des librairies, des concerts à tous les coins de rue' (Bulle 2018, 244) ['in Paris, there were cinemas aplenty, theaters, bookstores, concerts on every street corner'] (Bulle 2022, 248). The enumeration of nouns in this sentence, which are connected with commas rather than conjunctions, builds up to demonstrate just how greatly Petit-Frère appreciates Parisian life. Like Lucinde, he is keen to shed his Antillean identity and to assert his Frenchness. Indeed, he describes life on the island, 'avec sa hiérarchie coloniale, son absence d'ouverture et le manque de perspectives professionnelles' (Bulle 2018, 244) ['with its colonial hierarchy, its closed-mindedness, and its lack of professional prospects'] (Bulle 2022, 248), as oppressive. Each of the siblings, then, has a different relationship with Guadeloupe and mainland France, and they engage differently with the concept of diasporic citizenship. While Antoine succeeds in negotiating her membership of both French and Caribbean communities, Lucinde and Petit-Frère prefer to prioritise their French identity.

Conclusion

The four novels analysed in this chapter offer a nuanced portrayal of the identitarian models upheld by BUMIDOM participants and their descendants. They demonstrate that the concept of diasporic citizenship offered a model of resistance for Antilleans in the face of racial discrimination, but that not all individuals were willing, or indeed were able, to maintain diasporic connections to the Caribbean. Instead, they chose to subscribe to models of national identity which privilege belonging to a single, homogenised entity. For them, the BUMIDOM equated to a rupture with the Caribbean past and an espousal of French values. In *Desirada*, *D'eaux douces* and *Là où les chiens aboient par la queue*, it is the generation who actually emigrated with the BUMIDOM who are the most eager to claim their French identity, while their children, who were born in France, shun both identities in search of a less historically loaded sense of self. The identity quest of characters in *Mon examen de blanc* differs somewhat, since the novel is set in Guadeloupe rather than on the French mainland, and the characters do not participate in the scheme themselves. Nevertheless, Manicom denounces the impossibility of being Black, Caribbean and French during the 1960s and explores the problems the BUMIDOM caused for those remaining on the island.

This chapter has demonstrated that the genre of the novel is particularly effective at transmitting memories of the BUMIDOM across generations. Creating polyphonic texts with alternating narrative voices and employing innovative literary strategies such as analepsis, the four authors provide us with different perspectives on

Caribbean emigration and allow us to reflect on generational differences in belonging and identity. Moreover, by bringing together texts by prominent Caribbean authors and those writing during the time of the BUMIDOM with new voices, the chapter has shown that the BUMIDOM still resonates with French Caribbean writers today. Emigration was a crucial issue for Manicom in 1975 when she published her novel because she witnessed first-hand the racial discrimination to which BUMIDOM participants were subjected. Yet the writing of Condé, Kanor and Bulle renders true Michel-Rolph Trouillot's assertion that 'the past does not exist independently from the present', but that our understanding of the past is always dependent on our memories and interpretation of the past in the present time (1995, 15). In this case, the novels demonstrate how people of Caribbean origin living in mainland France remain haunted by inherited memories of state-sponsored mass migration and the sentiments of non-belonging the BUMIDOM inevitably provoked. They can thus be considered as postcolonial realms of memory, as sites and symbols of postcolonial memory which help to distinguish between history, 'a primary preoccupation with recovering what actually happened in the past', and memory, 'a term that encompasses diverse forms of representation of that past' (Achille, Forsdick and Moudileno 2020, 8).

Notes

1. For Glissant, *errance* is a positive concept which moves away from stable, homogeneous identities and brings about cross-cultural encounters (1990, 33).
2. Confiant first wrote this novel in Antillean Creole; it was published in 1987 under the title *Marisosé*.
3. 'Câpresse' refers to a mixed-race category on the middle rungs of the ethnoclass hierarchy, a system that continues to structure Antillean society today. It describes a woman with one Black and one mixed-race parent. As Hardwick observes, the etymology 'reveals an inherent animalisation' because it comes from the Latin *capra* meaning goat (2014, 401).
4. In 1997, Condé also published a collection of short stories entitled *Pays mêlé: nouvelles* [*Land of Many Colours*]. In two of the short stories, 'Pays mêlé' ['Land of Many Colours'] and 'Trois femmes à Manhattan' ['Three Women in Manhattan'], Condé evokes the BUMIDOM when discussing the political, economic and demographic changes faced by Guadeloupeans in the 1970s and 80s.

5. In 2008, Kanor collaborated with Emmanuelle Bidou on *Jambé dlo: une histoire antillaise* [Jambé Dlo: An Antillean History], a documentary about post-war Antillean migration.
6. For a discussion of Marie-Noëlle's rejection of the traditional family unit, and her attachment to female friends who provide her with a sense of community, see Celia Britton, *The Sense of Community in French Caribbean Fiction* (2008).
7. For an examination of how this colonial discourse operated, see Jacqueline Couti, *Sex, Sea, and Self: Sexuality and Nationalism in French Caribbean Discourses*, 1924–1948 (2021).

Chapter 4

Racism and Classism in Film and Television

In *Memory Activism: Reimagining the Past for the Future in Israel-Palestine* (2017), sociologist Yifat Gutman studies organisations in Israel which document silenced Palestinian memories of conflict and displacement and incorporate them into the dominant collective memory. Gutman terms this process 'memory activism', which she defines as 'the strategic commemoration of a contested past outside state channels to influence public debate and policy' (2017, 1–2). For Gutman, these memory practices, or practices of counter-memory, have a specific political goal: 'to change people's understanding of their shared past beyond the dominant national frame' (2017, 2). This chapter questions the extent to which the three film directors whose works of fictional film are analysed here – Pascal Légitimus, Jean-Claude Barny and Christian Faure – can be considered as memory activists. Do they succeed in incorporating the BUMIDOM into France's collective memory and changing the ways people conceive of post-war Caribbean emigration and the French Caribbean community more broadly? Or do they reveal the limitations of cultural works in the production of collective memory and demonstrate that representation does not necessarily equate to commemoration?

Film is a particularly productive medium through which to analyse the concept of collective and cultural memory. As Jennie M. Carlsten and Fearghal McGarry argue, 'film's impact lies less in its empirical qualities than in its powerful capacity to influence public consciousness, mould collective memory and retrieve suppressed or marginalised histories' (2015, 1). Departing from a focus on the textual in the previous chapters (whether in life writing or in fiction), this chapter instead examines the visual, interrogating how the accessibility, the immediacy and the pictorial qualities of cinema enable films to transmit memories in ways in which textual sources cannot. I interrogate the formal and stylistic devices and techniques used by the three directors to transmit memories about the BUMIDOM. In each film, these memories are memories of racism and classism to which BUMIDOM participants and their descendants were subjected in mainland France. For these people, being Black meant being a minority in society. Their experiences of Blackness correspond to Pap Ndiaye's definition as 'l'expérience sociable partagée selon le marqueur socialement négatif de la peau noire' (2008, 55) [the shared social experience of having the socially negative marker of Black skin].

I analyse the three films chronologically, beginning with *Antilles-sur-Seine*. This mainstream comedy film was funded by Légitimus's own production company Marie-Galante Productions, in collaboration with TF1. The plot centres on the mayor of Marie-Galante, Horace Sainte-Rose, whose wife is kidnapped in Paris in a plot orchestrated by the white Sauveur family who want to stop their land from being developed. The film is set in the 1990s and not in the BUMIDOM era, but the mass migration of Antilleans is evoked frequently in the film, particularly since it is thanks to the sizeable Antillean community who emigrated to Paris through the BUMIDOM and who continue to work in transportation and public service that Horace's wife is found. The second film I consider is Barny's *Le Gang des Antillais*, a cinematic adaptation of Loïc Léry's autobiographical novel of the same title.[1] The film follows the trajectory of the protagonist, Jimmy Larivière, a fictionalised version of Léry, who arrived in France at the age of thirteen in the early 1970s, when mass migration through the BUMIDOM was at its height. As he grows up, he becomes increasingly disillusioned with life in continental France. This disillusionment leads him to join a group of criminals in committing armed robbery, and he is eventually sent to prison for twenty years. The final film I examine is Faure's *Le Rêve français*. Unlike the other two works, this is a television film composed of two 90-minute episodes.[2] It seems that the filmmakers were primarily targeting a Caribbean audience given that it was first screened on the islands. It was projected at the Rex cinema in Guadeloupe on 13 March 2018 and at the Madiana complex in Martinique on 15 March 2018, and then shown on television over two separate weeks – on 20 and 27 March 2018 in Martinique and Guadeloupe via La 1ère and on 21 and 28 March 2018 in mainland France on France 2 (Chazeau 2018). *Le Rêve français* follows the love story between two Guadeloupeans, Samuel and Doris, from their childhood in the 1960s to the present day. The story is told against the backdrop of significant political and historical events that bind Guadeloupe and France together, such as the BUMIDOM. Very little scholarly attention has been dedicated to these films; following one of the overarching aims of this book, the chapter thus aims to shed light on these important but underexplored examples of French Caribbean culture.

Of course, these three films are not the only examples of French Caribbean cinema to pay attention to the BUMIDOM, or to Caribbean emigration more broadly. Indeed, some of the very first films from the French Caribbean in the 1970s and 80s – cinema came very late to the Caribbean islands –[3] tackled the issue of emigration. Examples of short films about emigration and return include Jacques Ferly's *Chronique d'un retour* (1971) [Chronicle of a Return] and Gabriel Glissant's *Le Pion* (1972) [The Pawn]. In the 1980s, Caribbean emigration became an important theme in feature-length films made by French filmmakers who did not have a personal connection to Martinique and Guadeloupe, such as *En l'autre bord* (1978) [On the Other Side] by Jérôme Kanapa, *Ô Madiana* (1979) [Oh Madiana] by Constant Gros-Dubois and *West Indies ou les nègres marrons de la liberté* (1979) [*West Indies: The Fugitive Slaves of Liberty*] by Med Hondo. These films are critical towards the BUMIDOM, as Sophie Saint-Just makes clear: the films 'critiquent les instances administratives françaises qui orchestrent cette migration, dénoncent l'aliénation et l'exploitation de la main d'œuvre antillaise et relatent les dures conditions de vie des Antillais en métropole' (Saint-Just 2016, 173) [criticise the administrative bodies which orchestrate this migration, denounce the alienation and exploitation of the Antillean workforce and recount the difficult working conditions Antilleans face in mainland France]. Since the 2000s, there has been a proliferation of documentary films about the BUMIDOM from a Caribbean perspective. Examples include *L'Avenir est ailleurs* (2006) [The Future is Elsewhere], directed by Antoine Léonard-Maestrati; *Jambé dlo: une histoire antillaise* (2008) [Jambé Dlo: An Antillean History], directed by Fabienne Kanor and Emmanuelle Bidou; and *BUMIDOM: des Français venus d'Outre-mer* (2010) [BUMIDOM: French from Overseas], directed by Jackie Bastide. The specificities of the Reunionese situation have also been explored through documentary film. Awarded the DOC Alliance Award for best short film in May 2022, Erika Etangsalé's *Lèv la tèt dann fenwar* (2021) [*In the Billowing Night*] is a recent example of a documentary which has very personal resonances, as the film is framed around the story of her father. These documentaries bring together archival footage, interviews and testimonies to create detailed factual and reflective accounts of what it was like to migrate through the BUMIDOM. Although these films would be fruitful sources for analysis, this chapter focuses instead on films of fiction or historical fiction (also sometimes called 'docudrama' or 'dramatic documentary'), those 'fictional accounts of history in a moving-image medium that purport to tell a more or less true story about, or provide a historically more or less accurate account of, some element of the past' (Plantinga 2021, 115).

Making Memory in Film

Carl Plantinga argues that 'the effect of historical fiction films, whether intended or not, is to create, change, and/or preserve the collective memory of a people or nation' (2021, 114). Of course, how films create collective memory depends on numerous factors, including who is watching the film and in which sociocultural circumstances the viewing occurs. In addition, the status of the collective memory of a particular people or nation – how it has already been promoted, marginalised or silenced by external actors – also affects how memory making occurs through film. Following Plantinga's reasoning, historical fiction film can be considered a form of memory activism which seeks to challenge the dominant narrative about the shared past of a group or community. Could the same be argued about fictional film, and specifically in the case of *Antilles-sur-Seine*, about comedy film? Although comedy films clearly have a very different purpose to historical fiction films – they are created to entertain rather than educate an audience – they are still situated in a particular historical, political and cultural setting and thus, like historical fiction films, contribute to raising awareness of the memory of a particular community, even if this occurs subconsciously.

Plantinga argues that historical fiction film creates collective memory in three principal ways: firstly, 'an ambiguous reference to historical reality'; secondly, 'medium characteristics that foster viewer immersion and a sense of "presentness"'; and thirdly, 'the use of conventional narrative schemes that elicit emotions that assist memory formation' (Plantinga 2021, 114–15). In relation to the first characteristic, Plantinga argues that these films intentionally blur historical truth (defined by Dorothy Haecker as a historical fact which is meaningful and evidenced and refers to the world as it once was (1985, 267)) and fiction in such a powerful way – through the use of vivid images, emotive rhetoric and poignant storytelling – that viewers may consider these fictional elements to be accurate representations of a historical event (Plantinga 2021, 120). As a collective memory becomes formed, it becomes altered and transformed as viewers accept these fictional qualities as more or less 'real'. Alison Landsberg claims that this collective memory is in fact created by viewers taking on these memories as if they were their own, in a form of memory transfer across generations. In *Prosthetic Memory: The Transformation of American Remembrance in the Age of Mass Culture* (2004), she argues that, through contact with experiential media such as films, television, monuments and museum exhibitions, an individual 'does not simply apprehend a historical narrative but takes on a more personal, deeply felt memory of a past event through which he or she did not live' (Landsberg 2004, 2). Controversially, Landsberg terms these memories 'prosthetic memories', a term which, to her, implies that these are unnatural, mediated and embodied memories which nevertheless are useful because they enable individuals to reflect on their relationship with the past and enact a form of social justice (2004, 20–1). Landsberg's theory has been critiqued by scholars in memory studies and film studies, not least for her use of the loaded term 'prosthesis'. Margaret-Anne Hutton argues that Landsberg's use of the term is ideologically fraught because she 'employs ableist language rooted in a medical model of disability' (2022, 234), and Hutton uses Landsberg's work on prosthetic memory as a case study to demonstrate the problematic use of metaphors in the field of memory studies more broadly. Nicki Hitchcott has also taken the concept to task. In her analysis of Terry George's 2004 film *Hotel Rwanda*, Hitchcott argues that survivors of the 1994 genocide against the Tutsi in Rwanda recall a very different account of what happened inside Hôtel des Mille Collines – where over a thousand Hutus and Tutsis were saved from genocidal forces – from the one depicted in the film (2021). It can thus be dangerous, according to Hitchcott, for people to 'take on' memories as generated through film because these can be revisionist memories, and would mean a sense of complicity with the perpetrators (Hitchcott 2021, 943). I would add that the notion of 'prosthetic memory' is insulting to survivors of trauma; a viewer can never claim to remember a trauma that they did not experience, no matter how much empathy they may feel for survivors. Critics agree that prosthetic memory is not really transferred memory because what viewers are accessing through film is a representation of memory and not memory itself. James Berger suggests that what Landsberg terms 'prosthetic memory' is really a combination of knowledge and empathy (Berger 2007, 605). Despite these various criticisms, Landsberg's concept is a useful way of thinking through the role of mass media in sharing histories of marginalised communities across cultures and generations.

The second characteristic outlined by Plantinga is the use of cinematic techniques which enable a viewer to become immersed in a film. As Anton Kaes explains, film is a powerful means with which to shape public opinion about historical events: films 'can make history come alive more readily than commemorative addresses, lectures, exhibitions or museums' because they can 'reconstitute past events in the immediate experience of the viewer' (Kaes 1990, 112). One way in which films make history 'come alive', as Kaes puts it, is through flashbacks, as they transport the viewer back in time through the memories of a particular character. Maureen Turim defines the flashback as 'an image or filmic segment that is understood as representing temporal occurrences anterior to those in the images that preceded it' (1989, 2). Turim theorises the flashback with reference to psychoanalysis and philosophy, but also embeds her work in literary concepts of narratology and temporality. For instance, she discusses Gérard Genette's delineation of narrative temporality to examine how the flashback can transport the viewer to a different temporal period to the rest of the narration, and this past event can vary in 'amplitude', in Genette's terms (that is, how much of the past is narrated by the flashback) (Turim 1989, 8). Turim also thinks through Roland Barthes's work on narrative coding to analyse why flashbacks are used in film. They can be employed as a device to find the answer to a question or enigma posed at the beginning of the film (the proairetic code); they can provide information about a character (the semic code); or they can provide historical, political or cultural information about the time period presented in the film (the referential code) (Turim 1989, 11–12).

Moreover, Turim shows how flashbacks grant the viewer access to memory on an individual and collective level. Flashbacks 'often merge the two levels of remembering the past, giving large-scale social and political history the subjective mode of a single, fictional individual's remembered experience' (Turim 1989, 2). Turim terms this process 'subjective memory', referring both to the 'rendering of history as a subjective experience' lived by a fictional character in the film, and 'the formation of the Subject in history as the viewer of the film identifying with fictional character's [*sic*] positioned in a fictive social reality' (Turim 1989, 2). This merging of fictional, personalised stories and contextual historical detail through the use of flashback enables viewers to become personally invested in the stories of the characters while also witnessing a retelling of a larger collective past. *Le Rêve français* in particular makes use of the flashback in this way to heighten viewers' emotional reaction to the story, as we will see in the final section of this chapter.

In each of the three films, flashbacks sometimes take a fictional form, as the viewer is exposed to an earlier episode in the protagonist's life which helps to explain current events as they are being told in the narrative present. For instance, in *Le Rêve français*, Samuel is in Paris watching the news about the protests of May 68, and this footage then segues into a flashback of violent protests in Guadeloupe in the late 1950s, which resulted in the supposed death of his brother Julian. The viewer is given a snapshot of Samuel's state of mind; he is triggered by this violence which evokes graphic images of the death of his brother. At other times, the flashbacks incorporate archival footage of historical events from news reels and periodicals, a technique borrowed from documentary filmmaking. *Le Rêve français* and *Le Gang des Antillais* also employ other formal-stylistic devices which are more often associated with the documentary genre, such as the use of a voice-over, in order to give historical veracity to their fictional accounts of the BUMIDOM and its afterlives.

The third method of creating memory in film, according to Plantinga, is through the use of storytelling. He argues that a narrative structure does not simply provide information to the viewer, but it also offers 'an embodied experience that consists of moods and emotions' such as drama and suspense which 'have the capacity to organise memory and sediment it through powerful affective responses' (Plantinga 2021, 123–4). He gives examples of different narrative structures which elicit emotional reactions from the audience, including the 'Hollywood narrative', in which a protagonist is faced with a conflict which is resolved by the end of the film (Plantinga 2021, 124). He then draws on Paul Connerton's work on collective memory to explain the connections between emotion and memory in film. In *How Societies Remember* (1989), Connerton explains that cultural memory is formed and preserved through rituals such as celebrations, parades and ceremonies because these are embodied emotional experiences – people clap, chant, march and sing, which enables memory to be 'sedimented, or amassed, in the body' (Connerton 1989, 72). In an argument reminiscent of Landsberg's notion of prosthetic memory, Plantinga posits that historical fiction films offer a fictionalised version of these rituals, meaning that the spectator has access to 'a kind of virtual or once-removed ritualistic experience that replicates the sights and sounds such rituals offer' (2021, 126). He also suggests that historical films themselves enact a type of ritual when they are viewed because of the repetition of structure, style and cinematic technique they employ, which in turn elicits an embodied emotional response from the viewer, helping to amass and preserve memory (Plantinga 2021, 126–7).

In the sections which follow, I show how the films connect history and memory through these different cinematic techniques. Aleida Assmann argues that 'history turns into memory when it is transformed into forms of shared knowledge and collective identification and participation' (2006, 216). Do *Antilles-sur-Seine*, *Le Gang des Antillais* and *Le Rêve français* succeed to the same extent at turning the history of post-war Caribbean emigration into collective memory?

Antilles-sur-Seine: A Failure to Commemorate the Past?

Antilles-sur-Seine is Légitimus's début feature film. Before its release he was best known as a member of French comedy act Les Inconnus [The Unknowns], alongside Didier Bourdon and Bernard Campan, a trio who specialised in satirising French cultural and political icons and communities living in France, including the Antillean community. Born in Paris of Armenian and Guadeloupean origin, Légitimus 'has a family connection to Antillean film history', as Louise Hardwick explains (2015, 51). Grandson of Darling Légitimus, who starred as M'man Tine in Euzhan Palcy's masterpiece *Rue Cases-Nègres* (1983) [Sugar Cane Alley], he is the son of Théo Légitimus, also a well-known Antillean actor.

The film deals with issues of race, migration and integration within a Caribbean context. The plot is driven by the kidnapping of Lucia Sainte-Rose in Paris, who is absent for most of the film. Her husband, mayor of Marie-Galante, and her two sons, Manuel and Freddy, travel to Paris to find her, enlisting the help of a white female police inspector, Herman, and her lieutenant, Henry. Initially hostile towards the family whom she repeatedly and openly mocks, Herman eventually becomes integrated into the Antillean community and engages in acts of solidarity to help them find Lucia, refusing to obey her superior Marin who has warned her off the case for its sensitive political nature. Herman is repaid for her solidarity when the Antillean community living in Paris rally together to help find her son, who has also been taken by the kidnappers. In a nod to the opening scene of the film, in which the Sainte-Rose family has been shown celebrating Horace's sixtieth birthday in Marie-Galante, the film ends in a large party, but this time, the party takes place in Paris and the two white police officers are invited. This signals, according to Sam Haigh, 'the acceptance of the two white French police officers into the Antillean community' (2007, 60). Légitimus thus reverts the notion of integration, which typically requires individuals of different origins to assimilate into the French cultural model, to suggest that it is the French community which needs to adapt to the racial and cultural diversity of the French Republic.

Yet this important message about integration and republicanism is undermined by the film's reliance on derision, satire and over-exaggeration, which led it to becoming a critical and commercial flop. Its first month at the box office was not a great success. It registered only 379,121 box-office entries in this period, according to the Internet Movie Database, a much lower figure than other comedy films released at this time (Haigh 2007, 60). This lack of interest in the film was mirrored by its lukewarm reception by film critics. Writing for Africine.org, a website collating articles and reviews about African and African diasporic cinema, Soeuf Elbadawi describes the film as 'un bon credo de départ, mais Légitimus pousse ses comédiens à trop en faire' (Elbadawi 2001) [a good starting point, but Légitimus pushes his actors to do too much], thus creating a film steeped in ridicule. Following such reviews, I argue that Légitimus uses satire and stereotype in his film to the extreme to evoke memories of mass migration, but that, ultimately, he is unsuccessful at converting the history of Caribbean migration into memory because it is not transformed into 'shared knowledge and collective identification and participation', to quote Assmann again. Rather, the film reinforces stereotypes about race and class, thereby revealing that not all cultural representation can be considered as a practice of commemoration and remembrance. The tone of the film contrasts with Légitimus's own self-perception as a socially engaged filmmaker who endeavours to raise awareness of the contributions of the Antillean community to French life. His comments in the interview on the DVD version of the film illustrate his political engagement. He asserts that his principal objective in making the film was to ensure that white French people would realise that 'autour il y a des Antillais, des domiens, et que ces gens-là il faut les respecter, ils sont là, et que grâce à eux, on peut aussi s'amuser' [around them there are Antilleans, people from the overseas departments who should be respected, and that thanks to them, they can have fun]. However, as I shall argue below, there is a mismatch between his apparent intentions as documented in this interview and the film itself, which fails to respect and commemorate the Antillean community living in mainland France.

Légitimus's stereotypical approach to the Antillean community is evident from the opening scene which, unlike the rest of the film, is set in the Caribbean, in Marie-Galante. The camera zooms in on two women walking down a road lined with palm trees, wearing traditional Caribbean dress and carrying baskets on their heads. We also see a man struggling to control his cows, and these images of rural Caribbean life connote a slow and unsophisticated way of life, in comparison to the urban, fast-paced style of living in Paris, as depicted in the rest of the film. The title of the film then appears in a font which matches that on the DVD box; the letters are created out of sugarcane in an allusion to the agricultural landscape of the Caribbean, and zouk music is playing in the background. The letters which make up the title dance about to the rhythm of the music under a bright blue sky, thereby portraying the Caribbean as an idyllic, tropical location where people can enjoy themselves. This party metaphor then becomes solidified in the birthday celebration in the next scene. Légitimus also plays on these stereotypes of exoticism through the subtitle (echoed on the DVD box and pre-release posters) which reads 'un film tropicalisé par Pascal Légitimus [a film tropicalised by Pascal Légitimus]. My reading of this scene concurs with Haigh's analysis, which points to the clichéd and stereotypical representation of the Caribbean as an exotic location for pleasure (2007, 50–1). In contrast, H. Adlai Murdoch argues that Légitimus intentionally overloads the viewer with stereotypes of Caribbean life in order to distort them. Drawing on Homi Bhabha's work on the stereotype as an arrested form of representation in his essay 'The Other Question', Murdoch argues that Légitimus reverses the 'colonially driven hierarchy of representation that inheres in externally imposed stereotypes of the Caribbean, exposing, extending and inverting its assumptions by playing on its superficialities' (2012, 331). Yet there is no indication in the film that Légitimus is intentionally using stereotypes in this way. The audience is not made aware through any kind of framing technique that Légitimus is playing with stereotypes to disrupt them. Rather, by portraying Antillean people as frivolous and carefree, he is in fact reinforcing these stereotypes about Caribbean peoples which originated during French colonialism.

Légitimus is somewhat more respectful towards the Antillean community, however, in his evocation of the BUMIDOM. Even though the film is set in the 1990s, when the scheme is no longer in operation, it repeatedly evokes memories of the Bureau through plot devices and an 'ambiguous reference to historical reality', to quote Plantinga. It integrates historical detail about mass migration into the fictional plot to attempt to create a form of collective memory with which Antilleans can identify. At the beginning of the film, Horace is arguing with two developers who want him to sell land in order to develop Marie-Galante. He refuses, but is reminded by the developers of the escalating unemployment rate on the island which is causing 'tous ces jeunes [à] déserter les Antilles pour engraisser la Métropole' [all these young people to desert the Antilles in order to fatten up the Metropole]. Here, Légitimus gives a nod to those who left through the BUMIDOM to escape from soaring unemployment, while also suggesting that this phenomenon has continued even into the early 1990s. Horace's aversion to young people helping to 'engraisser la métropole' implies that he is firmly against France profiting financially from the Antillean community. However, this is offset by his own bourgeois respectability as mayor and his commitment to the French Republic, made clear in the film by the close-up of France's motto 'Liberté, égalité, fraternité' [liberty, equality, fraternity] which is inscribed at the top of the town hall building, and by the camera's emphasis on the French flag placed at the back of his office. His assimilation to the French Republic is thus unquestionable, and so the viewer is unsure whether Horace really does oppose the emigration of his citizens. The BUMIDOM is evoked explicitly later in the film when Horace is invited to a meeting by Gertrude Boisec, an Antillean newspaper vendor, to help find his wife. This meeting takes place in a disused theatre, and Gertrude and his friends are sitting on the stage playing dominoes. Haigh terms this scene 'Antilles-sur-scène', explaining that it is a 'staging – a literal *mise en scène* [. . .] of the size and diversity of the Antillean community in Paris, its crucial role in the very functioning of the city, and most of all, its solidarity' (2007, 58) [original emphasis]. This solidarity is made evident in the dialogue between Horace and the other Antillean men. Gertrude asks Horace how many Antilleans are currently living in France; he estimates 100,000 but Gertrude thinks the number is closer to 800,000. The others then cry out the sectors in which Antilleans are employed; the list seems endless, and many abbreviations are used to designate all the public service sector roles carried out by Antilleans from the BUMIDOM era to the present time of the film. Horace recognises the importance of the Antillean community who are carrying out necessary jobs which white people refuse to do; he comments that 'si tous ces gens-là arrêtent de travailler la France est bloquée' [if all those people stop working France is stuck]. For Gertrude, their value is in the solidarity that they offer, and he reassures Horace that they will find his wife 'avec [s]es 800 000 cousins' [with [his] 800,000 cousins]. Through this scene, Légitimus does seem to challenge the stereotypical narrative of Antilleans as lazy and uneducated by demonstrating that those who arrived through the BUMIDOM have then stayed in France to work in crucial jobs in the public sector, without whom the country would not be able to function.

However, this respectful attitude towards the Antillean community and their histories and memories is not borne out by the rest of the film. On the contrary, they are constantly mocked and stereotyped by the white people in power, and particularly by the police. For instance, when Inspector Herman goes to the hotel to investigate Lucia's disappearance, she goes into the bathroom and remarks 'c'est humide ici. Tropical comme ambiance' [it's humid here. A tropical environment]. This adjective 'tropical' is repeated throughout the film, and also alludes to the subtitle and marketing strategies employed by Légitimus to package the film. It contributes to stereotyping and essentialising Caribbean communities living in mainland France and overlooking the very real difficulties they encountered because of their race and class. In another early scene involving Herman, the film reinforces the notion of Black communities as an othered minority. As the Sainte-Rose family are arriving at the police station, Herman is recounting to Henry in an exaggerated fashion a holiday she once had in the Caribbean. Again, she uses vocabulary with essentialising undertones, and then proceeds to imitate Antillean women, mocking their accent and the way they pronounce the French 'r', dancing and touching her breasts to connotate the oversexualisation of Antillean women. To make matters worse, when they arrive in her office she introduces them in racist language by comparing the family to an African tribe: 'bonjour, je vois que toute la smala est là. Enfin la tribu. Le clan' [hello, I see that the whole brood is here. I mean the tribe. The clan]. In this way, Herman defines the family as a racialised minority, even though they belong to a relatively privileged social class. The ways in which she categorises the family chimes with Ndiaye's critical stance towards Blackness, for whom being Black equates to being a minority, regardless of class or gender: Blackness is 'une situation sociale qui n'est ni celle d'une classe, d'un Etat, d'une caste ou d'une communauté, mais d'une minorité' (Ndiaye 2008, 24) [a social situation which is that of neither a class, a state, a cast nor a community, but a minority]. Despite the episode's derogatory stance towards race, it does try to tackle gendered stereotypes. Horace initially addresses his concerns towards Henry whom he presumes to be in charge because he is male. Herman calls this out and remarks 's'il vous plaît, je suis le commandant' [excuse me, I am the inspector]. Murdoch claims that this gendered stereotype made by the Sainte-Rose family cancels out the previous one made by Herman about race (2012, 338). Yet these constructed images work on very different levels, and while Horace's comment is harmful as it dismisses Herman's professional expertise, it does not intentionally other and ridicule her, as her own racist comments about the Sainte-Rose family do. While Légitimus's concern to address damaging attitudes towards gender should be acknowledged here, his lack of critical focus on Blackness and how it has been constructed is highly problematic.

In an interview for BFM TV on 14 September 2016, Légitimus admitted that the over-the-top, exaggerated nature of the film was its primary downfall: 'son défaut, c'est qu'il y a trop de choses: trop de méchants, trop de gentils' (Lachasse and Légitimus 2016) [its flaw is that there is too much of everything: too many baddies, too many goodies]. I would argue that the film is not only exaggerated and stereotypical but also offensive and insulting to Antillean communities, whether through the use of blackface and disguise to portray Antilleans as lazy, overweight and gossiping busy-bodies,[4] or through the attempt to offset racist remarks with humour rather than calling them out.[5] These devices humiliate Antillean communities rather than preserving memories of how they arrived in France in the 1960s and 70s to plug the labour gap in public service. *Antilles-sur-Seine* is therefore not an example of memory activism because it does not act 'in the service of reconciliation and democratic politics', to quote Gutman (2017, 2). It is a comedy film, and its prime objective is to make people laugh, but this does not mean that it cannot also be a vector of collective memory. However, the film seems to be directing the audience to laugh at the Antillean community rather than at the antagonists, and it certainly does not treat Antilleans or their past with the respect they deserve. In the following section, I analyse how and why Barny is a more successful memory activist with his film *Le Gang des Antillais*.

Memories of Racism and Violence in *Le Gang des Antillais*

Unlike Légitimus, the actor and director Barny is concerned with examining, through cinema, French colonialism and its impact on the contemporary politics, economy and society of France and the Caribbean. His debut film, *Nèg marron* (2005) [Black Maroon], predates the strikes of 2009, in which Guadeloupeans and Martinicans protested about 'la vie chère' [the high cost of living], but it deals with many of the issues at the heart of the protests, such as poverty, marginalisation and racism. In 2007, he made the television film *Tropiques amers* [Bitter Tropics] about the history of enslavement in Martinique, and in 2015 he directed *Rose et le soldat* [Rose and the Soldier], a television film which recounts life in Martinique in the Vichy period when the island was governed by Admiral Georges Robert. His latest film project – *Fanon* (2023) – is a biopic about Frantz Fanon. *Le Gang des Antillais* is thus no exception in its engagement with crucial episodes of Caribbean history. In media interviews, Barny has spoken about the role of the BUMIDOM in his own life. His mother arrived in France via the Bureau aged twenty. Life was difficult for her in mainland France, and although emigration enabled her to 'se cultiver' [become educated], she also experienced economic precarity and racism; so much so that she sent her son, who was born in France, back to the Caribbean to live with her mother until the age of six (Diarrassouba and Barny 2017). The film spotlights the difficult experiences of Antilleans living in mainland France in the 1970s, its characters turning to violence to cope with poverty, racism and exploitation.

Winner of several international awards including the Caribbean Spirit Award for the best feature-length film at the CaribbeanTales International Film Festival in Toronto in 2017, *Le Gang des Antillais* tells the story of single father Jimmy Larivière who becomes involved in a gang and robs a series of banks and post offices. During his first raid, he is spotted by Nicole, a white, middle-class woman who used to employ his godmother as a cleaner when she first arrived from Guadeloupe. Nicole is then threatened by the gang on numerous occasions for her silence until Molokoy, one of the gang members, beats her so badly she ends up in hospital. Jimmy returns to Guadeloupe to visit his mother. Leaving his daughter with her, he returns to France to carry out a final raid, but along with the rest of the gang is caught by the police. Jimmy ends up in prison where he is visited by a fictionalised Patrick Chamoiseau, in a nod to the writer's parallel career as a prison educator. The film is peppered with famous faces who act in cameo roles, including Jocelyne Béroard (lead singer of zouk band Kassav'), who plays Jimmy's godmother, and actor and director Mathieu Kassovitz as the bartender who helps Jimmy to fight off the police.[6] The film is not without its problems, notably in its depiction of female characters. Women such as Linda (Jimmy's girlfriend) and Marraine (his godmother) lack depth and seem to exist only in order to spotlight difficulties encountered by the male characters; they are not characters in their own right but are always relational to men. Yet the film is successful at transmitting the memories of racism and classism which lead to the violence the gang members commit. *Le Gang des Antillais* is careful not to excuse the men for this violence – for instance, it shows very clearly the consequences that being part of a violent gang have on the members' personal lives, and they are punished for their actions at the end of the film. Yet it also reveals that this violence stems from the racial and classist oppression to which they have been subjected in continental France. The film makes use of a number of formal and stylistic devices, such as employing documentary footage, emotive music and flashbacks, in order to incorporate the BUMIDOM into the French and Caribbean collective memory.

The first of these devices is the use of documentary footage which, I argue, lends historical veracity to the film and reinforces the place of the BUMIDOM in collective memory, while also blurring boundaries between reality and fiction. The film begins with a caption in white text on a plain black background which reads 'cette histoire est inspirée d'une histoire vraie' [this story is inspired by a true story]. This allusion to the notion of historical truth, reinforced by documentary footage about Général de Gaulle's visit to the Caribbean in the 1960s and the establishment of the BUMIDOM, positions the rest of the film as a form of documentary about the social and political condition of life during this period, even though the viewer knows through paratextual material that the film is a fictionalised account of Léry's life. Robert Burgoyne argues that incorporating documentary footage into a fictional film means that historical events are re-enacted 'from a fictional or speculative perspective', meaning that it is unclear to the viewer whether these archival images are an accurate record of the past (Burgoyne 2003, 222). Drawing on Paul Ricœur's work on the 'document' as division between history and fiction, Burgoyne concludes that the veracity of the archival image is 'placed in doubt' (2003, 222). Barny seems to be aware of the capacity of documentary footage to cross the line between history and fiction: on the DVD sleeve, he acknowledges that using archival footage was a deliberate strategy to 'prendre à témoin l'histoire et de rentrer dans la fiction' [take history as witness and enter it into fiction]. The documentary footage Barny includes, taken from Bastide's film *BUMIDOM: des Français venus d'outre-mer* in a palimpsestic layering of different memories, primarily emphasises the disappointment and disillusionment experienced by those who emigrated through the BUMIDOM. For instance, as the camera pans over the city of Paris, we hear, in a voice-over, a woman talking poignantly about her desire to return to the Caribbean until she realised that the Bureau had not provided her with a return ticket. Through this documentary footage, Barny creates a causal link between the BUMIDOM and the violent exploits of the gang members, as fictionalised in the film. Like the woman talking in the documentary clip, the protagonists feel betrayed, coerced and oppressed, and they respond through violence and robbery. This sense of betrayal is evident early in the film after the gang has committed its first robbery, when the camera zooms in on a large sign written in red paint in capital letters which reads 'BUMIDOM TRAHISON' [BUMIDOM BETRAYAL]. Yet before this scene, the film continues its documentary-like quality. The credits are written in black-and-white text which, like that of the caption, has an archival, historical, feel. The title of the film breaks with this colour scheme as it appears in red, white and black. These colours give a nod to the republican Tricolour, but the blue band is replaced by a more sinister black one, perhaps suggesting that republican notions of liberty, equality and fraternity as embodied by the national flag did not hold true for BUMIDOM participants.

They did not hold true for Jimmy either, for whom France was not a land of equality and opportunity. At the beginning of the film, he is sleeping rough with his young daughter in a shed until he is told in hostile terms by the landowner to leave. Jimmy recounts his difficult experiences in a reflective voice-over, in a further nod to the documentary style of filmmaking. As Bill Nichols explains, there are different forms of documentary voice. In a direct address, the audience is told directly about the state of the world through embodied practices (such as a reporter or interviewee speaking) and disembodied practices (such as a voice-of-God commentary), while in an indirect address the audience is directed towards a particular viewpoint but in a less overt manner, either by observing social actors go about their lives or by interpreting the film's form (Nichols 2017, 55). Barny's use of a disembodied, voice-of-God commentary, told by

Jimmy himself, once again positions the film in the factual realm and suggests that the experiences of racism of the fictional character of Jimmy were shared by many Antilleans living in the Hexagon during this period. In the voice-over, Jimmy explains that he left for France when he was only thirteen, three days after the death of his father, with whom he had a complex relationship. In emotive language, he describes his life as one of constant struggle, acknowledging that 'toute ma vie je me suis battu' [I have fought all my life]. He goes on to explain his motives for joining the armed gang, noting his frustration at the racial discrimination he encountered:

> j'en avais marre de chercher des boulots mal payés. Quand ils me voyaient arriver les patrons me disaient que la place était déjà prise. Il y en avait qui étaient moins hypocrites. On n'embauche pas les Nègres.
>
> [I was fed up of looking for badly paid work. When the bosses saw me arrive they told me that the post was already taken. Some were less hypocritical. We don't hire Black people.]

In his speech, Jimmy places emphasis on the insulting proper noun 'Nègres' to highlight the disdain and contempt with which Black people were held by white metropolitan citizens.

This racism is also apparent in another scene, after Jimmy has committed his first armed robbery with the gang. He is concerned that the group did not wear masks when they robbed the post office and is worried that they will be recognised, but Molokoy tells him 'non, t'as rien à perdre. Un Nègre est un nègre. Ils se ressemblent tous' [no, you've nothing to worry about. A Black man is a Black man. They all look alike]. Here, Molokoy is being ironic by suggesting that he shares the views of white French people who think that all Black people look the same. Through this character, Barny positions Black Antilleans as a minoritised group who are constantly stereotyped, pigeonholed and essentialised because of the racialised phenotypes they share. Molokoy's ironic attitude is reminiscent of Ndiaye's comment in *La Condition noire* that 'les Noirs de France sont individuellement visibles, mais ils sont invisibles en tant que groupe social' (Ndiaye 2008, 17) [Black people of France are individually visible, but they are invisible as a social group].

To return to the form of the film, voice-over is not only employed in the film to signal historical veracity but also to solicit emotion from the viewer, allowing the audience to identify with the plight of the characters and share in their fictionalised personal memories. For instance, Jimmy talks to the audience in a voice-over when he returns to Guadeloupe to visit his mother. He walks along the beach with her, the voice-over filling the silence between the two characters. In a wistful, nostalgic tone, he explains how he tried to fit into metropolitan society by forgetting his old life in the Caribbean, and he evokes the sensorial pleasures that used to fill him with joy in Guadeloupe, for which he feels nostalgic: 'je me suis efforcé d'oublier ma vie d'avant. La chaleur, les senteurs, le bruit des vagues' [I tried hard to forget my old life. The heat, the scents, the sound of the waves]. Furthermore, the voice-over gives detail about the expectations his mother had for him on his departure for France; she dreamed he would become a successful civil servant, but he left school because he refused to obey authority. Through the voice-over, the audience participates in Jimmy's sentiment of failure and self-pity. This scene is also important because it gives an insight into the complex relationship Jimmy has with his mother. His mother asks him for forgiveness for sending him away to avoid tensions escalating between Jimmy and his violent father, adding that 'je savais pas que ce serait si difficile pour toi' [I didn't know it would be so difficult for you]. In this emotional scene, the camera zooms in on each character in turn, enabling the audience to witness a reconciliation between mother and son. The action then moves back in time to Jimmy's childhood as Jimmy watches in a flashback the cockerels they used to own fighting. Jimmy's family used to participate in this popular Caribbean sport until his mother was forced to sell the cockerels, in an illustration of the financial precarity experienced by those who remained on the island in the 1960s and 70s. The flashbacks to this sport in this scene, repeated elsewhere in the film, provide the viewer with more information about Jimmy's character in an example of Barthes's 'semic code', as theorised by Turim (1989, 11). They allude to the Caribbean heritage of his past, while their fleeting nature suggests that he is becoming further and further removed from his Caribbean identity through his emigration to mainland France.

The final stylistic device worthy of note is the music Barny incorporates into the film to reinforce plot points and transmit memories about the BUMIDOM. Music takes on a particularly emotional and melancholic quality when Jimmy has returned to Paris after his visit to Guadeloupe. He and his girlfriend Linda are stopped by the police, who demand to see their papers. Despite Linda's instance that they are French citizens from the overseas departments and not immigrants – 'on est Français, monsieur, lui est né en Guadeloupe et moi je suis née en Martinique' [we are French, sir, he was born in Guadeloupe and I was born in Martinique] – the police become violent, handcuffing Jimmy and sexually harassing Linda. Jimmy storms off, and then we see him sitting on the rooftops looking out across Paris. Rap music provides the soundtrack to this scene. The lyrics to the song 'J'aurais dû' [I Should Have] by French rapper Tito Prince, written specifically for the film's soundtrack, summarises accurately Jimmy's sentiment of exile, alienation and disappointment because life in Paris does not correspond to the promises he had been sold: 'où sont les villas qui m'étaient promises, où est mon cash monnaie, la vie classe qui m'était promise?' [where are the villas I was promised, where is my cash, the classy life I was promised?]. The repetition of the verb 'promettre' in these poignant lyrics reinforces the notion of disenchantment experienced by Jimmy and his fellow BUMIDOM participants. In this scene, music gives emotion to the plot and helps to convert the history of Caribbean emigration into collective memory by transforming this history 'into forms of shared knowledge and collective identification and participation', to quote Assmann again (2006, 216).

On 30 November 2016, Barny and Vincent Vermignon (who plays gang member Liko in the film) gave an interview for *Couleurs tropicales* [Tropical Colours], a podcast which celebrates African music on RFI. During this interview, Vermignon acknowledged the importance of film in creating collective memory out of difficult histories to enable communities affected to move forward. He stated:

> je pense que c'est bien de dire la vérité, parce que c'est le seul moyen pour nous d'aller de l'avant. Lorsque les choses sont reconnues, lorsque les choses sont acceptées, lorsque les choses sont analysées, après on a le recul suffisant pour se tourner vers le futur. (Siar 2016)
>
> [I think it's good to tell the truth, because it's the only way for us to move forward. When things are recognised, when things are accepted, when things are analysed, then we have the necessary distance to turn to the future.]

It is through the formal and stylistic devices employed by Barny that the film is able to offer this degree of acceptance and reconciliation with the past, and enable Antilleans to move towards the future. This engagement with both the past and the future is also the primary concern of *Le Rêve français*, to which I now turn.

Le Rêve français: A False Promise?

Writing for the television section of French news magazine *Obs* on 21 March 2018, Maryse Condé described *Le Rêve français* as a television film which 'veut mettre au jour des faits souvent inconnus des Antillais eux-mêmes' (Condé 2018) [wants to bring to light facts which often Antilleans themselves do not know]. Divided into two parts, the film uncovers important episodes in French Caribbean history which have been marginalised and silenced, but it does this through the love story between Guadeloupeans Samuel and Doris. The childhood sweethearts drift apart when Doris becomes pregnant by Armand, a white French man who works for Doris's father at his factory. Shunned by her family, Doris emigrates to mainland France through the BUMIDOM. At the training centre in Crouy-sur-Ourcq she meets Martinican girl Prisca with whom she strikes a friendship. Frustrated with the mundane domestic tasks they are forced to undertake, the pair run away from the centre and get a job working as ticket inspectors for the metro in Paris. Meanwhile, Samuel and his brother Julian become involved in the GONG, the Guadeloupean clandestine independence movement. In May 1967, they go on strike with other workers in Pointe-à-Pitre.[7] The police soon open fire on the protestors, supposedly killing Julian. However, Samuel later learns that his brother is still alive and has been working for the police as a spy. Samuel is arrested for his role in the protests and is taken to France where he is tried and eventually found not guilty. He decides to become a lawyer, and later a politician, to defend other people like him who are accused of crimes that they did not commit on grounds of their race and social background. Both Samuel and Doris marry and have children, but neither is happy with their prospective partner. The end of the film sees them return to Guadeloupe and reconcile their relationship, after Doris reveals it was her father who denounced him to the police following the May 1967 protests.

Although it is set against the backdrop of these significant historical events, the film does have a melodramatic quality, with characters at times seeming exaggerated and sensationalised. Moreover, the film has been criticised by some media outlets for starring non-Antillean actors. Aïssa Maïga, who plays Doris, is a Senegalese-born French actor, while Yann Gael, who plays Samuel and who won the 'Best actor' award at the Festival de la Fiction TV de La Rochelle 2017, is French-Cameroonian (La Dépêche 2018). However, the writing team did consist of people from the overseas departments who had a personal connection with Caribbean and Reunionese history. *Le Rêve français* was written by Faure in collaboration with Sandro Agénor, of Reunionese origin, and Alain Agat, of Martinican origin, both of whom grew up in Île-de-France after their parents migrated through the BUMIDOM. Agénor's mother also worked on the project as a consultant alongside Michel Reinette, director of the documentary film *L'Avenir est ailleurs*. This expertise has lent authenticity and accuracy to the project, even if the principal actors are not personally connected to this history.

Despite its melodramatic quality, the film succeeds in transmitting memories of emigration which chime with the lived experiences of many Antilleans, as evidenced in the letters they sent to the BUMIDOM authorities, analysed in Chapter 1 of this book. These are memories of disappointment and disillusionment as characters such as Doris feel they were sold an idealised version of mainland France. Sitting on the beach in Guadeloupe with her friends as a teenager in an early scene, Doris explains her desire to go to Paris to '[se] promener sur les grands boulevards ou dans les Jardins du Luxembourg, monter en haut de la Tour Eiffel, [s]'acheter du parfum sur les Champs Élysées' [walk along the great boulevards or in the Jardins du Luxembourg, climb the Eiffel Tower, buy perfume on the Champs Élysées]. Doris's romanticised vision of Paris is also evident on the DVD cover, which features a close-up of Doris and Samuel looking wistful against the Parisian backdrop; under the film title, however, we see a depiction of reality as the characters are surrounded by violent protests. The characters were keen to experience 'the French dream', to quote the title of the film. Doris wanted to leave behind a repressive family environment, while Samuel wanted to escape his precarious living conditions – he was living in a hut with a corrugated-iron roof which was frequently destroyed by hurricanes. However, they are disappointed with the reality they encounter in Paris. Doris finds herself in a low-paid job and living in the outskirts of the city, meaning that her middle-class, bourgeois status which protected her in Guadeloupe does not carry over to the metropole. Samuel, in contrast, does succeed professionally but is frequently subjected to racial discrimination, as many Guadeloupeans and Martinicans were during this period.

Faure adopts several cinematic techniques to convert this history into memory. Firstly, the film employs a cyclical structure. It begins with Samuel as an old man attending the opening ceremony of the Mémorial ACTe in Pointe-à-Pitre, a museum and cultural institution which opened in 2015 to preserve the memory of those affected by slavery and the transatlantic slave trade, and the film closes with these same scenes to show the repetitious, cyclical nature of life. The opening is poignant as Samuel meets his long-lost son for the first time at the museum. Slow, emotional piano music plays in the background as the camera pans around the museum and then zooms in on the young child's face, who is learning about the history of enslavement for the first time. During this scene, and in a nod to the documentary style of filmmaking that was also present in *Le Gang des Antillais*, Samuel's voice appears in a voice-over as he reflects on how best to transmit his own past to his son and wonders 'comment lui expliquer les liens qui nous unissent' [how to explain to him the bonds that unite us]. The camera pans across the statues in the museum of enslaved people whose feet are tied together in chains until the image becomes blurred and we see the feet of young Samuel preparing to run in a race. The narrative time thus changes as the audience is transported back in time to summer 1962, when Samuel is a young child living in Guadeloupe with his mother and brother Julian. The rest of the film continues in flashback as we follow Samuel's life chronologically until we arrive once again in the present day at the Mémorial ACTe. This extended flashback is an example of both the semic and referential code, picking up again on Barthes's terminology as theorised by Turim; it gives more information about Samuel's fictional past, but it also provides historical, political and cultural detail about what life was like in France and Guadeloupe from the 1960s to the present day. By intertwining the personal, fictionalised memories of Samuel, Doris and their families with larger-scale historical events through the use of flashback, Faure brings us into the realm of what Turim terms 'subjective memory'. By identifying with the fictionalised and emotive memories of the characters, the audience in turn engages with these broader historical memories which then become crystalised into a collective form of memory.

The BUMIDOM is highly present in the early memories of both Samuel and Doris, as revealed through this extended flashback. Samuel remembers Julian's anger at seeing young girls queueing up outside the BUMIDOM office. The camera zooms in on the BUMIDOM sign and then pans down to focus on the racialised and gendered aspect of the scene. We see a white, male *fonctionnaire* [civil servant] trying to convince two young Black girls to participate in the scheme. He tells them: 'ils te donnent un billet d'avion pour la France pour rien! Ils te trouvent un travail! Et quand même un logement! Profite, ça ne peut pas durer longtemps!' [they give you a plane ticket for France for nothing! They find you a job! And even housing! Make the most of it, it won't last long!]. Julian is furious that Guadeloupeans are being treated as 'des étrangers' [foreigners], and here the film makes an important comment on how French citizens of colour from Guadeloupe and Martinique were being denied their Frenchness by being considered as foreigners. Yet we are also reminded here that *Le Rêve français* is a fictional film which at times has an 'ambiguous reference to historical reality' which transforms fictionalised history into memory, to quote Plantinga again. In this episode, we see a BUMIDOM official trying to promote the scheme, and later he visits Samuel's mother and gives her a leaflet to convince her to send Samuel to France (which she refuses). However, according to policy documents held in the Archives nationales, the BUMIDOM did not advertise its services in this way. In March 1975, an independent report was produced on instructions of the government to improve the services of the BUMIDOM. The report criticises the BUMIDOM for taking too literally the ban on promoting its services by not giving prospective migrants any information at all; the BUMIDOM responded to this criticism by remarking that it decided not to advertise to avoid being accused of 'd'avoir pesé sur les décisions des migrants et de faire de la propagande' [having weighed in on the decisions of migrants and carrying out propaganda] (BUMIDOM 1975a, 3). This slight historical inaccuracy reinforces the fact that, although it does draw on real-life events, it is above all a fictionalised film about personal and collective memory rather than a historical documentary.

A further way in which the film transmits memory is through emotion and storytelling which enables the audience to identify with the plight of the characters. Emotion is particularly heightened in early episodes which narrate how Doris employed the services of the BUMIDOM. Although her family is relatively well-off – her father runs a rum factory and they live in a large, elegant house – and therefore could afford to send her to France without relying on state assistance, she is disowned by her family after the birth of her son Rudy, and so she is forced to turn to the BUMIDOM. She receives an envelope containing her plane ticket, and she announces to her sister that 'je pars le premier décembre' [I leave on 1 December]. Here, Doris's fictional experiences do chime with those who participated in the BUMIDOM; their plane tickets were booked for them, and they had little choice about when they would leave for France. This is borne out by the archival records. A letter from the president of the CASODOM to the prefect of Martinique on 5 December 1969 confirms participants' lack of agency. The president explained that the CASODOM had to inform Antilleans that the dates of their voyage could not be changed (CASODOM 1969). Returning to the film, the screen then goes black to signal a change in setting, and a small white caption reads 'Paris'. The camera travels with the bus on which Doris and her fellow female compatriots journey to the training centre in Crouy-sur-Ourcq. Nostalgic music provides the backdrop to this scene, and while the other girls stare out of the window with amazement at the snowy landscape, which is so different from the bright and sunny environment of Guadeloupe, Doris looks wistful and lonely. On arrival at Crouy, however, the girls' excitement turns to disappointment as they realise that they are far removed from the glamour of Paris. Shivering in their flimsy dresses, one girl asks incredulously 'c'est ça Paris?' [is that Paris?]. They are then met by the manager of the centre, a stern-looking woman who tells them that 'c'est une grande chance pour vous d'être ici' [it's a great opportunity for you to be here]. This sense of 'opportunity' is not shared by Doris and Prisca, however, who engage in small acts of rebellion against the domestic training they receive. For instance, when practising how to serve guests at a dinner party, Prisca intentionally pours the drinks from the right instead of the left, and then rolls her eyes when she is scolded by the centre manager. Furthermore, in a disturbing episode which recalls memories of the buying and selling of enslaved people during the transatlantic slave trade, the girls parade in front of rich, bourgeois men and women who then select them to work as housemaids. Prisca deliberately plays up in front of them and saunters down the corridor to avoid being chosen, and then the two girls climb out of the roof and run away. These scenes do not simply provide factual information about what life was life at Crouy-sur-Ourcq, but they also offer 'an embodied experience that consists of moods and emotions' which enable memories of Caribbean migration to be organised through the viewer's 'powerful affective responses' to the film, in Plantinga's terms (2021, 123–4).

Finally, the film incorporates different media which give both the characters and the audience information about historical events. This then triggers the characters' memory of how these historical events impacted on their own fictional world, and the audience is given the opportunity to reflect on their own possible memories of these events. Some of these items originate from real-life sources. For instance, in a *mise-en-abyme*, we observe Samuel watching the news following his release from prison, during which a news broadcaster relays the story of the BUMIDOM offices being ransacked in May 1968. The camera pans around the offices and we see graffiti sprawled on the walls which reads 'non au BUMIDOM' [no to the BUMIDOM] and 'à bas la traite des nègres' [down with the slave trade]. The audience presumes that this news footage is real because it appears in a news-like broadcast and recounts an event which has been well documented by scholars such as Germain (2016, 147–55). Indeed, footage of the occupation of the BUMIDOM office, taken from the news bulletin on 2 June 1968, is freely available on the website of the Institut national de l'audiovisuel [National Audiovisual Institute], and it seems as though the filmmakers incorporated this footage into their fictional film. In contrast, other media items draw on historical sources but are fictionalised to fit into the plot of the film, such as the newspaper article in which Doris learns of the charges against Samuel for his supposed involvement in the GONG. The heading of the article reads 'verdict dans le procès des indépendantistes guadeloupéens' [verdict in the trial of the Guadeloupean independentists]; this is a likely heading from a newspaper from 1968 which recounted the trial, but fictional information about Samuel has been added to the article so that it responds to the plot of the film. Memory works on different levels in some of these episodes. Not only do these media items crystallise historical events into the characters' memory (and also into the audience's memory) but they also trigger flashbacks as the characters are transported further back into their own memories of the past. This is particularly the case when characters are confronted with violent, traumatic memories. For instance, Samuel is watching the news about protests in France in May 68 and is reminded in a flashback of his own role in similar protests in Guadeloupe.

The power of *Le Rêve français* is its ability to weave accurate historical detail about little-known episodes in French Caribbean history into an emotional and believable love story between two Guadeloupeans. The film thus succeeds in intertwining the personal and the political, the individual and the collective. In other words, the film fulfils its objectives, as outlined on the DVD sleeve, to show how the characters 'ont franchi le cap de leur "rêve français"' [have reached the milestone of their 'French dream']. It does this through various mnemonic devices. It distorts narrative time through the use of the extended flashback and employs emotive storytelling techniques, while also integrating media items as intertexts in innovative ways.

Conclusion

This chapter has sought to question what films about Caribbean emigration offer in terms of representation and commemoration that other forms of creative production do not. I have argued that film is a powerful medium in the creation and transmission of memory because of its visual impact, its emotive and affective qualities and its ability to blur fact and fiction and history and memory in potent ways. This certainly rings true for two of the films analysed in this chapter, and *Le Gang des Antillais* and *Le Rêve français* are important vectors of memory about the intersecting racial and classist discrimination to which BUMIDOM participants and their descendants were often subjected. Not all films about the BUMIDOM are successful in incorporating the Bureau into the French collective memory, however. *Antilles-sur-Seine*, for instance, relies on stereotype and cliché to mock Antilleans and their history rather than preserve their memories. The chapter has thus revealed the limitations of cultural production in this regard. It is not enough for a film to simply represent a past for it to be considered a commemoration of that past; it must actively engage in practices of memory making through the types of devices outlined here, such as the use of flashbacks, documentary footage and emotive music, in order to transmit this memory. *Le Gang des Antillais* and *Le Rêve français* do this very effectively. Unlike *Antilles-sur-Seine*, they can be considered as examples of creative work which act as strategies of recovery, restoring Frenchness to BUMIDOM participants and their descendants who have often not been able to engage in familial or community-led memorial practices because they have felt too ashamed of having to rely on state assistance to finance their emigration and wanted to forget their painful experiences of racism and discrimination. These two films offer BUMIDOM participants a vehicle through which they can remember their past.

Notes

1. Léry wrote his autobiography while in prison for committing several armed robberies. *Le Gang des Antillais* was published in 1986 by Caraïbéditions. Léry has since returned to Fort-de-France and now divides his time between writing crime fiction and working as a healthcare worker. He was a consultant on the film (Marivat 2016).

2. According to Alain Agat, one of the screen writers, the project was initially structured into six episodes of fifty-two minutes. France 2 insisted that the structure was changed and material on Réunion was cut (Humbert Wozniak 2019, 192).
3. Mbye Cham argues that the French Caribbean has had a long history with cinema, not as producers but as consumers of foreign, imported, colonial films which 'exploit(ed) the natural/physical endowment of the tropical islands and invented other endowments to manufacture an image of the Caribbean radically at odds with the people of the Caribbean' (Cham 1995, 242).
4. Herman disguises herself as an Antillean cleaner to break into her superior Marin's office, while Légitimus himself is involved in disguise and cross-dressing as he plays an overweight, Black female postal worker.
5. For instance, when Herman and Manuel go for a coffee after he treats her son, she calls him 'le grand noir' [the big Black man], and then apologises by conceding that 'vous êtes pas noir noir noir quoi' [I mean, you're not Black Black Black]. Instead of calling this out, Manuel replies: 'moi, je vous trouve plutôt pale, pale, pale' [I find you pale, pale, pale].
6. Kassovitz and Barny have worked with each other on numerous occasions – for instance, Barny was casting director on the films *La Haine* (1995) [*Hate*] and *Assassin(s)* (1997).
7. The strike, which began on 24 May 1967, involved construction workers who were protesting for an increase in salary, but the protest was also supported by the GONG. Protestors agreed to meet with their superiors and the governor of Guadeloupe on 26 May, but the police opened fire before this meeting could occur. French officials reported that eight people were killed in the clashes. Witnesses have reputed this figure, estimating that approximately two hundred people were killed, but this remains unconfirmed. Eighteen members of the GONG were arrested and put on trial in 1968. They were supported by numerous anti-colonial public figures, including Aimé Césaire and Jean-Paul Sartre. Twelve men were acquitted but six were sent to prison for up to four years (Bonilla 2015, 28).

Chapter 5

Migration, Memory and Pedagogy in Graphic Novels and Children's Fiction

In an interview on radio station RCI Guadeloupe on 23 April 2018, Jessica Oublié spoke in detail of her motivations for co-authoring, with illustrator Marie-Ange Rousseau, the *bande dessinée*[1] *Peyi an nou*. She explained that 'il existe déjà un certain nombre de thèses, d'essais et d'écrits scientifiques très complexes sur le sujet, et j'avais vraiment envie de vulgariser l'information scientifique' (Oublié 2018) [there are already quite a few theses, essays and academic texts on the topic which are very complicated, and I really wanted to make this academic information accessible]. Alongside her desire to render this complex historical detail available to the general public, she also wanted to pay tribute to those whose migration through the BUMIDOM was particularly difficult. For Oublié, 'l'image permet ça plus que les mots peuvent le faire' (Oublié 2018) [images allow this more than words] because the graphic form invites an empathetic response from readers who can identify with the plight of characters more easily than through the written form. While the aesthetic qualities of the text must not be overlooked, it is clear from these comments that Oublié was driven to create *Peyi an nou* out of a desire to teach adults and young people about an episode of French and Caribbean history which has been marginalised both in historical discourse and in national commemorations of twentieth-century migration to France.

Yet what is particularly striking about *Peyi an nou* is that it does not only offer the reader historical information about how the BUMIDOM operated. The didactic nature of the graphic novel operates on another level, because it also teaches readers about the slippages and overlaps between history and memory. It reveals how migration through the BUMIDOM in the past continues to hold influence over Guadeloupean and Martinican families in the present, and therefore acts as a reminder about why the BUMIDOM should be memorialised, because of the significant demographic, social and cultural impacts the Bureau continues to have on Caribbean people today. Aleida Assmann reminds us that acts of remembering must 'reclaim the past as an important part of the present' and 'reconsider, revalue, and reassess it as part of individual biographies and the way individuals position themselves in a wider historical perspective' (Assmann 2008, 54). *Peyi an nou* connects the past and the present in different ways; it links Oublié's present to her family's past through her grandparents' story of migration, but it also unites the present of the wider Caribbean community with their collective past. By combining historical methods, including the use of oral testimonies and archival material, with artistic decisions such as writing themselves into the text as characters in the story, Oublié and Rousseau demonstrate effectively the differences between history as a subjective representation of the past and memory as a collective interpretation of this past in the present to create a shared, common identity.

This chapter moves on from purely textual and visual representations as analysed in the previous chapters to investigate how written and graphic forms work together in graphic novels and children's fiction. Alongside *Peyi an nou*, I analyse *Maman-Dlo*, a book aimed at children aged between six and nine and written and illustrated by Guadeloupean writer and artist Alex Godard, and *Emil'Patt à Paris*, a text which explores the history of the BUMIDOM through Antillean folktale, written by Marie-Louise Danchet and illustrated by José Gladone. These two children's books speak to the graphic novel because of the ways in which the textual and the visual overlap, even though they are written with a different audience in mind. The chapter asks how these three texts not only transmit memory but also transform memory into pedagogy, pedagogy about the BUMIDOM but also about memory itself.

These texts have been selected for their sustained focus on the BUMIDOM and Caribbean migration and their emphasis on debates surrounding history and memory. While *Peyi an nou* is to date the only graphic novel to be produced about the BUMIDOM in the Caribbean context, it invites comparisons with Tehem's *Piments Zoizos: les enfants oubliés de la Réunion* (2020) [Piments Zoizos: The Forgotten Children of Réunion], a graphic novel which charts the lives of two children who were removed from their Reunionese parents and resettled in France as part of the 'Enfants de la Creuse'.[2] In both of these graphic novels, the reader participates in the process of historical research alongside the protagonists because the reader witnesses them going to archives, interviewing participants and writing up their findings. Moreover, *Peyi an nou* sits in a line of graphic novels to emerge recently which address important social and historical issues afflicting the islands. Examples include *Tropiques toxiques* (2020) [Toxic Tropics], a collective volume by Oublié, Nicola Gobbi, Kathrine Avraam and Vinciane Lebrun about the chlordecone scandal;[3] *Frantz Fanon* (2020), a graphic biography of the Martinican anti-colonial thinker by Frédéric Ciriez and Romain Lamy; and *Nengue: l'histoire oubliée des esclaves des Guyanes* (2018) [Nengue: The Forgotten History of Slaves from the Guianas] by Stéphane Blanco and Samuel Figuière, which uncovers the history of maroons in French Guiana. There is also a rich strand of recent *bandes dessinées* which examine the penal colony in French Guiana, some of which has been published in the Caribbean (Forsdick 2019). These texts can be defined as 'bande dessinée de reportage' [graphic journalism], a genre which is 'une voie non conformiste de se confronter à la réalité' (Dabitch 2009, 91) [a non-conformist manner of confronting reality].

Children's fiction is also an emerging genre of literature in the Caribbean which tackles similar themes of social and historical concern, even if this literature remains underexplored in academic scholarship on Caribbean writing, as Véronique Bonnet deplores (2017, 1). Key themes addressed by picture books and illustrated books written in a range of genres include histories of enslavement and forced displacement, the environment, local Caribbean traditions and migration. Many of these texts are written by established and prolific authors such as Maryse Condé, Gisèle Pineau and Dany Laferrière. While they do not necessarily examine migration through the BUMIDOM in detail, a considerable number of books do explore the theme of displacement from the Caribbean, either during the BUMIDOM era (Pineau's *Un papillon dans la cité* (1992) [A Butterfly in the Housing Estate]) or in a more contemporary period (Condé's *Rêves amers* (2001) [Bitter Dreams] and Pineau's *Caraïbes sur Seine* (1999) [The Caribbean on the Seine]). The BUMIDOM is explored, though, in children's books through a Reunionese lens, such as in Ahmed Kalouaz's *Enfants de l'exil: de l'île de la Réunion à la Creuse* (2016) [Children of Exile: From Réunion to La Creuse] and Olivier Trotignon's *Ella – Dada Tom* (2008) [Ella-Brother Tom]. For Bonnet, such books allow children and adolescents to fully enter into a global and connected history (2017, 8). As this chapter will demonstrate, they enable children to become memory activists alongside the authors because they participate in reinterpreting and valuing memories of the BUMIDOM.

A Pedagogical Approach to Memory in Graphic Novels and Children's Fiction

At the heart of practices of memorialisation and commemoration is the notion that we learn about the past in order to build a better future. According to Claudia Mitchell and her colleagues, the primary function of remembering is to learn from the past so that the same mistakes will not be repeated (2011, 1). For them, memory is about activating personal and social change in a future time. However, Roger Simon, Sharon Rosenberg and Claudia Eppert contend that the phrase 'learning from the past' is too simplistic because it does not take into consideration what lessons are being learned, who is teaching and who is learning, and how this learning actually occurs (2000, 2). They argue that remembrance is always inherently pedagogical, and not only when it is situated within an educational framework such as in schools or in museums: 'rather, whatever its site and social form, remembrance is an inherently pedagogical practice in that it is implicated in the formation and regulation of meanings, feelings, perceptions, identifications, and the imaginative projection of human limits and possibilities' (Simon, Rosenberg and Eppert 2000, 2). Drawing on Foucault's dialectic of 'knowledge/power', they create the 'remembrance/pedagogy' couplet to signal the interconnectedness between the two terms; all formations of memory are implicitly involved in thinking through issues related to pedagogy – who remembers, who teaches, how this is taught and what is the purpose (Simon, Rosenberg and Eppert 2000, 2). They then conceive of three forms of pedagogy related to memory: 'remembrance as a strategic practice', which consists of efforts to mobilise knowledge to serve a particular social and political function, such as institutional apologies and state-led compensations; 'remembrance as difficult return', which aims to honour significant individuals and value their deeds in the present; and a remembrance of hope which suggests a more positive attachment to the past and a recalibration of our ideas surrounding community and identity (Simon, Rosenberg and Eppert 2000, 3–5).

Bill Niven, in contrast, is critical of what he terms 'didactic memory'. Analysing the remembrance of the Nazi past in Germany, he argues that 'didactic memory', which denotes learning lessons of World War II 'in a manner which presupposes their (Germans'] need for ethical instruction', is no longer necessary because Germans today have learned the lessons of Nazism (Niven 2017, 31). He proposes a move towards 'post-didactic memory' which operates on trust; 'Germans must be given more freedom to determine their own ways of thinking and feeling about Nazism' (Niven 2017, 31). For Niven, people need to be trusted to enact their own practices of remembrance on their own terms. Post-didactic memory does not seem entirely applicable in the case of the BUMIDOM, however. Remembering on a state level has not yet occurred, and the French government has not made any significant attempt to right the wrongs committed during this period. While it is important to grant individuals the space to create their own memory practices, national initiatives of commemoration are also needed in order to indicate to communities that their memories are valued and respected by the nation.

Graphic novels and children's fiction are the ideal space to carry out this more independent type of pedagogical memory work. The reader is guided to interpret the past by the author and illustrator through different techniques such as the incorporation of intermedial sources and the combination of text and image. However, these different materials allow for numerous interpretations of the past, meaning that the reader has a degree of freedom in how he or she connects the past to the present and turns history into memory. This, of course, occurs on different levels, depending on the audience; children are not necessarily conscious of their participation in this memory work, but it can occur on a subconscious level. Considering graphic novels and children's books in turn, I now examine the formal devices used in each genre which favour a pedagogical approach to memory transmission.

As Golnar Nabizadeh argues, graphic novels are particularly effective at representing and memorialising complex human experiences such as migration because they 'rely on exploratory, experimental, and unorthodox modes of representation to raise their readers' awareness of social, political, and historical issues, and ontological approaches to these concerns' (Nabizadeh 2019, 1). They allow readers to consider histories and memories from different perspectives and often spotlight the experiences of marginalised communities (including women and migrant groups) whose past has been overlooked in more conventional methods of storytelling. Nabizadeh's comments here ring true in the case of *Peyi an nou*. While, as I have shown in this book, there has been a recent surge in cultural works in a variety of genres about the BUMIDOM, these items have tended to explore the Bureau from a very personal perspective and have not fully considered how the BUMIDOM operated within its political and social context or its impacts on society. *Peyi an nou*, in contrast, succeeds in uniting the voices of men and women, children and elderly people, experts and lay people, and those who left the islands and those who stayed, providing detailed historical context to explain why the BUMIDOM was created but also recovering the memories of those who were the most greatly affected. Nabizadeh argues that there are three principal reasons why graphic novels are effective at transmitting memory. Firstly, she contends that the ways in which graphic novels are structured into a series of panels, separated from each other by a gutter or a blank space, enables both remembering and forgetting to take place; remembering occurs within the panels themselves, while the gutters act as a 'sea of forgetting' (Nabizadeh 2019, 4). As we shall see, the layout of panels in *Peyi an nou* is unconventional, in that sometimes they are separated by a gutter but not always, particularly when an expert is providing historical detail about the BUMIDOM (such as in the second chapter, where historian Monique Milia-Marie-Luce is speaking). Oublié and Rousseau thus play with textual spaces of remembrance. Remembrance occurs in *Peyi an nou* in spaces where it would not necessarily occur in other graphic novels, and this is representative of their overarching approach to memory transmission, as they seek to transmit memory among audiences where this has not previously occurred. Secondly, Nabizadeh proposes that graphic novels work on a process of inclusion and exclusion through their fragmented nature, and it is thus up to the reader to participate in the process of remembering by filling in the blanks of the story (2019, 4). Finally, she argues that panels in the graphic novel move the reader through time, and therefore act as a visual representation of how the past is connected to the present and the future (Nabizadeh 2019, 4). *Peyi an nou* certainly fulfils these last two criteria. As I shall demonstrate in the following section, a strength of the text is its ability to show how the history of the BUMIDOM continues to have resonances for French and Antillean communities in the present.

An additional factor in the potential for graphic novels to transmit memory in a pedagogical manner is in the combination between text and image. Hillary Chute and Marianne DeKoven define graphic novels as 'cross-discursive' because the words and images do not 'simply blend together, creating a unified whole, but rather remain distinct' (2006, 769). The images do not only illustrate the written text but also work on another level to offer an additional narrative to the reader. It is the tension between the text and the image, and the narrative threads they both offer, that helps to generate meaning and transmit memory. Maaheen Ahmed and Benoît Crucifix, meanwhile, contend that memory is transmitted not only through the content of the images and photographs (which they term 'polygraphy'), but also through the style of the lines and the drawings (termed 'graphiation'). Polygraphy 'interweaves knowledge of different media' while graphiation 'calibrates readers' involvement and emotional responses' (Ahmed and Crucifix 2018, 6). *Peyi an nou* makes use of both polygraphy and graphiation: it incorporates different media such as images, newspaper articles and archival documents to teach the reader about the layered, polyvalent memories of the BUMIDOM, while the bold lines and bright colours of the drawings draw the reader in to the narrative.

Practices of archivisation are also important in turning memory into pedagogy. Jared Gardner suggests that comics and graphic novels can actually be considered as archives themselves which contain 'forgotten artefacts and ephemera', items which 'were never meant to be collected' (Gardner 2012, 150). Chute sees this archivisation process as taking place in a more orderly fashion; the job of the graphic novelist, she contends, is to select and sort material and then contain it in boxes, just like an archive (Chute 2016, 192). Following this line of argumentation, *Peyi an nou* as a whole could be considered a literary archive of the BUMIDOM, because Oublié and Rousseau sort through a whole range of historical material in order to create a coherent narrative, which they then put into panels, or *cases* in French, on the page. The documents they incorporate from the BUMIDOM files held at Pierrefitte-sur-Seine add another layer to the archivisation process inherent in *bande dessinée*, and acts as a reminder of the text's pedagogical function because the documents are primary sources which offer historical detail about the BUMIDOM operations.

Memory transmission works in similar ways in picture books and illustrated books for children, given the connections between text and image; unlike in graphic novels, though, image and text usually come together to offer a single, unified narrative. Julia L. Mickenberg and Lynne Vallone distinguish between illustrated books as those in which 'pictures supplement the text but are not integral to it', and picture books as those 'where the text, if any, is incomplete without reference to illustrations' (Mickenberg and Vallone 2011, 10). Both *Maman-Dlo* and *Emil'Patt à Paris* fall into the former category. While the images are instrumental in the transmission of memory about the BUMIDOM, the narrative would still function without access to these images. The images in the two books help the child reader to grasp the narrative thread, but also offer numerous ways of interpreting the narrative action. They thus point towards the complexity of children's illustrated fiction: 'the old cliché that a picture tells a thousand words simultaneously suggests the form's appropriateness to children and childhood but also reminds us of visual imagery's beguiling complexity and the challenges of acquiring vocabulary sufficient to analyse it' (Mickenberg and Vallone 2011, 11). The fact that images offer a multiplicity of interpretations is useful for children learning about memory through these texts because it increases the number of memories to which they have access.

The connections between memory and pedagogy also operate on an extratextual level within children's fiction. Ulrich Knoepflmacher and Mitzi Myers have introduced the term 'cross-writing' into scholarship on children's fiction; 'cross-writing' refers to texts which interest both children and adults, either together through a shared reading practice, or separately when they engage with a text on different levels (1997, vii). I argue that when children read texts of which the primary function is to transmit memory with adults, they have the possibility to engage in dialogue and exchange with the adult reader not only about the content of these memories, but also about the nature of memory itself; its limitation, its unreliability, its productive and restorative potential. This intergenerational learning process through children's literature is particularly important when it comes to the BUMIDOM because children do not have sufficient formal opportunities to learn about what the BUMIDOM was or how it operated. The BUMIDOM is not a compulsory part of the school curriculum at primary or secondary levels either in mainland France or in Guadeloupe and Martinique, and nor does it feature in history textbooks aimed at children of these levels. It is thus crucial that texts such as *Maman-Dlo* and *Emil'Patt à Paris* enable such a learning experience to occur.

Peyi an nou, *Maman-Dlo* and *Emil'Patt à Paris* can thus be considered pedagogical tools which teach adults and young children about what it was like to migrate through the BUMIDOM and what it was like to stay behind on the Caribbean islands. The pedagogical nature of the texts operates on an additional level because they offer a commentary on how Caribbean communities remember their histories of migration today. For Oublié and Rousseau, this didactic approach to memory is at the heart of their writing practice. In an interview with me in December 2022, Oublié commented that she and Rousseau wanted to teach their readers about how the collective memory about the BUMIDOM has been created in the present, but they also wanted to give readers methodological tools of research and investigation so that they too could begin their own process of uncovering familial memory (Oublié 2022). The authors thus feel they have an ethical responsibility to transmit their historical knowledge and research skills to the subsequent generation to enable individual memory work to occur on a larger scale.

Memory, Testimony and the Archive in *Peyi an nou*

Peyi an nou won the Prix étudiant de la BD politique France Culture [France Culture's Student Prize for a Political Graphic Novel] in April 2018. This prize was awarded by a judging panel of eleven students and presided over by David Amiel, advisor to President Emmanuel Macron at the time (Pujar 2018). Although this prize gave increased visibility to the graphic novel and granted it political endorsement – in addition to Amiel's involvement, the prize was awarded to the pair at the Assemblée nationale in Paris – there has not been any concrete political action as a result in terms of valuing the histories and memories of the Antillean community living either in continental France or in the overseas departments. The text narrates the discovery of Oublié's family history as one of migration. It opens with the narrator-protagonist Jessica[4] learning about her grandfather's cancer diagnosis, which sparks her desire to travel to Guadeloupe to learn more about her family's past while her grandparents are still alive. During a family meal in Guadeloupe, she hears the acronym 'BUMIDOM'; she knows nothing about the Bureau, but is intrigued to learn more about why so many Antilleans (including her own grandfather) made the journey to France to find work in the 1960s and 70s. We then witness the meeting between Jessica and Marie-Ange as they decide to work on a *bande dessinée* together, and the reader follows their process of historical research and creative production. They interview experts about Antillean migration such as historians, sociologists and demographers, but they also spend time listening to the testimonies of people directly affected by this mass migration. Diverse voices and perspectives are incorporated into the text: those who left for France, those who remained on the islands and those who have inherited this history of migration through their family network. Interspersed between these interviews and testimonies are Jessica's personal reflections as she thinks through what her family's migratory past means for her own present. The structure of the graphic novel thus reveals what is at stake in the memorialisation process – memorialisation does not only mean preserving and honouring the memories of oppressed groups, but also bringing these memories into the collective imaginary of communities in the present so that intergenerational healing can begin. In other words, memorialisation involves the sharing of traumatic histories across generations to help each generation to understand and process the psychological effects of the trauma, whether experienced directly or indirectly, and begin to look forward to the future.

This emphasis on memory and pedagogy is also visible in the paratext, the fringe between the text and what lies beyond it, a fringe which is 'always bearer of an authorial commentary either more or less legitimated by the author', to quote Gérard Genette (1991, 262). The title of the graphic novel, written in Guadeloupean Creole, means 'our country', but as Oublié remarked in an interview for the podcast series *#MaParole* on La 1ère on 18 January 2022, the affective ties towards France and Guadeloupe differ depending on the positionality of the person speaking (Oublié 2022). When she spoke to people in Guadeloupe, they were keen to stress their connection to France to prove the legitimacy of their French identity; when she interviewed people of Guadeloupean origin living in Paris, they emphasised Guadeloupe, the country they had left behind, as their homeland. This brief but evocative phrase, then, captures the complexity of creating a collective memory out of the individual personal memories of a particular generation, which differ depending on personal circumstance, social class, gender and race. Interestingly, the title is not translated from Creole into French.[5] This strategy differs to the approach taken in the book itself: each chapter is entitled with a Creole proverb or idiom which is then translated into French in a footnote, and other culturally specific items which appear in Creole (such as 'dombré', referring to a traditional Antillean dish) are also glossed in French to ensure comprehension and to teach a francophone audience about Antillean culture. Perhaps Oublié and Rousseau thought that the linguistic structure of the phrase in Creole was close enough to the French to be understood by francophone readers, or perhaps they wanted to give value to the Creole language by using it in the text's title (Wimbush 2018, 17). The epigraph, a quotation taken from Françoise Ega's 1966 autobiography *Le Temps des madras*, further reveals connections between memory and pedagogy. Ega is describing her personal memories of watching the boats arrive from France, transporting people from what she describes as 'l'autre pays' [the other country]; Oublié and Rousseau use Ega's personal memories to open the text and to frame it as a pedagogical quest to understand why so many boats were transporting people between the Caribbean and Europe during this period. Finally, the paratext contains a dedication to Oublié's grandparents Somène and Paul, whose memories of migration trigger Oublié's own process of learning and reflection about the BUMIDOM (2017, 2). While her grandfather migrated of his own accord rather than through the Bureau, he was the catalyst for her desire to learn more about this institutionalised form of migration and to connect the past to the present to learn for the future.

Within the graphic novel itself, the interviews and testimonies carried out with family members, BUMIDOM participants and experts in migration act as pedagogical tools to teach the reader about how the BUMIDOM operated, but they are also instructive in what they reveal about the blurring between history and memory. These are interviews undertaken by Oublié and Rousseau during the research process, and inscribed into the text as part of the storyline. In order to provide the reader with accurate historical information, Jessica and Marie-Ange interview historians Milia-Marie-Luce, Serge Mam-Lam-Fouck, Françoise Vergès and Anton Perdoncin to discover why the BUMIDOM was created; they speak to Philippe Pierre-Charles, founder of the Groupe révolution socialiste [Socialist Revolution Group], and sociologist and political activist Ary Broussillon, to find out about resistance to migratory policies in the overseas departments; and they talk to sociologists Alain Anselin and Stephanie Condon to discover the social impacts of the BUMIDOM and how this migration was gendered from its inception. This material is highly detailed; dates, statistics and thorough explanations are included in the text to render it intellectually rigorous and to ensure that it is an effective pedagogical tool for people with no prior knowledge of the BUMIDOM. For instance, in chapter 2 we are introduced to key figures instrumental in the departmentalisation law of 1946 (Léopold Bissol, Gaston Monnerville, Raymond Vergès and Aimé Césaire) and learn of the very difficult socio-economic conditions of the period, when unemployment rates hovered at 40 per cent (Oublié and Rousseau 2017, 25). The layout of these sections providing historical detail is significant. When Jessica gives the narrative voice to the expert, the text is not structured in conventional panels, but the information takes over the whole page in order to maximise the space available and emphasise the historical detail. When Jessica and the expert are in dialogue, at times the speech bubbles cross over and it is not always easy to work out which speech bubble belongs to which character (Oublié and Rousseau 2017, 24). The boundaries between Jessica and the expert thus become blurred, as Jessica slowly becomes an expert in her own right by listening to the specialists and exchanging ideas with them. This occurs on another level, too, as the hierarchies between protagonist and reader also become distorted. The pedagogical aspect of the text is subtle, and because readers learn about the BUMIDOM alongside Jessica and Marie-Ange, there is little risk of them feeling judged for their lack of knowledge about Antillean migration.

Alongside this detailed historical contextualisation appear the personal testimonies of people directly affected by the BUMIDOM in different ways. These personal accounts add a level of intimacy to the narrative, as the reader learns more about the private lives of Jessica's family. The authors pay attention to gender dynamics in chapter eleven when Jessica interviews her grandmother to discover why she stayed in Guadeloupe when her husband left for mainland France in 1974. The grandmother's simple, matter-of-fact response that her place was 'à la maison, avec les enfants' (Oublié and Rousseau 2017, 149) [at home, with the children] reveals that Guadeloupean society was dominated by patriarchal discourse at the time, meaning that men and women did not have the same prospects for professional opportunities. Moreover, the gendered nature of the work offered to BUMIDOM participants is apparent when Jessica interviews Léo and his friends in the eighth chapter, and the gendered divide the characters speak of is borne out in BUMIDOM policy documents, as analysed in Chapter 1 of this book. The two men were given work installing telephone lines and in the postal service, while the women worked as cleaners in private houses and hospitals (Oublié and Rousseau 2017, 113).

These testimonies are highly effective at teaching readers about the BUMIDOM because they offer personalised examples of migration which make the historical information provided by the experts come to life. They also offer a commentary on memory because the characters are enacting the process of remembering in the textual space, which then allows the reader to reflect on the difficulty of remembering traumatic events. For example, in chapter 8, one of Léo's friends is reluctant to recall her experiences because they were painful, explaining that 'ah non, moi, je préfère me souvenir des bons moments' (Rousseau and Oublié 2017, 116) [oh no, I prefer to remember the good times]. For her, evacuating difficult memories is too traumatic, but Jessica explains the importance of learning about these memories, no matter how hard they may be to recall, in order to 'mieux comprendre votre histoire' (Oublié and Rousseau 2017, 116) [better understand your history]. Oublié and Rousseau thus demonstrate the need to foreground individual memories to create a more nuanced and complex history of an event, while also acknowledging that recovering difficult memories can be traumatic. The graphiation at work in the text, to borrow Ahmed and Crucifix's term, reinforces differences between the past and the present. When characters are talking about memories of their past, or when experts are providing historical context, the background colours of the images change from different bright colours to a pale green and pink to signal that the characters are referring to the past. The graphiation is enhanced by the polygraphy employed to signal memory transmission between characters, thus teaching the reader about what it means to remember. A recurrent and prominent image in the panels in which characters are interviewed is a tape recorder. Sometimes it is placed next to Jessica and Marie-Ange as they listen to stories and memories of the BUMIDOM, while at other times we see Jessica holding it for participants to talk into. It also appears in a panel on its own, used as a temporal marker to distinguish between the conversation between Jessica and the interviewee Anselin in the present and the historical detail he recounts about the past (Oublié and Rousseau 2017, 131). For Jennifer Boum Make, the tape recorder is more than just a symbol of oral exchange between interviewer and interviewee, but also an aesthetic marker of the circulation of difficult memories between the BUMIDOM generation and the post-BUMIDOM generation (Boum Make 2022, 123). *Peyi an nou*, therefore, teaches readers not only about the history of post-war migration, but also the differences and overlaps between history and memory; that collective memory is a shared history of a group 'which exceeds the boundaries of one individual's life span', to quote Assmann (2008, 52). The post-BUMIDOM generation, represented in the text by Jessica, is able to participate in shared practices and discourse through the act of collecting testimonies, and the image of the tape recorder operates as a metonym of this process.

A further mnemonic device employed by Oublié and Rousseau is the incorporation of themselves as characters in the story. While this technique enables readers to understand more about the process of historical research and the production of the graphic novel, it also allows them to see how Jessica's present is connected to her family's past, and thus how history becomes memory when it is 'reconfigured into a particular and emotionally charged version of "our history" and absorbed as part of a collective identity' (Assmann 2008, 65). In the first chapter, following her trip to Guadeloupe, we see Jessica discussing her ideas for the project with Marie-Ange. She remarks that she had always heard people talking about the Bureau without really knowing what it was, and she describes it as '. . . le grand absent qui hanterait toutes les familles antillaises . . .' (Oublié and Rousseau 2017, 17) [. . . the conspicuous absence that would haunt every Antillean family . . .]. The ellipses at the beginning and end of this phrase which appears, like the rest of the dialogue, in a speech bubble, illustrate Jessica's sensation of bewilderment because it suggests a silencing of information. Her confusion is also emphasised graphically in the next panel by the ghosts floating above her head. She has always been aware that her present is affected by her past without fully understanding why. This is the case for Oublié, too, who talks of incorporating her self-identity into the Antillean collective memory through the creation of *Peyi an nou* as a transformative and therapeutic act: 'listening to my grandparents narrating their childhood to me, seeing my father and mother break their silence, questioning my sisters about their lives, was by far the best way for me to be reborn' (Oublié 2021, 120). For Oublié and her narrative persona, remembrance is a hopeful practice of critical learning. By listening to her family's stories, collating testimonies and bringing them together in the form of a graphic novel, they undergo a process of 'continual unsettling and an interminable asking of pedagogical questions regarding what it means to be taught by the experience of others' (Simon, Rosenberg and Eppert 2000, 6).

Finally, *Peyi an nou* can be considered a pedagogical tool in the ways in which it is intermedial. The text incorporates newspaper articles, archival documents and transcriptions of letters sent by migrants in order to provide accurate and authentic historical information. These documents appear on double-page spreads at numerous times in the book to separate one chapter from another. The items overlap each other, as if to point towards the overwhelming quantity of information that Jessica and Marie-Ange had to sift through to create a coherent narrative about the BUMIDOM. Indeed, we see a sketched image of Jessica and Marie-Ange in the right-hand corner of these spreads as they consult the documents, becoming experts in the process. On one level, these images are visual representations of the research process they undertake to find out about the BUMIDOM, and on another, they represent what Chute describes as the archivisation process of turning history into memory through *bande dessinée*

(2016, 192). The pedagogical nature of *Peyi an nou* falls down slightly in that there is no documentation to explain where these historical sources have originated from, nor in which archives they are situated (Wimbush 2018, 24). However, it could also be argued that the emphasis of the authors is not so much on the factual contents of the BUMIDOM archives; rather, Oublié and Rousseau seek to give the reader a more holistic impression of what it is like to carry out historical research when confronted with so many different and at times conflicting sources. They endeavour to teach the reader how to negotiate between formal historical sources, such as archival documents and newspaper articles, with the oral histories and memories of those who experienced migration first-hand.

By combining testimonies from first-hand witnesses and emotive sketched images with detailed historical information from a range of experts in twentieth-century Caribbean migration, *Peyi an nou* succeeds in teaching the reader both what the BUMIDOM was and how it has been remembered. While Oublié wanted the graphic novel to interest both children and adults alike,[6] I would argue that it is most likely to be read by a more mature reader, given the level of detail at work in the historical contextualisations and the relatively complex language employed both in the speech bubbles and in the narrative voice-overs. The album, however, has had a large readership, and Oublié has developed various initiatives to extend the reach of the work, helping to inscribe the BUMIDOM into the Antillean collective memory. For instance, several book signings and debates were held when the album was released in 2017 in Paris and Guadeloupe, and Oublié and Rousseau also curated the travelling exhibition 'Memwa', taking panels from the graphic novel and providing additional historical context.[7] Are the works of children's fiction as successful at incorporating the BUMIDOM into collective memory? How does the interplay between history and memory work in these texts?

The Textual and the Visual in *Maman-Dlo*

The work of author and illustrator Alex Godard is steeped in history, memory and Caribbean tradition. Born in Marie-Galante, Godard moved to Lyon in 1984 to continue his artistic training at the École Émile Cohl. Since 1990, he has written and illustrated nine books for primary-aged children, as well as illustrating three books for other

French writers, including for Fabienne Kanor, whose prose fiction for adults is explored in Chapter 2 of this book.[8] These texts address themes relevant to a young Caribbean readership wishing to explore their history and cultural heritage through literature; they focus on the Caribbean landscape, traditional folktales and histories of migration, enslavement and incarceration.

Maman-Dlo is thus no exception in its evocation of Antillean history and culture. The book weaves the story of a family separated by the Atlantic Ocean between the Caribbean and Europe in the 1960s with the traditional folktale of the *mama-dlo*, a mermaid considered to have protecting and healing qualities in the Caribbean but who terrifies the young protagonist, Cécette. The title is polysemic; it clearly evokes the emblematic Antillean figure of the *mama-dlo*, but it could also read 'maman de l'eau' [mother of the water], referring to Cécette's mother who is separated from her child by the ocean. The title thus signals the importance of the maternal figure and the *mama-dlo* for Cécette and for the Caribbean community more broadly. The text is narrated by a third-person omniscient narrator, following the style of traditional Antillean folktales, but occasionally Cécette's voice is heard through an internal monologue. The story is set in Godard's native island of Marie-Galante and centres around the daily life of Cécette who lives with her grandparents. Her grandmother Man Ninie takes care of the domestic tasks, while her grandfather Papoli spends all day at sea, fishing and waiting for his son, who disappeared one day at sea, to return. In this way, Godard makes a similar comment about the gender norms at work in patriarchal Guadeloupe during the 1960s as Oublié and Rousseau. In both texts, labour is highly gendered, and women are expected to stay at home to look after (grand)children while men carry out physical work on the sugar plantations, in factories or at sea. Cécette spends most of her time waiting for her mother to come home from continental France. She is disappointed when she receives a letter from her mother telling her she will not be able to return this year, so she goes to visit the local storyteller Racik to cheer her up. However, he frightens her with tales about the *mama-dlo*, and so when she eventually receives a more positive letter from her mother inviting her to stay in France, Cécette fears that the boat on which she will travel will be destroyed by the mermaid. The text ends poignantly with Cécette promising her grandparents she will return to Marie-Galante. The repetition of the verb 'revenir' [to return] in the future tense, coupled with the ellipsis at the end of the first use of this verb, emphasises the young child's sorrow at leaving behind her grandparents and her beloved Caribbean island (Godard 2014, 38). This is mirrored visually by a double-page spread of an empty beach and the sea shaded in different hues of bright blue, with a small boat in the background to symbolise that her affective ties lie more with the Caribbean than with France. While Cécette is excited to see her mother in France, her home is with her grandparents in Marie-Galante.

As this summary makes clear, *Mama-Dlo* approaches the topic of the BUMIDOM from a different perspective to *Peyi an nou*. While the latter seeks to transmit detailed historical information about why the BUMIDOM was established and how it operated, the former provides almost no factual material about the Bureau. Indeed, it is not altogether clear whether Cécette's mother used the services of the Bureau to migrate to France, or whether she migrated of her own accord or through another conduit. The narrative focus does not lie on the mother or on her experiences in France; in fact, the mother is never given the narrative voice, apart from in the two letters she sends to Cécette. Rather than questioning what it was like to migrate to France in the 1960s and 70s, the book asks what it was like to remain in the Caribbean when separated from close family. While the book is situated in a specific space and time, the themes it evokes are so universal that it has the potential to resonate with any child who has been separated from a loved one. The pedagogical objectives of *Maman-Dlo* – teaching young children about loss, separation and longing during the BUMIDOM era and today – are thus different from those of *Peyi an nou*. In fact, *Maman-Dlo* is one of the only cultural items explored in this book to place the spotlight on those who were left behind in the Caribbean rather than on those who left in search of a better life in France; as this text shows, their experiences are equally worthy of commemoration.

Maman-Dlo is pedagogical in a different sense, too. On the back cover of the book, we read that the text is an 'ouvrage sélectionné par l'Éducation nationale pour le cycle 3' [text selected by the National Curriculum for cycle 3].[9] The text is used in schools in France and the Caribbean as a reader to help develop the literacy and comprehension skills of young children, and teaching tools to support their learning can be found online.[10] Storybooks not only enhance children's linguistic knowledge and their capacity to empathise with others, but also 'provide children with new information about the world' (Pulimeno, Piscitelli and Colazzo 2020, 13). In this case, the book provides children with new information about a location with which they or may not be familiar, depending on the context in which the book is read. Furthermore, the book has a memorial function, as it teaches children what it means to live with the memories of someone rather than with their physical presence. It thus fulfils Simon, Rosenberg and Eppert's category of 'remembrance as difficult return'; honouring the mother figure who undergoes the sacrifice of separation in order to give financial stability to her family, remembrance is, for Cécette, 'a learning to live with loss, a learning to live with a return of a memory that inevitably instantiates loss and thus bears no ultimate consolation, a learning to live with a disquieting remembrance' (2000, 4). The text also demonstrates why it is important for these experiences of departure and stasis to enter the French and Caribbean cultural memory, because this mass migration which began in the BUMIDOM era has continued in the present day, and so children need to learn to connect their present to this not-so-distant past.

One way in which these connections between memory and pedagogy become clear is through the combination of the textual and the visual. The front cover is striking; it is framed as a photo frame or postcard, and we see the back of a young Black girl looking out to sea. The colours are bright – blues, greens and reds dominate the scene – and the image is framed by shells which complete the tropical ambiance (at risk of exoticising life in the overseas departments). The title of the text appears in a brown luggage label at the top of the image, connoting themes of travel, departure and migration. Even from the front cover, then, the reader learns of the overpowering weight of the memory of her mother from beyond the sea. In the rest of the text, prominence is given to the image in order to create this evocative atmosphere and teach children about remembering a lost family member, a trauma conjured more powerfully through images than words. Images which illustrate the storyline either take up the whole page and are placed alongside the page of text, or they form the centrepiece of a double-page spread, and the text appears in relatively small font at the bottom. Images are also used to mark time in the narrative and move the story on; chapters are not given a title, but at the beginning of each chapter a small image appears which neatly summarises the content of that particular chapter. In addition, the colour scheme employed in the text is significant and helps to convey the pain of remembering someone who is not physically present. Nicole Brissac observes that the colour scheme changes in the text: the pastel browns, pinks and blues, which connote calmness and tranquillity, give way to darker colours when Cécette is afraid of the *mama-dlo* and fears that she will never see her mother again (Brissac 2007, 45). These images of fear are further emphasised by the text that accompanies them. At the beginning of the story, as Cécette looks out to sea for her mother, the narrator explains that 'l'horizon reste désespérement vide. Ce n'est pas encore aujourd'hui qu'elle viendra . . .' (Godard 2014, 4) [the horizon remains desperately empty. She won't come again today . . .']. The use of the adverb 'déspérément' conveys Cécette's bitter disappointment that her mother has still not returned, and here again we see an ellipsis, employed frequently throughout the book, to emphasise further her distress at her familial separation.

The format of the written text also reveals much about memory and pedagogy. On two occasions in the book, the structure of the prose departs from the conventional paragraph structure as the two letters sent from the mother to Cécette are transcribed, taking over the whole page. These letters are significant didactically because they situate the narrative action as taking place in the BUMIDOM era – the two letters date from April 1967 – and thus provide some factual detail about this period. For instance, the reader learns that the mother's departure is a labour migration to find work, and that she intends this displacement to be temporary, given that she has left Cécette with her own parents and is upset not to be able to return (Godard 2014, 18). During the 1960s and 70s, it was common for young women to leave their children in Martinique and Guadeloupe to be raised by the grandmother, and the women would either send money back home to support their family, or send for their children once their financial position in mainland France was more stable. This is borne out by correspondence between the directeur départemental [president of the department] and the administrateur délegué du BUMIDOM [chief executive of the BUMIDOM] about prospective migrants, stored in the Archives départementales de la Guadeloupe. In one particular case, following the survey carried out by the social worker, it was concluded that the young woman should stay in Guadeloupe and look after her children herself, rather than go to Paris and leave her children with her parents, because the latter did not have the physical or financial capabilities of looking after two more children (27 May 1968). As Louise Hardwick observes, this process of 'othermothering', in which a female relative or friend acts as a substitute mother in times of crises, occurred frequently in the Caribbean in the twentieth century, and it appears as a common trope in French Caribbean literature (Hardwick 2013, 194).

These letters thus provide important historical and contextual information to explain why Cécette was living with her grandparents. They are also significant for what they reveal about memory.

Memory operates here on a personal level. Unlike the rest of the text, in which Cécette is thinking about and remembering her mother, here, it is the mother who is remembering her daughter and communicating her affection towards her through the form of a letter. Janet Gurkin Altman posits that 'given the letter's function as a connector between two distant points, as a bridge between sender and receiver, the epistolary author can choose to emphasize either the distance or the bridge' (1982, 13). In this instance, the letters act as a bridge between mother and daughter. They also connect Cécette to her grandmother in a different way: the grandmother is illiterate as she never went to school (Godard 2014, 10), and so Cécette reads the letter aloud to her, further cementing the bond between them. This practice of reading the letters aloud can occur extratextually, too, as the child reader can share their reading practice with an adult. As Mickenberg and Vallone explain, children access books through their relationships with adults, because it is adults who buy or provide them with the book, and reading together is a means of developing affective bonds further (2011, 11). While this shared reading can take place throughout the whole text, the format of the letter, its brevity and the fact that letters are often read aloud to other people mean that the letters are the most suitable elements of the text to be shared between children and adult readers. This shared reading practice can facilitate discussion between adults and children beyond the text itself about the BUMIDOM era, about why it is important to learn about and remember this difficult period, and about how migration between Europe and the Caribbean in the present is connected to the organised migration in the 1960s, 70s and 80s. This reading practice, and the cross-generational dialogue it engenders, enables the BUMIDOM to enter the collective memory of French and Caribbean children today.

Maman-Dlo thus combines word and image in innovative ways to spotlight the personal memories of those who remained in the Caribbean during the BUMIDOM era, and to create a shared memory of Caribbean migration among child readers. It illustrates effectively how the 'visual collages not only function as narratives in their own right but together with the textual ones act as thresholds that can transport readers into the worlds of storytelling and memory' (Attarian 2011, 158). In the case of *Emil'Patt à Paris*, the world into which the reader is transported through word and image is one of myth and folklore which is transposed onto a history of the BUMIDOM.

Emil'Patt à Paris: The BUMIDOM as Caribbean *Conte*

Author of novels, poetry collections and children's fiction which engage with Caribbean histories of deportation and enslavement,[11] Marie-Louise Danchet is also the current director of Lanmou Ba Yo, an association for the commemoration of the abolition of slavery which was founded in the town of Le Moule on Grande-Terre in 2005. Her commitment to restoring historical memory and creating a space for Caribbean people to honour the suffering of their enslaved ancestors is thus evident both in her literature and in her political activism. Moreover, she takes a critical stance towards more contemporary examples of inequality, oppression and subordination in Martinique and Guadeloupe through her writing, and her criticism of France's continued colonial project in the Caribbean is evident in *Emil'Patt à Paris*. While on the surface this text is a colourful book for children[12] and appears to be a fun, enjoyable read because the protagonists are anthropomorphised insects, on a deeper level, it transmits a much more serious and critical message about the BUMIDOM as an experience of disappointment and false promises. Indeed, Danchet denounces the BUMIDOM very explicitly in the dedication of the book. She dedicates *Emil'Patt à Paris* to 'nos aînés qui ont vécu le BUMIDOM' [our elders who experienced the BUMIDOM], for whom she employs humour to 'apaiser les douleurs qui demeurent encore en eux, sans mésestimer leur courage face à cette tragédie' (Danchet 2018, 3) [ease the pain they still feel, without underestimating their courage faced with this tragedy]. For Danchet, migration through the BUMIDOM was a difficult ordeal rather than an opportunity or adventure, and this is borne out in the narrative by the experiences of centipede protagonist Emil'Patt.

As Aisha Takiyah Spencer explains, 'in the Caribbean, children are always being told stories' which often focus around the exploits of a trickster hero to present 'the cultural practices, beliefs and history of peoples and societies across the Caribbean' (Spencer 2020, 170). Danchet taps into this storytelling tradition by adopting the form of an Antillean *conte*, or folktale, for her text, a popular form of oral storytelling in Martinique and Guadeloupe which narrates the exploits of anthropomorphised animals and mythological figures such as the devil (Demasy 2001). The insect protagonists are each given different character traits and are dressed in human clothes. They are also given black skin colour and Afro-Caribbean hairstyles so that they are easily identifiable for a child reader as being a part of the local Caribbean environment. Emil'Patt the centipede is depicted as being sensitive and inquisitive; Vonvon the hornet likes to sing; Zandolivio the lizard is joyful and carefree; and Germa Bouy the gecko is wise and sensible. A list of the characters and the insects to which they correspond is placed at the beginning of the book (Danchet 2018, 4), alongside an explanation of the acronym 'BUMIDOM' in a nod to the pedagogical objectives of the text, although very little factual information about the Bureau actually appears in the narrative. Emil'Patt overhears Man Nenné, under whose bed he has made his home in Le Moule, talking about the BUMIDOM in very positive and grateful terms. Emil'Patt does not know what the BUMIDOM is; he thinks it must be a place from the ways in which Man Nenné talks about it, and he is eager to go there so that he too can participate in these conversations. Enlisting the help of his friends, he climbs into a fruit and vegetable box which is transported to mainland France. He is bitterly disappointed on his arrival – he encounters a cold, inhospitable place, and he learns from the other insects he meets there that he has been deceived because 'Bibidonm ou BI.MU.DOM dans la langue de la capitale n'était pas joyeux' (Danchet 2018, 44) [Bibidonm or BI.MU.DOM in the language of the capital wasn't joyful]. So great is his distress that he returns to Guadeloupe at the end of the text.

The text is pedagogical in that it is an allegory. Children's literature often makes use of allegories and extended metaphors to bring difficult ideas to young readers in more accessible ways and to allow children to construct an interpretation of the text themselves (Ash 2012, 91). In the case of *Emil'Patt à Paris*, children learn about the journey made by BUMIDOM participants through Emil'Patt's own journey to France to find out more about the BUMIDOM. Some of his experiences map exactly onto those of the Martinicans and Guadeloupeans who arrived in France, such as his culture shock on his arrival and the extremely cold weather to which he was not accustomed in Guadeloupe. Other details operate more figuratively – for instance, the assistance he receives from his new friends to help him hide in a cardboard box in the hold of a plane to return to Guadeloupe is representative of the solidarity of the Antillean community in mainland France which helped people to maintain diasporic connections to the Caribbean and ultimately to return if they so wished. Danchet's decision to create a Caribbean *conte* allows children to learn about the BUMIDOM in a fun and enjoyable manner, and it also teaches them about the structure and style of the traditional Caribbean fable, and about the ways in which it uses allegory to transmit an important message. Just like *Maman-Dlo*, *Emil'Patt à Paris* is not informative in a factual sense. Readers do not learn about how the BUMIDOM operated from the book nor about how many people migrated during this period. What the reader does learn, however, is what it felt like to move to new, unfamiliar surroundings and be overwhelmed with sentiments of loneliness and alienation. These feelings are universal, and children of all ages and backgrounds can identify with them, even if they occur in a different context to the one described in the book.

Furthermore, *Emil'Patt à Paris* connects pedagogy and memory, because it creates new interpretations of history through the imagined characters of the centipede and his friends so that children can learn from the past and move forward in the present and future. Initially, the centipede is excited to learn more about the BUMIDOM after hearing humans talking about it in a positive light. His desire to participate in a shared Caribbean experience – he thinks to himself that 'tout le monde en parle, j'aurais bien aimé en parler moi aussi!' (Danchet 2018, 8) [everyone is talking about it, I would really like to talk about it too!] – is representative of those who left for France primarily to undertake an exciting adventure. His naivety – he wonders whether the BUMIDOM is actually 'un pays enchanté' (Danchet 2018, 16) [an enchanted country] – is indicative of the inexperience of BUMIDOM participants who did not know what awaited them on the other side of the Atlantic, as well as the lack of knowledge about the Bureau among French and Caribbean populations today because of the government's unwillingness to commemorate it. Man Nenné, however, subscribes to government rhetoric which emphasised the economic and social opportunities that migration through the Bureau would provide, particularly for young people. She prays to God that the BUMIDOM will save her child from the misery and precarity that reigned on Marie-Galante in the 1960s and 70s, suggesting that she saw the BUMIDOM as a conduit for social promotion. The opening pages also teach children about the linguistic landscape of Guadeloupe at the time. When Man Nenné speaks or prays in the text, her words first appear in Guadeloupean Creole and are then immediately translated into French within the body of the text. This linguistic decision adds to the pedagogical nature of *Emil'Patt à Paris* because it introduces Guadeloupean and metropolitan French children to Creole, a language with which they may not be familiar, but also ensures comprehension through translation into French, the primary language in which the text is written. Significantly, Man Nenné is not the only character to speak in Creole in the text, as the insects also speak to each other in both French and Creole. The use of both languages by all characters, young and old, disrupts stereotypes of Creole as a language used only in domestic spaces by the older Antillean population, and in this way Danchet reinforces the value of the Creole language among young children.

Throughout the rest of the text, the BUMIDOM is depicted in a much less positive light. The journey to reach France, which Emil'Patt thinks is a country named BIBIDOM, is an ordeal; he is frightened in the cardboard box in which he travels, and when he arrives he is so overwhelmed by the cold that he hides down the nearest hole he can find, which leads him to the Parisian sewers. The centipede's fear and culture shock on his arrival mirror the experiences of many Antilleans, who have documented their sentiments of isolation and alienation in autobiographical accounts of migration through the BUMIDOM (explored in Chapter 2 of this book). The images add an additional layer to this allegory. Emil'Patt is depicted as being squashed by a foot of a large white man; the difference in skin colour of the human protagonists indicates that he is now in mainland France, and the towering skyscrapers in the backdrop confirm his location in Paris. The fact that he is trodden on by a white man represents the oppression and discrimination to which Antilleans were frequently subjected in mainland France. The centipede is lonely and confused because he still does not understand what the BUMIDOM is. Eventually, he realises that he has been tricked by the BUMIDOM, just like the other insects he meets who tell him that the Bureau is a 'stupidité qu'ils ont inventée pour tromper les imbéciles' (Danchet 2018, 36) [a stupidity that has been invented to trick imbeciles]. He is taken to see Caffa the cockroach who explains to him what the BUMIDOM is, and here Danchet offers her most explicit textual denunciation of the BUMIDOM. The omniscient narrator explains that Antilleans 'avaient abandonné leur famille, leur vie paisible avec l'espoir de trouver mieux' (Danchet 2018, 42) [had abandoned their family and their peaceful life in the hope of finding something better] but were disappointed to find that life was no better in Paris.

Emil'Patt à Paris, therefore, makes use of anthropomorphised insect characters to appeal to young readers while also making a damning statement about the ways in which the BUMIDOM did not deliver what it promised to young Antilleans, and the ways in which the state apparatus has been reluctant to memorialise the BUMIDOM through official practices of commemoration. In addition, the text makes a comment on the unreliability of memory and questions whether the personal memory of individuals can fully be trusted. Man Nenné's comments about the BIBIDOM (the Creole term used for BUMIDOM) becomes 'BIMUBOM' or even 'BIBIDONM' in Emil'Patt's memories of these conversations (Danchet 2018, 8), evoking a memory of Caribbean emigration which is constantly changing and in flux. These memories can be activated among children through the process of cross-writing, sharing their reading with adults and engaging in extratextual dialogue about the content of the book. There is the potential for children who read the book alongside an adult to engage in discussion about what the BUMIDOM was, why it is important to remember this significant migratory phenomenon because of the connections with displacements between the Caribbean and Europe in the present day, and how stories such as *Emil'Patt à Paris* can facilitate this memory retrieval. Indeed, in an interview with me on 30 January 2023, Danchet explained that she wanted children to 'poser des questions aux grands-parents' [ask their grandparents questions] about their own experiences of life at this time while reading the book, bringing different generations together through the reading process and sharing stories and memories.

The recovery and discovery of memory about the BUMIDOM also occurs through the structure of the text. The narrative is organised like a Caribbean folktale, in that there are five distinct stages: situation, turning point, action, obstacles and final resolution (Damasy 2001, 293). A brief description of Emil'Patt's life and environment is followed by a specific event – Emil'Patt overhears discussions about the BUMIDOM and wants to know more. We then follow the centipede on his journey to France, where he meets new friends but also encounters difficulties in his new environment. The text ends with an ambiguous resolution – Emil'Patt is pleased to be home, but he is also bitter because he realises that 'BIBIDOM n'avait été que misère et amertume, j'avais connu le froid, la faim; la peur s'était installée dans mon être, j'avais frôlé la mort' (Danchet 2018, 66) [BIBIDOM had only been misery and bitterness, I had been cold and hungry, fear had invaded my body, I had had a brush with death]. This structure enables the text to fulfil its pedagogical and memorial objectives because, like in *Peyi an nou*, readers learn about the BUMIDOM and the associated sentiments of disappointment and disillusionment alongside the protagonist. Readers are thus not made to feel ignorant about their potential lack of knowledge about the Bureau because the protagonist does not know anything about it either. The emphasis on Emil'Patt's confusion and simultaneous desire for knowledge about the BUMIDOM demonstrates the lack of official memorialisation of the Bureau (as it is an unknown entity for the centipede), but it also reveals just how deeply engrained the BUMIDOM is in the Caribbean collective imaginary, because the insect characters are desperate to find out why humans are talking about the BUMIDOM so much. As Maeve McCusker notes, the Antillean *conte* 'harnesses together both individual and collective memory' because the *conteur* [storyteller] embodies a 'heroic individual who personifies memory', while the community is void of memory because of the 'amnesiac blow' delivered by the Caribbean's traumatic past (McCusker 2010, 159). By adopting the form of the Antillean *conte*, Danchet succeeds in bringing the BUMIDOM into these debates about personal and collective memory, enabling young children to reflect on histories and memories in France's past which have been concealed or erased by the state.

Conclusion

Rachel Falconer argues that children's literature is innovative not only in its 'hard-hitting content', but also in the hybrid, playful form it employs to convey important historical and social matters (Falconer 2009, 6). This chapter has taken Falconer's comment further by demonstrating that children's fiction is innovative not only in form and content, but also in the ways in which it teaches young (and older) readers about the slippages between history and memory. It does this through a variety of techniques, such as by combining text and image in the case of *Maman-Dlo*, and by employing the structure of the Caribbean *conte*, in the case of *Emil'Patt à Paris*. Falconer's comment can also be applied to graphic novels, as my analysis of *Peyi an nou* has shown. The chapter has drawn out the opportunities offered by the selected graphic novels and children's fiction to teach readers about the BUMIDOM and to facilitate reflection on how Caribbean communities interact with memories of migration in the present. The three texts are not linear narratives, though, and they do not provide a chronological, factual account of post-war emigration from Martinique and Guadeloupe to mainland France. Rather, their fragmented and non-linear aesthetic means that readers have to piece together the past themselves, and thus the texts encourage readers to resist the notion of history as a single account of what actually happened. Instead, they 'urge readers to envision polyphonic, diverse, complicated narratives of history – versions of history that enable not only recitation of past trauma but also a revaluation of what is at stake in the envisioning of history itself' (Cutter and Schlund-Vials 2018, 16).

Notes

1. The French term 'bande dessinée' is used to refer to both comics and graphic novels, although 'roman graphique' is also employed for the latter. Jan Baetens and Hugo Frey note distinctions between comics and graphic novels in terms of form, content, publication format and production and distribution (2014, 8–19).
2. Gilles Gauvin, historian and member of the national commission investigating the 'Enfants de la Creuse', was a consultant on the project.
3. The graphic novel follows Oublié's investigation on the use of chlordecone pesticide on banana plantations in Guadeloupe and Martinique between 1972 and 1993.
4. I make a distinction between Jessica and Marie-Ange, the characters in the graphic novel, and Oublié and Rousseau, author and artist respectively.
5. A new edition of the graphic novel was published in 2024. The title has been kept in Guadeloupean Creole but the French subtitle 'un exil vers l'hexagone' [an exile to France] has been added, presumably to provide more information about the book's principal theme to a non-Creole-speaking readership.
6. In the interview with me in December 2022, Oublié explained that she wanted *Peyi an nou* to be accessible to both adults and children, and that she wrote the book so that her young cousins could learn about their own history.
7. Oublié and Rousseau also created a website for the album to promote the work further: https://peyiannou.wordpress.com/ [accessed 15 September 2023].
8. See Godard's personal website for more information about his biography and his published works: https://www.alexgodard.com/ [accessed 21 December 2022].
9. In the French education system, 'cycle 3' consists of CM1, CM2 and Sixième. It is the equivalent of Key Stage 2 in the United Kingdom.
10. See, for example, https://www.i-profs.fr/litt-c3-Maman_Dlo.php [accessed 22 December 2022]. I-prof.fr is an official government website which provides teaching resources and administrative support to teachers in France at all levels.
11. Danchet's first two novels, *Mawy* (2012) and *Ida, la Créole* (2013), tell the story of the young African woman Mawy, who is captured, enslaved and transported to the Caribbean to work on the plantations,

and her daughter, Ida, who is born into enslavement. Other publications include the poetry collection *Aux portes de la sagesse* (2014) and the illustrated book for children *Tikòk, le maître coq, Tikòk, majo savann* (2022), a bilingual edition in French and Guadeloupean Creole.

12. In an interview with me on 30 January 2023, Danchet explained that the text is aimed at children aged seven or eight, although adults have also enjoyed reading the text with younger children.

Chapter 6

Music as Memory: The Legacy of the BUMIDOM

The album *Histoire d'un expatrié* (2019) [Story of an Expat] by French rap/hip-hop artist BUMIDOM tells the story of a family's arrival in mainland France from Guadeloupe. The album fuses tradition and modernity, as exemplified in one of the tracks entitled 'La gwadk-oup' Malad' [Sick Guadeloupe]. BUMIDOM takes the title and the chorus of gwoka singer Guy Konket's 1970 hit about the economic problems facing Guadeloupe and adds his own rap to it, offering a commentary on the ills of contemporary Guadeloupean society. Sung in a mix of French and Guadeloupean Creole (like many of the songs on the album), the opening track, 'BUMIDOM', focuses explicitly on the Bureau. It follows the trajectory of a young man who leaves his family behind in Guadeloupe to make a new life for himself, but who encounters exploitation and racial prejudice in France. His family are especially critical of the BUMIDOM, described in the track as 'une arnaque' [a scam], for the promises it failed to deliver. Throughout the song clips from Bastide's documentary *BUMIDOM: des Français venus d'outre-mer* can be heard.[1] These extracts have been selected for their denunciation of the Bureau as an exploitative system which (in the interviewees' view) tricked Guadeloupeans and Martinicans into coming to France, a theme in keeping with the overall critical tone of the song. Moreover, peppered throughout the track are political speeches from the BUMIDOM period, including Charles de Gaulle's infamous speech delivered during his visit to Fort-de-France in 1964, when he declared 'Mon Dieu, comme vous êtes Français!' [Goodness me, how French you are!].[2] This palimpsestic layering of different voices from history and from screen lends historical veracity to the song while also offering different perspectives on the BUMIDOM, most of which criticise the Bureau. From this point of departure, the final chapter of this book interrogates how music contributes to a collective remembering of the past among the Antillean community. What do we learn about the BUMIDOM by studying the music that was produced when the Bureau was in operation and its reception? How and why has music produced in the twenty-first century, decades after the BUMIDOM was closed down, transmitted memories of migration to subsequent generations of Antilleans?

The Caribbean has a long history of musical tradition. As Peter Manuel points out, music is both an important feature of the national identity of Caribbean countries and regions, and a significant cultural export which provides economic capital for the region (1995). In other words, music is 'the most visible, popular, and dynamic aspect of Caribbean expressive culture' (Manuel 1995, 2). Caribbean music has been formed through a process of creolisation, as contact with African and European music through colonisation and forced displacement has enabled Caribbean peoples to forge new musical styles. Indeed, African cultural practices have provided much of what makes Caribbean music distinctive today, such as the use of drums, complex rhythm patterns and participatory practices of clapping, singing and dancing. Music was particularly important for enslaved African people. Martin Munro argues that music and rhythm was often a source of comfort for the enslaved on the ships and enabled communication between them (2010, 13). While drums were banned on the Caribbean plantations as they were seen as a dangerous and submissive tool for resistance, they were nevertheless used, and a new form of music was created through the fusion of African and European musical traditions (Munro 2010, 8). The British, French and Spanish colonisers imported a range of musical styles including classical music, folk songs, church hymns, social dances and military marches. During the twentieth and twenty-first centuries, these European styles have been adapted into new musical expressions in the Caribbean.

In Martinique and Guadeloupe, contemporary music has developed from three popular European dance forms (the biguine, the quadrille and the mazurka) and two types of drums (the bèlè from Martinique and the gwoka from Guadeloupe). Brenda Berrian notes that there is a racial and class distinction in the popularity of these musical forms; dance forms were more popular in urban areas among mulattos and white elites, whereas the drums were played in rural areas by Black agricultural workers (Berrian 2000, 2). The biguine enjoyed international success in Africa and Latin America as well as in mainland France until the 1960s when dancehalls were replaced by discotheques. International music, such as the Haitian compas and the Dominican cadence-lypso, then became more popular.

Berrian argues that, 'as a result, pride in local music ebbed drastically as Martinican and Guadeloupean musicians functioned within a creative void' (2000, 3). It was not until the Guadeloupean band Kassav' emerged onto the scene with their dance music of zouk – which combines fast percussion rhythms, romantic lyrics and a strong horn section – that Martinicans and Guadeloupeans could claim their place at the forefront of Caribbean music. As we will explore later in this chapter, Kassav' is arguably one of the most successful Guadeloupean bands of all time – the group was the first Antillean band to sell over 100,000 copies of their 1983 album, *Zouk La Sé Sel Médikaman Nou Ni* [Zouk is the Only Medicine We Have], and they have since recorded over twenty studio albums (Pareles 2021). Despite the international success of Kassav', Berrian argues that, in general, French Caribbean artists have not succeeded in gaining recognition beyond Martinique and Guadeloupe. She argues that:

> musicians and singers from the French Caribbean islands struggle to be produced and heard, recreate themselves and their songs, and speak from an informed small physical space with a larger cultural consciousness while taking control of their Caribbean identity as it evolves. (Berrian 2000, 9)

Their lack of an international profile replicates the broader political marginalisation of the French Caribbean departments which continue to be overlooked in economic policy, educational programmes and environmental strategies. Nevertheless, music does provide an autonomous space in which Caribbean resourcefulness is deployed. French Caribbean music has long been a Creole popular form over which French culture has had less control, unlike, for example, the novel. Although, as Berrian rightly points out, there are clear problems in the production and distribution of French Caribbean music (due to a lack of musical infrastructure on the islands), I argue in this chapter that musicians from Martinique and Guadeloupe *have* succeeded in creating an important musical tradition which has spread across the Atlantic Ocean. Their identity, culture and political convictions are represented in the music they create, through different rhythms, lyrics and musical styles.

The first part of this chapter asks how music was used during the 1960s and 70s both to respond to BUMIDOM policies initiated by the French government, and to create an ethnic Caribbean identity among the Caribbean diaspora living in mainland France. The second part shifts the focus to the present day, interrogating the role of music today in preserving memories of the BUMIDOM and keeping this sense of Antilleanness alive in mainland France. In order to do this, I analyse the song lyrics and performances of selected musicians of Guadeloupean and Martinican origin who engage with a range of musical styles, from gwoka and zouk to rap and hip-hop. In addition, I examine the discourse surrounding these recordings and performances through media interviews and discussions with me and other scholars, such as Jérôme Camal. My approach is thus informed by research in ethnomusicology which interrogates what music means to individuals and to society. In the second volume of *Ethnomusicology: A Contemporary Reader* (2017), Jennifer Post defines the discipline of ethnomusicology as 'the study of human music-making' through a methodology of fieldwork (interpreted broadly as digital or physical fieldwork) (2017, 1). Following this definition, I question how and why music has been made by musicians of Antillean origin for identity formation and community building, and how different audiences have responded to this musical project.

This chapter, like the rest of the book, examines musical representations of the BUMIDOM from Martinique and Guadeloupe, but it must not be forgotten that music was also produced about the Bureau by Reunionese artists too. Songs were mostly written to denounce the system, but some music did reflect more positive aspects of migration. A salient example is Michel Admette's 1970 song 'BUMIDOM', which appeared on his album *Folkore de la Réunion* [Folklore from Réunion]. In this song, he emphasised the opportunities the BUMIDOM offered young people to find work and escape from precarity. A more critical perspective can be found in Jacky Lechat's 1979 song 'Là-bas l'est pas la lune' [It's Not Paradise over There] from the album *Joyeux Noël* [Happy Christmas]. As the title makes clear, the song critiques the false promises given to people who soon found that life was no better in mainland France than on Réunion. Severe criticisms of the Bureau can also be found in the song 'BUMIDOM', written by maloya (traditional Reunionese percussion music) band Ziskakan in 1980 but never recorded.[3] The chorus deplores what the musicians considered to be the forced departure of young people from the islands, who were tricked into leaving their families behind: 'BUMIDOM, BUMIDOM, tu voles nos frères; BUMIDOM, BUMIDOM, arrête de nous mentir' [BUMIDOM, BUMIDOM, you're stealing our brothers; BUMIDOM, BUMIDOM, stop lying to us]. Music was thus an important means of contestation about the BUMIDOM in Réunion as well as in the Caribbean.

Above all, this chapter interrogates how music has become a vector of cultural memory about the BUMIDOM. It argues that songs and music create a shared understanding of what the BUMIDOM was, how it was received at the time and how it has impacted on Caribbean communities today. To do this, I first need to examine how diasporic communities deploy music to create a shared identity and preserve the collective memory of a community.

Music, Memory and Diasporic Identity

Music has long been considered an articulation of collective identity because it helps to unite individuals and ensure social cohesion. According to Thomas Turino, music is 'at the heart of our most profound social occasions and experiences' as it creates communities through knowledge of and participation in a shared cultural practice (Turino 2008, 1). Music also enables people to understand their own identity, communicate their emotions and convey a particular political message. It is not only making music which binds people together; listening to music and participating in musical practices can have the same outcome. In other words, social formation occurs through a process of 'musicking', defined by Christopher Small as taking part 'in any capacity, in a musical performance, whether by performing, by listening, by rehearsing or practising, by providing material for performance (what is called composing), or dancing' (Small 1998, 9). By being involved in music in different ways, emotional, social and cognitive ties can develop, according to Kay Kaufman Shelemay (2006). Individuals become aware that they form part of a larger social group which is united through a common collective identity and memory. Music thus succeeds in bringing the individual and the collective together.

Music has been particularly important for BUMIDOM participants and their descendants because of its significant role in the identity formation of people living in the diaspora. It has enabled them to construct a common sense of identity which they may have lost following their initial dispersal from their home community when they migrated to mainland France through the Bureau, or which they may not have felt being brought up in France and surrounded by white metropolitan culture. According to John Baily and Michael Collyer, music enables individuals to connect with their past and keep their memories of their home country alive (2006, 173–4). Rolf Lidskog, meanwhile, identifies four different ways in which music develops the identity formation of diasporic groups: it strengthens the cohesion of a diasporic community; it acts as a space for recognition and recovery; it brings about remembering and historical consciousness; and it is used for political purposes, to demonstrate subordination or resistance (Lidskog 2016). I examine each category in turn to investigate how diasporic groups are able to construct and negotiate their identity through music.

Firstly, music helps to create a sense of diasporic consciousness among members of a particular group. For Paul Gilroy, music has long been a method of communication and a symbol of cultural identity for Black people since the time of enslavement. In *The Black Atlantic: Modernity and Double Consciousness* (1993), he argues that Black identity in Europe, the Caribbean and Africa was formed through an ongoing process of travel and exchange across what he terms the 'Black Atlantic', that is 'one single, complex unit of analysis in [. . .] discussions of the modern world' which unites the three continents in a transnational and rhizomatic framework (Gilroy 1993, 15). In this Black Atlantic world, music became 'the primary expressions of cultural distinctiveness which this population seized upon and adapted to its new circumstances' (Gilroy 1993, 81). More than the written or spoken word, it allowed Black people to share in their common histories of forced deportation and enslavement but also to create a distinctive cultural identity, inflected by the impacts of their social, historical and political contexts on their lived experience of Blackness. For Gilroy, then, music unites diasporic communities, enabling them to recognise that they belong to a particular group through the music they share.

Ethnographical studies have examined how this community building through music works in practice. Scholars have investigated how music helps to keep connections alive between diasporic groups and their home country, and between members of the same diaspora now scattered across different countries and continents (Boura 2006). Different generations within the diasporic community respond to this music differently, depending primarily on whether they had direct contact with this music in their homeland. However, as Adam Chapman notes, these generational attitudes are shifting, given developments in technology; online platforms and music streaming sites are enabling young people who did not grow up with this music to access these traditions and to discuss their musical tastes with other diasporic members (Chapman 2005). Research has also confirmed that music strengthens the social cohesion of a diasporic group living in a particular country, despite the social, political and economic differences between members. Rose Mary Allen's study of the migration of people from Curaçao to other Caribbean islands reveals that music, sung in Papiamentu, unites people living in the same country across different social groups, and even connects them to the broader diaspora composed of people originating from Curaçao but now spread across the Caribbean (2012). Of course, the music created by the diasporic community is not the same as the music created in the home country because musical elements of a new culture are absorbed, as demonstrated by Ray Allen's analysis of the hybridisation of music performed at Trinidad-inspired carnivals in the United Kingdom in the early 2000s (2019). The music from the home country is thus transformed by transnational flows to create a new type of music, destabilising notions of a fixed cultural identity. This was the project of Kassav', as we shall see later in this chapter; they sought to redefine what it meant to be Antillean and living in France through their music.

The second way that music is used by diasporic groups as identified by Lidskog is as a form of therapy, giving diasporic groups a platform for healing in the wake of catastrophe and disaster. Lidskog argues that 'listening to and performing music facilitates the articulation, shaping and acknowledgement of a particular cultural or ethnic identity' (2016, 28). This is particularly important in the wake of disaster, as Diane M. Grams demonstrates. Following the devastation of Hurricane Katrina in New Orleans in 2005, public parades emerged during the Mardi Gras festival in which performers danced and created music in a display of freedom, survival and cultural recovery (Grams 2013). Furthermore, music can play an important role in a politics of recognition. In her case study of Afrocuban cultural practices in New York City in the early 2000s, Lisa Maya Knauer shows how Black Cubans formed their own parades during New York's annual Cuban Day festivities because they felt excluded from the official New York parade (Knauer 2008). These performances enabled the Cuban immigrants to 'engage in a politics of mutual recognition and visibility' while countering fixed notions of Cuban identity (Knauer 2008, 1258–9). In these two examples, music is used in an 'outer-directed manner', because it helps to establish the cultural identity of a diasporic group in the eyes of others (Baily and Collyer 2006, 175). Music grants recognition for these communities, and this was also the case for people migrating to mainland France during the BUMIDOM era. As I shall argue in the following section, music enabled them to assert themselves as proudly Antillean. Musicians such as Konket and Éric Cosaque sang in Creole to reclaim their difference as members of an Antillean diasporic community living in mainland France.

The third role of music in diasporic identity formation, according to Lidskog, is its ability to shape the collective memory of a community. Music enables collective memories to be formed, preserved, defended and transmitted to subsequent generations. Hannah Lewis examines the case study of Kurdish refugees in Leeds to demonstrate how music and dancing, and associated performative elements such as costumes and accessories, create what she terms 'community moments', allowing them to connect with memories of their homeland, find a community in the hostland and negotiate their own place between these two locations (Lewis 2010). Scholars in musicology have analysed how music transmits and preserves collective memory. For instance, Steven Feld draws on Kaluli song from Papua New Guinea to examine the relationship between vocality, emplacement and memory (1996). He argues that using place names in these songs foregrounds emotional connections to places, times and events of the past. These place names 'magnetise memory' in Feld's words, connecting the listener to his or her own history in a fusion of time and space (Feld 1996, 107). For Tia DeNora, music operates as a narrative of self-identity, allowing listeners to recapture the agency they once possessed in the past and create a new structure in the future (DeNora 2000, 66). The past trajectories of the individual fuse together with others, creating a form of collective memory through music. Diana Taylor, meanwhile, distinguishes between the 'archive' and the 'repertoire' in the storage of memory. The archive consists of written or recorded documents (including music) which represents hegemonic power, while the repertoire denotes memory embodied through performance which counters hegemonic discourse (Taylor 2003). In the final section of this chapter, I shall show how the archive and the repertoire operate in tandem to circulate musical memories of the BUMIDOM.

The final function of music for the diaspora is its ability to convey political messages. This is the most striking aspect of the music produced during the BUMIDOM era; overtly political lyrics denounced the BUMIDOM for its exploitative nature and to criticise the government for neglecting the economic, political and social development of the islands. For Jean-Marie Donegani, music is a shared experience which 'mobilises and unifies groups, contributes to their movements and accompanies celebrations and rites. It excites to violence and combat, as it does to fervour and effusion' (Donegani 2004, 5). It can be used to denounce particular political practices, as was the case with the BUMIDOM participants, but it can also be used in more exclusionary ways, to create boundaries between those who belong to a particular group and those who do not (Levy 2002). Political messages are conveyed through the lyrics and the language in which these lyrics are sung. In addition, rhythms are imported from other cultures and used in different contexts for political purposes. Performative elements, such as costumes, staging and even the place in which the performance occurs, all add to the contestatory nature of music (Martiniello and Lafleur 2008). For musicians singing about the BUMIDOM, these three elements all came together to produce a catalogue of highly damning songs about the organised migration scheme. In contrast, the music produced by West Indian migrants to Britain during the post-war era offers a different story. Calypso artists such as Lord Beginner, Lord Kitchener and Lord Invader produced a more utopian and upbeat narrative which nevertheless 'presented an imperially conscious perspective on British society and identity' (Bidnall 2017, 106). It is for this reason that Kitchener's 'London is the Place for Me' (1948), sung on camera for reporters on Kitchener's arrival at Tilbury Docks, has been recuperated in political discourse for nostalgic British purposes.

For diasporic communities, then, music is highly influential for the formation of individual and collective identities, but it also helps groups to remember their original homeland, to recover from trauma and to become mobilised in support of a particular social or political issue. The following section investigates how music was used to criticise the BUMIDOM and create a diasporic identity among those who had migrated through this system.

Music in the BUMIDOM Era

In the 1960s and 70s, the most popular form of Caribbean music was gwoka. There are seven principal rhythms in gwoka, which are played on 'at least two, barrel-shaped, single-headed drums': tumblack, graj, kaladja, padjanbèl, léwòz, woulé and menndé (Camal 2019, 16). During the BUMIDOM period, these rhythms were fused with other musical traditions that artists encountered in mainland France to create a transnational, diasporic form of music. Gwoka has decreased in popularity in recent years, despite attempts to preserve it; in 2014, it was recognised by UNESCO as an intangible cultural heritage. In the mid-twentieth century, however, it was seen as a symbol of anti-assimilation and anti-colonialism, particularly because the gwoka drum was banned by the Code noir [Black Code] during the period of enslavement. Laura Donnelly describes gwoka as a 'spontaneous music of the proletariat' (2017, 88). It is an inherently political style of music which encourages spectators to dance to the rhythm of the drums and become mobilised around a political cause.

It is therefore unsurprising that gwoka music was used to express disapproval of the organised migration scheme, given its political undertones. One of the best-known musicians to denounce the BUMIDOM through his music was Konket (also known through different spellings of his surname as Conquête or Conquet). He was born in 1950 in Baie-Mahault in Basse-Terre island, Guadeloupe, and died on 23 May 2012. Music was very important to him from an early age. His mother was the famous gwoka singer Man Soso, and she transmitted to him her love for all kinds of traditional Caribbean music. Konket began his music career in the 1960s working for record labels in Guadeloupe such as Henri Debs and Célini. He then sought to adapt gwoka to create his own style, by incorporating musicians who played the biguine into his repertoire and experimenting with musical patterns of call-and-response (Camal 2019, 101–2). His conceptualisation of gwoka was thus quite different from that of Gérard Lockel, another Guadeloupean musician famous for the 'gwo ka modèn' (a new form of gwoka developed by Lockel which combined traditional percussion instruments with the electric guitar and the saxophone). As Camal argues, both musicians endeavoured to develop the genre but for different purposes and to transmit different political messages: 'whereas Lockel was involved in a self-conscious and ideologically driven effort to tame Western modernity, Konket is perhaps best heard as a chronicler of the experience of modernity in post-departmentalisation Guadeloupe' (Camal 2019, 102). This is particularly evident in Konket's later music which addressed social issues – songs such as 'Lapli ka tonbé' [Rain May Fall], recorded in 1968, highlighted his concerns about the working conditions of local agricultural labourers. Social themes continued to play an important role in his collaborative work, such as with the group Soukoué Kô Ou in 1994. Following his death in 2012, a tribute was paid to him in September 2013 at Théâtre Claude Lévi-Strauss, Musée du quai Branly in recognition for his contribution to Caribbean music (France Antilles Martinique 2013). This event was testimony to the high regard in which Konket was held by his fellow Antillean compatriots.

Konket moved to France in 1978 but he did not use the services of the BUMIDOM. He left Guadeloupe of his own accord in order to widen his networks and gain greater recognition for his music. Indeed, according to Camal, he was the first Caribbean musician of his generation to move to Paris explicitly to play music (2019, 109). Even though he did not have personal experience of migration through the Bureau, a denunciation of the BUMIDOM comes across in the lyrics and musical style of his best-known songs. This critique also goes beyond the specific policies of the BUMIDOM. Konket used music to incite his fellow Antilleans to resist French and European hegemony, in songs such as 'La Gwadloup malad' (1970) [Sick Guadeloupe], a critique of the social and political issues facing Guadeloupe, and 'Kenbé rèd' (1987) [Stand Strong], a call to Guadeloupeans to stay true to their Caribbean roots.[4]

While the Bureau was not necessarily mentioned by name in his songs, then, an Antillean audience would certainly have been able to pick up on the latent political messages hidden in his music. As Martiniello and Lafleur posit, it is not necessarily the case that songs in which the political message is more explicit are more openly political than songs in which the political agenda is hidden behind more 'harmless lyrics' (2008, 1196). Musicians who fear state censorship may decide not to declare their political agenda openly. Konket certainly experienced governmental censorship – 'La Gwadloup malad' was banned from being played on national radio for its revolutionary nature (Marmande 2012), and he was also arrested during the strikes of agricultural workers in 1971 for supposedly inciting workers to strike by playing his gwoka music on a picket line (Camal 2019, 104). This might explain why he was reluctant to name the BUMIDOM openly, although it is also true that, despite the repression he experienced from the French state, he continued to record and perform music which criticised French and European policies and decisions (albeit in Creole and not French). Perhaps, then, a more convincing reason to explain why he did not often mention the BUMIDOM was that he saw it as one specific example in a long line of others which highlighted the lack of financial and social investment in the overseas departments by the French government. Indeed, according to Isabelle Theillout, flautist and partner of Konket, the musician's political engagement went much further than defending the cause of the overseas departments. In a documentary produced about the musician's life in 2013, Theillout stated that Konket did everything he could 'pour defender les plus vulnérables' [to defend the most vulnerable], no matter what the cause (Ladal and Bordy 2013).

The BUMIDOM was mentioned for the first time in Konket's song 'Zèzèle', produced in 1970 on the same recording as 'La Gwadloup malad'. The song tells the story of two parents who are looking for their daughter Zèzèle. It is not until halfway through the song that Konket tells them she has left for France through the BUMIDOM, repeating the Creolised form of the word 'BIBIDOM' eight times against the beat of the gwoka drums. Konket thus criticises the migration policy for taking young people, and particularly young women, away from their families, culture and traditions. It is significant that Konket, like many of the gwoka singers of his generation, sung this song (and most of his other tracks) in Creole rather than in French. This was a political decision which had specific political consequences. Martiniello and Lafleur argue that 'choosing the language of the country of residence or singing in the home-country language, which is sometimes only spoken by the migrant community, has different consequences on the audience that will be reached and on the diffusion of the political message' (2008, 1196). In Konket's case, the song seemed to address Antillean, creolophone audiences living in both mainland France and Guadeloupe to encourage them to resist migrating through the BUMIDOM, rather than inciting French officials to change their policy in some way. Returning to the idea of censorship, singing in Creole could also be interpreted as a way to conceal the true political message of this song from the French authorities.

For Martiniello and Lafleur, the public performance of music also plays a crucial role in the ways in which music can transmit political messages. The place of performance can have an impact on the composition of the audience and the extent to which musicians succeed in transmitting their political agenda – a festive space such as a disco may not necessarily be the most conducive place to sing about politics (Martiniello and Lafleur 2008, 1198). Konket's decision to perform his politically motivated music in concert halls and discotheques could be seen to undermine his political agenda, but, at the same time, it did allow him to spread his message to a large, heterogeneous audience. The place of performance can also have political ramifications, and Konket's first concert in France, where he performed 'Zèzèle', illustrates this very clearly. In an interview with Camal and Christian Dahomay on 4 August 2008, he explained that this concert took place in the Salle Wagram, a grand auditorium located in the seventeenth arrondissement of Paris, built in the early 1800s and used over the years for international congresses and political conferences as well as music concerts. During the rehearsal for this event, the venue was evacuated by the police and the performance was halted: 'something about a bomb threat. It wasn't true, right? But because I arrived like a revolutionary, with [my message], so right away: "He's a revolutionary. Why did he come to this country?"' (Camal 2019, 106). It seems that the French authorities not only took offence at the lyrics of this song which criticised the BUMIDOM for exploiting young people, but they were also angry that this 'revolutionary' Guadeloupean artist with ideas about resisting French hegemony was allowed to perform at such a historical space which symbolised the French nation, a space in which, in the eyes of the French state, he did not belong. For Konket, then, conveying political messages through his music became even more urgent, given his own treatment at the hands of the French authorities.

Music's role in unifying and mobilising diasporic communities was shared by another important gwoka musician – Cosaque. Cosaque was born in 1952 in Capesterre-Belle-Eau in Basse-Terre island, moving to Pointe-à-Pitre with his family so his docker father could find work. Like Konket, he was initiated into gwoka music from an early age – his father would take him to working-class districts in the capital, where he would meet influential musicians such as Vélo, René Perrin and Alfred Labasse (Michel 2021). Cosaque's political commitment to producing music about the BUMIDOM stemmed from his personal experiences of the Bureau. In 1969, he used the services of the BUMIDOM to move to mainland France to join his sister, who had already settled in Paris. He then returned to Guadeloupe to complete his military service and worked for a short period for the postal service in Pointe-à-Pitre, before returning definitively to mainland France in 1973 (Dicale 2019). His migratory trajectory thus did not only consist of one displacement but a cycle of departures and returns until he ultimately decided to settle in France. It is unlikely, however, that he was able to apply to the BUMIDOM to help pay for these additional trips, given that participants could usually benefit from only one paid trip to the French mainland.[5] Migration to mainland France did not only provide Cosaque with content to include in his songs, but it also enabled him to encounter a range of musical styles and to meet and collaborate with other musicians. For instance, he began playing with the folklore band Karibana, allowing him to discover alternative musical styles. In 1980, he created the band X7 Nouvelle Dimension. According to Camal, the band's name 'combines the letter X to indicate that it consisted of ten musicians and the number 7 in reference to the seven rhythms of the swaré léwòz' (2019, 91). While their name asserts gwoka as the principal musical reference, the band also fused their music with other sounds and rhythms they encountered in Paris.

Cosaque's project was to create songs with lyrics which made an important political and socio-economic statement and combine them with up-tempo rhythms and beats to which Antilleans could dance. In this way, he was able to critique the BUMIDOM for its exploitative nature while simultaneously bringing Antilleans in mainland France together, creating what Gilroy describes as diasporic consciousness. This community building enabled Antilleans who shared similar problems of underemployment, exploitation and racial discrimination to benefit from a sense of solidarity to help them to face their problems. The most striking example of this musical strategy is 'A koz don biyé san fwan' [Because of a Hundred-franc Bill]. First released in 1987 on the album *Erick Cosaque – X7 Nouvelle Dimension* five years after the closure of the BUMIDOM, the song is told in the first person as Cosaque draws on his own experiences of migration. The lyrics are highly damning. The narrator warns Guadeloupean women hoping to find a better life 'an lòt koté' [on the other side] to be wary of falling into drugs and prostitution and advises them not to trust French men, and by extension France itself, for promises that are never delivered (Camal 2019, 91). The phrase 'an lòt koté' is repeated throughout the song, as Cosaque alludes to the fact that life was no better for many Antilleans in mainland France than it was in Guadeloupe or Martinique. The political statement made by the song is offset by its musical style. It opens with a guitar solo by Patrick Parole which is inspired by rock and roll, and the song continues in a mid-tempo speed, accompanied by drums and percussion instruments. This song, like others produced by Cosaque, was played in nightclubs in Paris and other French cities 'once or twice during an evening', according to Jocelyne Guilbault (1993, 34). Antilleans could dance, have a good time and enjoy a feeling of connectedness with other Antilleans living in France, while also being reminded of the need to be politically active to counter France's oppression of them.

The majority of Cosaque's songs are sung in Guadeloupean Creole. Like Konket, he used Creole to make a political statement, to show solidarity with an Antillean audience. The song 'Guadeloupe, île de mes amours' (1987) [Guadeloupe, Island of My Loves] thus takes a different approach as it is sung in French. Through the content of the song and the language in which it is written, Cosaque demonstrates the stakes of cultural assimilation and reveals what happens when

Antilleans adapt to French culture: they lose their Caribbean identity. Like 'A koz don biyé san fwan', the song is autobiographical. It tells of Cosaque's nostalgia for his life in Guadeloupe after migrating to Paris, a city described as 'une ville d'enfer où l'hiver sévit [a city of hell where winter rages]. Guadeloupe appears as an apostrophe in the song, as the singer lists all the natural elements of the island that he misses: 'Guadeloupe, où donc sont tes champs de cannes, tes bananiers, tes cocotiers; où sont donc tes plages et tes rivages' [Guadeloupe, where are your sugarcane fields, your banana fields and coconut trees, where are your beaches and your shores]. Again, Cosaque combines politically oriented lyrics with an upbeat tempo. The song opens with a soprano saxophone solo played by Édouard Labor, and drums and percussion are played in the background while musician Claude Danabé recites the poem written by Cosaque. It is a slower song than 'A koz don biyé san fwan' and not necessarily one to which people would dance in a nightclub, but it is certainly catchy. It is likely that Antilleans would come together to listen to the song and reflect on its meaning, thus embracing a sense of diasporic consciousness.

Interrogating what it meant to be Antillean living in mainland France was also at the heart of the project of Kassav', the best-known musical artist from the French Caribbean during this period. Kassav' was founded in the 1970s by Pierre-Édouard Décimus, a former sound technician and bass player for the jazz Creole band Vikings de Guadeloupe, who wanted to create a new sound to counteract the popularity of Haitian compas. The origins of the band – to create a more authentically Antillean type of music – are reflected in its name. Kassav's only female soloist, Jocelyne Béroard, explains that the name:

> refers to a crushed cassava mixed with coconut and sugar to make a cake . . . There is a kind of poison in it. You've got to know how to extract this poison before you eat it . . . So because they had to extract what was poisoning Martinican and Guadeloupean music, they called it Kassav. (Ampigny 1992, 61)

To find this new genre of Antillean music, Décimus began experimenting with different Caribbean styles with his brother George and another musician, Jacob Desvarieux. After a few carnival records, they began to call the type of music they produced 'zouk', meaning 'party' in Martinican Creole (Berrian 2000, 44), connoting freedom, excess and escape. Indeed, zouk is best defined as a form of dance music, even though the lyrics often address social issues such as male/female relationships, exile and nostalgia. The original rhythm of zouk was fast, although a slower form has since emerged called 'zouk-love' as other artists have sought to develop the musical project initiated by Kassav'. Their success has been astounding, and they continue to make music today, despite the untimely death of Desvarieux who passed away from COVID-19 in July 2021 (Bourdier 2021). Their success can be understood by the fact that although there are core members of the band, others come and go, bringing new styles and techniques with them. Indeed, Desvarieux has just been replaced by a young Guadeloupean singer and guitarist named Karim Verger, alongside singer and songwriter Patrice Hulman from Marie-Galante (Étienne 2023). Meanwhile, the founding members of the band are increasingly involved in other projects alongside their music career, reflecting the excellent esteem in which the band are held among an Antillean but also French and African public. Both Béroard and Pierre-Édouard Décimus, for instance, have recently published their memoires, in which they reflect on how music has shaped their lives.[6]

For Kassav', the function of music was not to make an explicit political statement, as it was for the other artists analysed thus far in this chapter, and they did not seek to make music with the intention of critiquing the socio-economic circumstances of Antillean life, including the BUMIDOM. This is perhaps because they were of a different generation from artists such as Konket and Cosaque, and therefore they had a different relationship to the Bureau. For instance, it was Desvarieux's mother who migrated through the BUMIDOM; he was only a young child at the time and so, although he accompanied his mother to France, he did not really understand the stakes of her migration. In an interview on 19 December 2013 for 'Générations BUMIDOM' [Generations of the BUMIDOM], a programme broadcast on France Ô to commemorate the fiftieth anniversary of the creation of the Bureau,[7] Desvarieux commented that, although his mother was disappointed not to receive exactly what she had been promised in mainland France, he was grateful for the opportunities that migration granted him. He stated that 'peut-être que si elle était restée aux Antilles, je ne serais pas musicien, j'aurais été coupeur de canne' (Ponchelet 2013) [perhaps if she had stayed in the French Caribbean, I wouldn't have been a musician, I would have been a cane cutter]. He was thus not as bitter about the BUMIDOM as Konket and Cosaque, and so he did not use music to criticise explicitly this governmental policy. Rather, Kassav' was more interested in bringing diasporic communities together, uniting people in mainland France with their Caribbean roots and facilitating a reconceptualisation of Antillean identity. Through their music, they encouraged people to rethink what it meant to be Antillean living in mainland France, whether these people had migrated through the BUMIDOM or not. For Kassav', music assisted Antilleans to engage in a politics of recognition in both an outer-directed and inner-directed manner, to quote Baily and Collyer (2006). It enabled them to maintain their own cultural identity for themselves but also to assert their identity as a coherent group in the eyes of others.

So how did they do this? Firstly, they adapted the musical style of traditional Antillean gwoka music. They abandoned the traditional drum and instead used electronic sounds to create the beat of the rhythm on albums such as *Vini Pou* (1987) [Come Here] and *Majestik Zouk* (1989) [Majestic Zouk]. In addition, they challenged traditional French Caribbean society through their lyrics and the themes they addressed, particularly in relation to gender roles. Paul Cohen explores how in 'Mari Mani Mélé' (2013) [Mani's Husband is in a Bind], the band mock men who are reluctant to pull their weight with domestic chores, while in 'Ki jan ké fè' (2007) [What Am I to Do], it is a man who is faced with heartbreak and despair, a condition habitually reserved for women in Caribbean culture (Cohen 2022, 334). Kassav' also drew inspiration from a variety of musical traditions across the Caribbean, even though their music remained resolutely French Antillean in rhythm. As H. Adlai Murdoch observes, Kassav' incorporated Jamaican reggae and Dominican cadence-lypso into their music, as well as Cuban and Puerto Rican salsa and Trinidadian soca, among other styles (Murdoch 2021, 196). In this way, Kassav' emphasised the fluidity and hybridity of Antillean identity, which was based on much more than its African heritage and French colonial tradition. For Kassav', being Antillean meant being pan-Caribbean. A further strategy to diversify their music was to sing not only in French or Guadeloupean Creole but also in English, in songs such as 'West Indies' (1982), sung by Patrick Saint-Éloi. According to Béroard, this crossing of linguistic boundaries was a deliberate strategy to show Antilleans living in both France and the Caribbean that Antillean culture was diverse, heterogeneous and linguistically hybrid, and that there was more than one way to be Caribbean. Kassav's intention was to 'faire réflechir [les Antillais] à leur identité, à une époque où il ne fallait pas parler créole' (Béroard 2013) [make [Antilleans] reflect on their identity in a period where they were not supposed to speak Creole]. This hybridity was also apparent in the racial composition of the band, which was made up of members of different skin colours from both Martinique and Guadeloupe.

For Kassav', then, music was less an opportunity to make an explicit political statement about the BUMIDOM as a specific example of inequality and oppression, and more an outlet to bring together communities that had settled in France via the BUMIDOM (and by other means) and enable them simultaneously to value and adapt their cultural traditions to their transnational environment. Of course, the musicians analysed above were not the only ones active in this period to sing about the BUMIDOM. Other tracks worth mentioning include 'Mwen domi dewo' (1975) [I Slept Outside] by Super Combo, a song in Creole which follows the trend of cultural production which condemns the Bureau. The song tells the story of a man who moved to Paris and ended up homeless, and thus it spotlights the mismatch between expectations and reality. This song appeared on the soundtrack of *Le Gang des Antillais*, analysed in Chapter 4 of this book, a further indicator of its importance in Antillean cultural tradition. In addition, 'A youskous pas fè fou' (1978) [You're Not Crazy] by Martinican band La Perfecta is another song which denounces the French government for neglecting to develop the Caribbean islands economically and socially, against an up-tempo beat. Turning now to music which has been produced more recently, what memories of the BUMIDOM are transmitted through music, and how does this occur?

Musical Memories of the BUMIDOM

In the past fifteen years, there has been a plethora of artists of Caribbean origin (living both in the French Antilles and mainland France) who have produced songs about the BUMIDOM. Some of these tracks are individual songs about migration in an artist's corpus which address wider social issues (as in the case of Kalme La Fournaise, who also sings about memory, labour conditions and life in the overseas departments). Other songs, meanwhile, form a more sustained discussion about the BUMIDOM in artists' musical oeuvre (the artist BUMIDOM, for instance, repeatedly evokes the legacy of this migration scheme on his album *Histoire d'un expatrié* (2019)). The extent of their musical engagement with the BUMIDOM reflects the weight the Bureau occupies in their family history. What is also noticeable about this contemporary music is that it adopts a variety of musical styles, depending primarily on the location in which the artists developed their musical career. Some musicians tap into Antillean and Caribbean musical traditions – Delgres, for instance, named after the revolutionary leader Louis Delgrès although spelled slightly differently, is a Creole blues and jazz band from Guadeloupe who mostly sing in Creole. Others, meanwhile, are inspired by metropolitan French tastes. For the French artist BUMIDOM, his preferred genre is rap and hip-hop. This is a preference shared by many French people; since the twenty-first century, 'France is second only to the United States' in its love for rap and hip-hop (Krims 2022, vii). I shall now look in more detail at three artists who transmit memories of the BUMIDOM through their music, working through their most substantial outputs about the Bureau chronologically.

One of the most successful bands to emerge from the Caribbean since the 2000s is the Guadeloupean band Soft. The band was created in early 2002 by frontman, singer and songwriter Fred Deshayes. The other core members are saxophonist Philippe Sadikala and bassist Joël Larochelle, although other musicians are involved in their live concerts. The band achieved success very quickly. Their first studio album, *Kadans a péyi-là* (Rhythm of the Country], was released in 2006 and sold more than 10,000 copies in Guadeloupe alone in the first three months of its release (Daoudi 2007). Deshayes is not only a musician; he has a PhD in public law from the Université des Antilles, where he currently teaches. He possesses an inherent sense of social justice, which is apparent in the lyrics he writes. In an interview for RFI Musique in 2018, Deshayes made his political commitment through music clear: 'il faut que les paroles soient profondes, sérieuses' (Lavaine 2018) [the lyrics must be deep, serious]. It thus seems that he draws inspiration from the great gwoka singers Konket and Cosaque analysed earlier in this chapter, for whom, as we saw, music was a political tool to express dissatisfaction with the status quo. Indeed, Deshayes has also acknowledged his debt to these earlier artists in terms of musical style, but he endeavours to do something different with his music. Claiming that 'j'essaie de construire une nouvelle musique, un nouveau chemin' [I'm trying to create a new style of music, a new path], his music draws on gwoka and zouk but also on other musical styles such as biguine and calypso (Deshayes 2020). His music is also slower and softer than that of these earlier artists, allowing more attention to be paid to his lyrics. Unlike the electronic sound of zouk, Soft's music is acoustic, created by saxophones, acoustic guitars and other percussion instruments.

A further difference is that, unlike artists from the previous generations, Soft's music offers a critique of Guadeloupeans' relationship with France, but also with the island itself. Camal sees *Kadans a péyi-là* as a project which 'departs from the nationalist rhetoric of the 1970s' because rather than encouraging fellow Guadeloupeans to rebel against the colonial oppressor, Deshayes and his musicians blame Guadeloupeans for subscribing to neocolonialist discourse and for being selfish and not helping each other to create a better future for Guadeloupe (Camal 2019, 157). I argue that this denunciation of Guadeloupeans' lack of solidarity is also evident in their later work, and particularly in the songs that transmit memories of the BUMIDOM.

Their second album, *Partout étranger* (2007) [Everywhere a Foreigner], is a clear critique of Caribbean migration organised by the French state. Indeed, the first song, 'Doudou o (on kat postal)', reveals that, for Soft, the Bureau needs to be remembered as a system initiated by the French state, but that Guadeloupeans themselves should be criticised for buying into governmental rhetoric that offered migration as a form of social promotion. The song begins with gentle rifts on the guitar and saxophone, while percussion instruments make the sound of flowing water, symbolising the crossing of the Atlantic. The words 'BUMI BUMI BUMI DOM DOM DOM' are sung quietly by a female backing singer, providing a rapid contextualisation of the song and giving it a nostalgic tone. This nostalgia also emerges through the song's lyrics. The song is a thwarted love story told from the perspective of a young Guadeloupean man who one day receives a postcard from his lover, leading him to recall the day she left for France. He tried to convince her to stay, but she wanted to live a new adventure in mainland France. The song is sung in Creole, like most of Soft's oeuvre. The phrase 'en diw en vlé rété; La lomblik an mwen téré' [I told you I want to stay where I was born] is repeated throughout the song, contrasting the young man's attachment to his native island with the young girl's desire for adventure and excitement.[8] On the surface, then, this seems to be a nostalgic love song, but there is a deeper message behind it. Towards the end of the song, Deshayes sings: 'fanmi aw yo pa enmé nom kon mwen; Yo pa enmén nèg a chivé kon mwen' [your family doesn't like men like me; they don't like Black people with hair like me]. He is thus critiquing people in Guadeloupe who have adopted negative metropolitan attitudes towards people of colour, in a process often described by people in the French Caribbean as becoming a 'négropolitain'. As Richard Burton explains, this term was used (and continues to be employed today) by islanders and residents of France to refer to Black people living in the metropole who have adopted Parisian attitudes and values and who retain this lifestyle on their return to the Caribbean (Burton 1995, 12). The song critiques those living in Guadeloupe rather than France, but whose values are distinctly metropolitan, because they are driven to migrate because of their capitalist intentions and their desire to shun their Black Antillean identity. It is important to acknowledge here that the album was written for the soundtrack of Antoine Léonard-Maestrati and Michel Reinette's documentary film *L'Avenir est ailleurs*. It is thus difficult to know exactly how much agency the band had when creating this song. Whether the song represents the band's own critique of the BUMIDOM, or whether it is more emblematic of the political message Léonard-Maestrati and Reinette wanted to convey is unclear from the interviews given by the band.

DeNora argues that music allows listeners to create a new self-narrative. The sounds they hear take them back to their past selves, which then become merged with their present self to create a new future self (DeNora 2000, 66). This process of tapping into personal memories through music becomes more complex when musical memories are transmitted to the next generation. In the case of Soft's *Partout étranger*, it is likely that much of the audience does not have direct experience of the BUMIDOM, given that the album was released in 2006. The album thus relies on more universal tropes such as love, loss and heartbreak to appeal to a younger generation. Yet the lyrics also provide historical contextualisation about the BUMIDOM, so that listeners familiar with the migratory scheme will connect these universal narratives to the history of the Bureau.

Soft's musical project is a collective one which unites individuals into a larger social group and creates affective ties between them. Indeed, Deshayes is very keen to point out in interviews that the memories portrayed in Soft's songs are not his own personal memories: 'ce n'est pas notre vécu [. . .] je n'ai pas connu le BUMIDOM' (Da Silva 2008) [it's not our experience . . . I didn't experience the BUMIDOM'. In contrast, the project of Delgres is highly personal. Although both bands consider music to be a vector for the intergenerational transmission of memories about migration, for Delgres frontman Pascal Danaë, his inspirations lie in his family's story of departure and return across the Atlantic.

Delgres is a Creole blues and jazz band composed of frontman, singer and guitarist Danaë, drummer Baptiste Brondy and saxophonist Rafgee. They first started playing together in 2017, releasing their debut album, *Mo Jodi* [Die Today], in 2018. Their music combines Creole blues with jazz, rock and African musical styles. Many of their songs are sung in Guadeloupean Creole, but French and English are also used as the language of expression, and thus Delgres mirrors Kassav' in the group's desire to transcend linguistic boundaries. In fact, in their 2024 album *Promis Le Ciel* [Promised the Sky], only three out of eleven tracks are sung in Creole while two appear in English, perhaps suggesting a linguistic and musical shift away from the Caribbean and towards Europe. Danaë was born in the Parisian suburb of Argenteuil in 1963 to Guadeloupean parents. He began playing the guitar aged fifteen and then studied musicology at Université Paris 8. He taught music in high schools for a few years while continuing to play his own music. In 1987, he moved to London to pursue his music career, where he collaborated with musicians such as Gilberto Gil, Peter Gabriel and Youssou N'Dour. He then moved back to Paris and in 2010 relocated to Amsterdam (Danaë 2020). It was during this period that he began to reconnect with his ancestral roots: he went to Guadeloupe for the first time where he discovered his family history of enslavement. He then began to reflect on the kind of music he wanted to create which would best represent himself and his family heritage, in an illustration of the connectedness between music and identity. It is significant that he named the band after Louis Delgrès, the revolutionary leader of the movement in Guadeloupe to resist French occupation and the reimposition of enslavement in 1802, as it reveals that the name of a musical artist can transmit a political message just as powerfully as the lyrics of a song. For Danaë, the struggle fought by Delgres for a fairer world is not over, and so they must take on this fight themselves:

> the name of the band is based on someone who was actually the victim of a great injustice. And he fought and he died fighting injustice. And it's very important for us to say that that kind of fight is never ended, of course, and it's all now, it's all today and more than ever. (Stewart 2022)

Delgres's second album, entitled *4.00am* (2021), is a salient example of the band's efforts to raise awareness of injustices and inequalities through music. It is a very personal record, particularly in its origins, and it evokes themes of migration, separation and racism. The album is dedicated to his father who migrated to France in 1958 to find work. A trained mechanic, he struggled to find a job in this sector and so ended up working in railway warehouses in Argenteuil, having to get up at 4.00 am. Although his migration slightly predated the BUMIDOM, then, he still suffered from underemployment and exploitation, in the same way as BUMIDOM participants. Danaë's mother and sister joined him in 1962, just as the Bureau was being set up (Volle 2021). The songs on the album are thus very much connected to his family history of displacement from Guadeloupe to mainland France. However, what is interesting is that the band fuse the past with the present by writing songs both about this very specific instance of internal migration within France's borders in the 1960s to 80s, and about contemporary experiences of migration which are not connected to the BUMIDOM. DeNora states that 'the past, musically conjured, is a resource for the reflexive movement from present to future, the moment-to-moment production of agency in real time' (2000, 66). *4.00am* moves the listener from past to present to future within the space of each song, carrying out the memory work for the listener. Danaë summarises his intentions as follows: 'ce qu'on veut dire c'est que ben, on peut être ensemble, s'éclater autour de valeurs qui réunissent tout le monde avec un peu d'histoire mais surtout beaucoup de présent' (Danaë 2021) [what we mean is that, well, we can be together, have fun based on values which bring everyone together with a bit of history but especially with a lot of the present].

The first song on the album, '4 ed maten' [4.00 am], demonstrates this very clearly. The song talks about the sacrifices made by a worker who has to get up at 4.00 am when everyone else is in bed, in order to send back money for his family living in the Caribbean. The phrase '4 ed maten' is repeated at the start of each verse to emphasise the hardships experienced by labourers working in very physical occupations.[9] The song makes use of tropes common to Caribbean cultural production about migration, such as complaints about the cold weather in France and laments about the loneliness felt by people living far away from their families. In addition, the song emphasises the resourcefulness of this community who use 'papié journal adan soulié aw; Pou pié aw pa two fwa' [newspapers shoved in your boots; to keep your feet warm]. The BUMIDOM is not mentioned specifically in this song. However, given the extensive interviews Danaë has given about the origins of the album, it can be deduced that the song makes reference to the workers who migrated during this period, and who did not receive the financial, administrative and emotional assistance to settle in mainland France that they expected. At the same time, the song universalises the experiences of any migrant arriving in France (or elsewhere) today and who struggles to adapt, thus bringing the past into dialogue with the present. This fusion between the past and the present comes across very strongly in the performance strategy of the band. The music video for this song was shot on the docks at Le Havre. The opening shot sees the camera pan down a caravan parked in the middle of a warehouse, and we see a man asleep until his alarm – of which there is a close-up shot – goes off at 4.00 am. Delgres plays music outside in the dark while the worker has his breakfast and gets ready. We then see him start work until, halfway through the video, the band sparks a protest, inciting other workers to join and protest against their working conditions. This video recalls the mass migration of Antilleans in the 1960s and 70s who arrived at the docks in Le Havre and worked in difficult physical jobs, but it is also relevant for contemporary experiences of labour migration, in which people suffer from the same sentiments of exploitation and loneliness. Indeed, as Brondy explains, it was important for the band, and particularly for Danaë, to perform the song there, not only as a tribute to Danaë's parents but also because 'ça donne cette lumière sur ces ouvriers' (Brondy 2022) [it shines a spotlight on these workers].

The band not only recorded the music video for '4 ed maten' at the port in Le Havre, but they have also performed there – for instance in February 2021, as they were touring with the album (Pias 2021). For Taylor, musical performances, as well as dancing, singing and movement, 'enact embodied memory' through a process she describes as a 'repertoire' (2003, 20). The repertoire works through the presence of other people who participate in the production and transmission of knowledge. Whereas the archive – consisting of written documents, films and musical records – remains more or less fixed and stable, the repertoire is in constant transformation, meaning that the memories provoked by these items are also continuously in flux. The fact that Delgres chose not only to record the music video for '4 ed maten' (an item of the archive) at the port, but also to perform there (an item belonging to the repertoire) reinforces the mnemonic capacity of the album in transmitting memories of migration, because memory transmission works on both levels.

As we have seen, Soft and Delgres share commonalities in the musical styles they adopt and the language in which they sing. Kalme La Fournaise, however, takes a rather different approach. He is not inspired by gwoka or zouk, like the other two artists. Instead, he draws on the sounds and rhythms of reggae music and fuses it with rap and hip-hop. Moreover, he sings in French (and occasionally English) rather than in Creole. Although he is of Antillean heritage (his father is from Guadeloupe and his mother from Réunion), he does not seem to be as focused on transforming French Caribbean music as Soft and Delgres. His cultural heritage is important to him, however, particularly the Reunionese traditions passed down to him by his mother. This is evident in his stage name. In an interview with me in April 2023, he explained the origins of his name: 'Kalme' emerged while talking to a friend as a play on words with the French expression 'au calme' [to be cool], and he added 'La Fournaise' as a tribute to Réunion, in a nod to the Piton de la Fournaise volcano situated on the eastern side of the island. A further difference can be discerned in the ways in which he promotes and circulates his music. He is not a mainstream, well-established artist like Soft and Delgres, and thus he does not have a manager or a team to help promote his music. He performs this task himself using social media such as Facebook, Instagram and Soundcloud to share his music with his fans.[10] He thus taps into digital memory practices, an increasing area of interest in memory studies (Hoskins 2018; Fridman 2022). In this case, sharing music via social media enables people in different diasporic locations to access the music connected to their homeland. He released his first solo album, *Bataille mi bataille* [Struggle My Struggle], in 2014 and his second album, *Cahier de vie* [Diary], in 2020. He is a socially engaged musician as his lyrics address social unrest, injustices and inequalities, both in a French context and in the wider world.

The track 'BUMIDOM', which appeared as the first track on the *Cahier de vie* album, thus sits alongside others which highlight the oppression and subjugation of a particular community of people. Indeed, this idea of seeking freedom from oppression comes through very strongly in 'BUMIDOM'. In the first line of the chorus, Kalme La Fournaise sings 'partout les opprimés chantent freedom, freedom, freedom!' [everywhere oppressed people sing freedom, freedom, freedom!]. The adverb 'partout' suggests that this is a general critique of contemporary society rather than about the BUMIDOM specifically. However, in the first line of the chorus he sings 'Bomayé, BUMIDOM', and other historical markers are peppered throughout the lyrics, such as a reference to 'les enfants de la Creuse', the children who were forcibly removed from Réunion during the BUMIDOM era. These references position the song as a clear denunciation of the Bureau, which removed people, described in the song as 'les déportés' [deported people], from their family networks and familiar surroundings. His intentions, however, were not really to denounce this system as an exploitative mechanism to provide cheap labour for mainland France. Rather, he sought to 'faire un témoignage de ce que pourraient ressentir les déportés et aussi ce que pourrait ressentir la famille' (La Fournaise 2023) [provide a testimony of what the deported people might have felt and what their family might have felt]. He considers music to be the ideal vector of these testimonies because of its accessibility; music allows people to learn about the past in an engaging and non-patronising manner (La Fournaise 2023). He is also compelled by 'un devoir de mémoire' [duty to remember] to commemorate France's past through music, an expression which is 'omnipresent in political discourse' when issues of collective memory and traumatic histories are raised (Ledoux 2013, 240). While this expression implies state-endorsed memory practices which recognises the state's role in committing and/or enabling violence, Kalme La Fournaise sees it as a personal project which helps him, and others, to better understand France's difficult history.

The legacy of the BUMIDOM is thus still very much present in French-language cultural production today, and music plays an important role in keeping memories of the Bureau alive. The three artists analysed above circulate memories of the BUMIDOM for different reasons. For Soft, music enables a critique of the BUMIDOM structure but also a judgement of Guadeloupeans who, according to the band, bought into this system too easily, and were too quick to assimilate to metropolitan life rather than working together to make Guadeloupe a more hospitable place. Meanwhile, Danaë from Delgres was inspired to tell his father's story of migration and to connect it to contemporary issues affecting people today. Kalme La Fournaise considers music to be a form of testimony, and he dedicates his song to his Reunionese mother who made sacrifices in order to have a better life. For other artists producing songs about this period, music is a means of learning about the past to compensate for the lack of formal knowledge about the BUMIDOM they received at school. In an interview with me on 1 August 2023, Bruno, the lead singer of jazz, slam and gwoka band Ginko Biloka explained that he wanted to record the song 'BUMIDOM' to teach himself and others about this important history: 'ce que je n'ai pas appris à l'école je le chante pour moi et pour d'autres qui ne connaissent pas vraiment cette histoire' (Bruno 2023) [what I didn't learn at school I sing for me and for others who don't really know this history]. In this case, music takes on a pedagogical function, teaching listeners about a historical episode that still remains marginalised in formal frameworks of remembrance.

Conclusion

The BUMIDOM has thus had a significant and long-lasting impact on the Antillean music produced both in mainland France and Martinique and Guadeloupe, in the mid-twentieth century and in the last fifteen years. The BUMIDOM was, in fact, the catalyst which enabled Antillean music to develop and be transformed in the Hexagon, because it brought Antilleans to the mainland and enabled them to encounter different musical traditions. Music then became an outlet for artists such as Konket and Cosaque to express their dissatisfaction with the scheme. For musicians producing music as the institution was coming to an end, it gave them the opportunity to reflect on what it meant to be an Antillean living away from the Antilles. The notion of Antilleanness was thus both affirmed and challenged through the music of bands such as Kassav'. Contemporary music has sought not only to transmit memories of the BUMIDOM to generations who may not be familiar with the scheme, but also to position these memories within a broader, global context of migration and exploitation. Antillean music is thus a powerful vector of social cohesion, diasporic identity and cultural memory.

Notes

1. Through a voice-over narrated by Martinican journalist and politician Audrey Pulvar, the film combines video footage, archival documentation and testimonials by BUMIDOM participants. One of these interviewees, Jéronise Gros-Désormeaux, is featured in the song 'BUMIDOM'. She describes her bewilderment on realising that she had been given only a one-way ticket to France.
2. According to Margaret Byron and Stephanie Condon, De Gaulle's visit to Martinique in 1964 was one of several trips to the Caribbean and Africa made by the president during a time of struggle for independence in the colonies. The visits 'were part of a strong assimilation policy aiming to maintain and reinforce the political and sentimental attachment of the populations to the French nation' (Byron and Condon 2008, 33). It became a common joke among Martinicans to change De Gaulle's comment to 'Mon Dieu, comme vous êtes foncés!' [Goodness me, how dark you are!], given the Creole pronunciation of the 'r' sound.
3. Although the song was never recorded, the lyrics appeared in the album sleeve of their record produced in 1981 (Générations BUMIDOM 2013).

4. Both songs appear on Robert Loyson, *Nostalgies caraïbes, accompagné par le tandem Vélo/Boisbant* (Disques Célini, 2007).
5. In a letter from Albert Bros to the general secretary to the Overseas Departments dated 2 September 1975, the chief executive of the BUMDOM explained that, although usually migrants were entitled only to a single paid trip, if young children had migrated at a young age as part of the family reunification scheme, an exception would be made (BUMIDOM 1975b).
6. See Jocelyn Béroard, *Loin de l'amer* (2022), and Pierre-Édouard Décimus, *Kassav'- Love and Ka-dance* (2023).
7. Other important cultural and political figures involved in this programme included George Pau-Langevin (at the time Junior Minister for Educational Success) and Monique Milia-Marie-Luce (historian and specialist of the BUMIDOM).
8. This is my translation, based on the translation into French of the lyrics on greatsong.net. See https://greatsong.net/TRADUCTION-SOFT,DOUDOU-O-ON-KAT-POSTAL,103841608.html [accessed 30 May 2023].
9. The song is sung in Creole, but on the band's official website the lyrics have been translated into French and English. See https://www.delgresmusic.com/lyrics2 [accessed 31 May 2023].
10. See his Instagram page: https://www.instagram.com/kalme974/?hl=en; and his Soundcloud page: https://soundcloud.com/kalme974 [accessed 24 May 2023].

Conclusion: Remembering the BUMIDOM Today

The year 2023 marked the sixtieth anniversary since the BUMIDOM was established by the French government. This significant anniversary led to an increased interest in the organised migration scheme among academics, artists and communities, both in mainland France and in the French Antilles. Examples of events which were organised to commemorate this anniversary include 'BUMIDOM: une migration réussie?' [BUMIDOM: A Successful Migration?], an event run by the Caribbean association Sonjé and held in Saint-Denis on 17 and 18 March 2023 (Jocksan 2023). The two-day event involved a round table with academics, a screening of the short film *BUMIDOM: une migration réussie?* (2022) by cultural activist Guilaine Mondor and the exhibition 'Partir pour la "métropole": une odysée populaire' [Leaving for the 'Metropole': An Odyssey of the Working Class], curated by Patrick Semiramoth and Willy Vainqueur.[1] Mondor also co-organised an event to commemorate the sixtieth anniversary of the BUMIDOM with Guadeloupean *député* Olivier Serva, held at the Assemblée nationale in Paris in December 2023.[2] Moreover, events were held in 2023 and 2024 in the Caribbean, such as an open-air film screening and discussion of *BUMIDOM, des Français venus d'outre-mer* in November 2023 in Le Gosier, Guadeloupe. In 2023, I worked with the graphic novelist Jessica Oublié, Brazilian artist Yure Romão and students at Université des Antilles in Saint-Claude, Guadeloupe, to create a compilation of oral histories of the BUMIDOM, which will be stored digitally on the website of the Archives départementales de la Guadeloupe. In addition, Semiramoth is collaborating with the departmental archives in Guadeloupe and Martinique to put on exhibitions there in autumn 2024. These events were complemented by academic conferences which examined the social, political and cultural legacies of the BUMIDOM project. On 25 and 26 May 2023, the conference 'Lot bo a – D'un bord à l'autre.

Des Français venus d'"outre-mer"' [From One Side to the Other: French People from "overseas"] was held at the Musée d'Acquitaine in Bordeaux, in collaboration with the Migrants de l'intérieur (MIGRINDOM) [Internal Migrants] network and the Centre international de recherches sur les esclavages et les post-esclavages [the International Centre of Research on Slavery and Post-Slavery]. I helped to bring these discussions to an anglophone audience through my conference 'The BUMIDOM in Interdisciplinary Perspectives', held at the University of Liverpool on 22 and 23 June 2023.

It is significant, then, that these examples of artist-led and community-led memorial practices are only just surfacing now, and that it has taken until 2023 for these memories of migration to be valued and deemed worthy of commemoration. There are several reasons for this. Firstly, there is certainly an urgency in the transmission of these memories, as older generations are keen to pass on their personal accounts of migration to their loved ones before they pass away. BUMIDOM participants are now in their 70s and 80s, and are thus likely to feel compelled to raise awareness of this history now in order to ensure that their family heritage is not forgotten. Moreover, as discussion about the BUMIDOM takes hold on both sides of the Atlantic, people are beginning to feel a little more at ease in discussing their difficult experiences of migration in public. The stigma surrounding the Bureau is slowly fading, and the more that community groups encourage Caribbean people to open up about their experiences, the less ashamed people feel to admit that they had to rely on state support to finance their journey to mainland France. A more significant reason is that until now, the memorial landscape of the French Caribbean has been consumed by commemorating the traumatic memories of enslavement and forced displacement, and so any other memories of the difficult history of the Caribbean in other contexts have been overshadowed by these debates. As I have argued elsewhere, Black Caribbean activists based on the islands and the mainland have, until recently, been mostly focused on ensuring that 'Caribbean people are active agents' in memorial practices surrounding enslavement, because the state-led initiatives – such as the announcement of 10 May as a national day of commemoration – 'promote a hexagonal, Eurocentric version of the past' (Wimbush 2022, 9). It is only now, in 2023, when sufficient progress has been made in commemorating the atrocities of enslavement, that community groups, artists and academics are able to turn to the BUMIDOM to denounce it as another, more recent instance of institutional racism. Through this collaboration, then, the BUMIDOM is gradually becoming a postcolonial *lieu de mémoire*; that is, an intentionally created memory because, in Nora's words, 'there is no spontaneous memory' (1989, 12). Nora argues that *lieux de mémoire* function through the 'push and pull' of history and memory – as moments of history are shrouded in silence and then emerge to the surface, realms of memory are produced. In fact, Nora goes as far to say that it is only through the simultaneous occlusion and release of histories that *lieux de mémoire* emerge (1989, 12). This is what is occurring in the case of the BUMIDOM; different groups are in a constant struggle to both conceal and release traumatic memories of migration from the suppressed histories of the Caribbean community. It must be made very clear, however, that this process is taking place on an individual and communal level, but not at a state level. The memorial events cited above are the fruit of individual activists, community organisations and research networks. They are not national, state-sponsored events and neither are they financially supported or endorsed by the French government. The BUMIDOM does feature in the new permanent exhibition at the Musée national de l'histoire de l'immigration [National Museum of the History of Immigration] in Paris, but it is only a small display and the history of the Bureau is primarily told through Oublié and Marie-Ange Rousseau's graphic novel and Jackie Bastide's documentary, rather than through historical records or oral testimonies.[3] There is still a long way to go before memories of migration through the BUMIDOM are fully respected by the French state.

* * *

The year 2023 was also an important one for the Caribbean community living in the United Kingdom – it marked the seventy-fifth anniversary of the arrival of the *Empire Windrush* ship in Tilbury Docks. This ship brought some 500 people from Jamaica to Britain and is heralded as the beginning of mass migration to the country after World War II.[4] What is often overlooked in this reductive discourse about the *Empire Windrush* is the fact that there was a sizeable Black community already living in Britain before 1948.[5] Indeed, the *Empire Windrush* was not even the first ship to dock in Britain in the 1940s; the SS *Ormonde* arrived first, docking in Liverpool in April 1947, followed by the SS *Almanzora* in Southampton in December 1947. As Alison Donnell explains, these ships 'were not subjected to the same cultural and political responses that hailed the arrival of the Windrush', and therefore these arrivals have subsequently been overlooked (Donnell 2019, 196). Despite the erasure of the specificities of this history, the British government has been keen to mark the anniversary of the arrival of the *Empire Windrush* through official, national practices of commemoration. It has thus reacted very differently to the French government, which has not funded or organised any event to commemorate the anniversary of the BUMIDOM. Since 2018, 22 June has been celebrated as an official National Windrush Day, following campaigns by Caribbean activists such as Arthur Torrington and Patrick Vernon.[6] For the 2023 iteration of this day, £750,000 was awarded by the government to forty-five different community projects across the country. These range from a photographic and alternative reality project in Birmingham and a cricket festival in Sheffield to the creation of an illustrated book for children in Endfield, London (Gov.uk, 2023). Remarkably, the royal family also became involved in the commemorations. King Charles III commissioned ten leading artists from the United Kingdom and abroad to create ten portraits of pioneering members of the 'Windrush generation', exhibited at the Palace of Holyroodhouse in Edinburgh from June to October 2023 and at Buckingham Palace from November 2023 to April 2024 (BBC 2023).[7] In addition, the Royal Mail commissioned eight stamps which feature artworks by Black British artists to commemorate the anniversary (Banfield-Nwachi 2023). In theory, then, the British government is committed to celebrating the contributions made by the Caribbean community to British life and to ensuring that the memories of the Windrush pioneers are honoured.

However, it is imperative to consider these national practices of commemoration within the context of the 'Windrush scandal', a phenomenon which casts these national initiatives in a rather different light. In 2017, it emerged that people born in the Caribbean Commonwealth and who moved to Britain in the 1940s, 1950s and beyond were being detained, denied their legal rights and even being deported. The 'hostile environment' policy initiated by the then Home Secretary Theresa May meant that migrants had to prove – often to excessive lengths – that they had the right to remain in the country. Many were unable to do so – they had no passport because they did not need one when they arrived in the country, thanks to the 1948 British Nationality Act which meant that Caribbean people were citizens of the United Kingdom and Colonies. The affair became mediatised after journalist Amelia Gentleman broke the story in *The Guardian*, and this media attention put pressure on the government to revoke the deportations, instigate a review of the scandal and create the Windrush Compensation Scheme to right the wrongs that the government had committed towards the Caribbean community.[8]

No official apology was ever given to the victims, however, and out of the thirty recommendations put forward by Wendy Williams in the Windrush Lessons Learned Review, published in 2020, three have been dropped, including organising reconciliation events with Windrush families (Gentleman and Syal 2023). In their manifesto for the 2024 general election, the Labour Party pledged to improve the compensation scheme by appointing a new Windrush commissioner, speeding up compensation payments and organising reconciliation events (Clinton 2024). It will be interesting to see whether these promises are upheld, now that the Labour Party are in power. The Caribbean community is thus rather sceptical about the real motivations for these commemorative events. It does seem disingenuous, and even hypocritical, that, on the one hand, the Conservative British government promoted a narrative of social cohesion and multiculturalism through the 'National Windrush Day' agenda, and on the other, made life extremely difficult for those who settled in the country from the Caribbean decades ago, and who consider the United Kingdom to be their home.

***

Why have governmental responses to these two anniversaries been so different, then? Why has the United Kingdom sought to shine a spotlight on Caribbean migration to the country, and the French government has ignored this important date? Firstly, I would argue that the British government is trying to promote the United Kingdom as a multicultural, multiracial and multireligious country for political reasons, to demonstrate that the policies implemented to ensure social cohesion in this culturally diverse society have been successful – even if prominent politicians and social commentators (such as former Prime Minister David Cameron) have criticised key aspects of multiculturalism (Ashcroft and Bevir 2018, 1). One way to show official support for multiculturalism is by providing financial assistance for the issues that affect specific communities, such as the memorialisation of migration from the Caribbean Commonwealth. Secondly, for the most part this group of people fits into the 'good immigrant' narrative, a trope which relies on the differentiation of citizenship and distinguishes between those who are worthy of belonging to a country and those who are not, depending on cultural and religious affiliation, legal requirements and economic status (Hackl 2022, 993). While those caught up in the 'Windrush scandal', who were often at the lower end of the social hierarchy, were not necessarily considered to be 'good migrants', many Caribbean people who arrived from the late 1940s to the early 1970s do correspond to this category. These are people who came to work for the nascent National Health Service and transportation systems such as London Transport Executive (now Transport for London). In fact, much of post-war Britain was rebuilt by migrants, and the 'Windrush generation' contributed enormously to reshaping the economy and social structures of the country. Their profile is thus very different from that of the migrants and refugees that the Conservative British government tried to crack down on through the draconian immigration and refugee policies introduced by then Home Secretary Suella Braverman.[9] Thirdly, there is a political expediency to these recent Windrush celebrations. The government used them to endeavour to move on from the 'Windrush Scandal', and the renewed efforts behind the seventy-fifth anniversary celebrations could be seen as some form of attempt to make amends for the dreadful treatment of this community. However, understandably many Caribbean people are angry that the government coopted these histories and memories for its own political purposes.

France, however, is governed by a very different political model. Embedded in France's national motto of 'liberté, égalité, fraternité' is the belief that all French citizens are equal, and that French citizenship transcends race, ethnicity, gender and religion. Unlike in the United Kingdom, dual or hyphenated identities, such as Afro-French or Arab-French, do not exist, and people are discouraged from identifying with a particular community because their identity is first and foremost French. The French government, therefore, cannot be seen to celebrate overtly the memories of its Antillean population because this would mean emphasising their Antilleanness over their Frenchness, thus undermining the model of republican universalism. More importantly, though, it would also mean highlighting the fact that those who migrated through the BUMIDOM scheme – who were French citizens – were not treated as such. It would mean shining a spotlight on the racial discrimination they often received from individuals and institutions in mainland France, and also admitting that the scheme was colonial in its conception and application. It is thus not in the French government's interests to right the wrongs of these past injustices. Instead, it is cultural practitioners, and increasingly community groups, who are honouring the memories of Martinicans and Guadeloupeans who bought into state rhetoric that they would have a better life in mainland France, but who often found themselves marginalised by French society.

***

By investigating cultural responses to post-war Caribbean migration in a variety of media and genres and relating these to key debates in memory practices in the French-speaking world, *BUMIDOM (1963–1982) and its Afterlives* hopes to contribute to a number of fields and disciplines. For scholars working in migration studies, the book has provided a detailed analysis of how the BUMIDOM operated in practice. It has revealed the colonial continuities of this scheme which was predicated on the notion of centre/periphery. It has also demonstrated the demographic consequences of governmental migratory and developmental policies currently afflicting the French Caribbean islands. For researchers in postcolonial studies, the study has uncovered what it was like to be a Black French citizen of Caribbean origin in the 1960s and beyond as represented by different forms of cultural production, and how experiences of Blackness, a subject of increasing debate in France today, have evolved into the twenty-first century. Finally, the book has contributed to debates in memory studies, because it has demonstrated how writers, filmmakers, musicians and activists have sought to create a different narrative of Caribbean migration than the one put forward by the French state. In this way, it has interrogated the role of the artist as a memory activist and examined the dynamics of memory on individual, familial and collective levels, analysing how these different modalities of memory work together to commemorate a migratory phenomenon which has long been overlooked, and even concealed, by the French state.

For the most part, the cultural production analysed throughout this book – whether texts of life writing, novels, films, graphic novels, children's fiction or music – offer a critical account of the Bureau. The works emphasise the mismatch experienced by participants between their expectations of what they would find in mainland France and the harsh reality they actually encountered. In addition, they focus on the racialised and gendered discrimination experienced by participants, and the false promises many feel they were sold. The works thus paint a damning picture of the BUMIDOM. However, it is important to recognise that not everyone who migrated through the scheme suffered in this way. In fact, some people today have expressed gratitude towards the BUMIDOM, without which they feel they would not have been able to combine a successful career in mainland France with their parental responsibilities. Out of the six people I interviewed in September and October 2022, two out of the six explicitly acknowledged that they owed their professional success to the Bureau (Wimbush 2023). This is not to disregard the more negative experiences of migration undergone by the people I interviewed, or indeed, to say that the cultural production is biased in any way against the state apparatus and should not be taken seriously. Rather, it is to acknowledge that each migration journey to mainland France during this period was idiosyncratic and the result of a complex set of decisions and outcomes.

What this study has also shown is that there is a certain exceptionality regarding representations of the BUMIDOM, in relation to the representation of other migration journeys to France from different geographical contexts. Firstly, the pedagogical nature of the works analysed in this book is striking. Some outputs are overtly pedagogical, given the audience to whom they are addressed and the form in which they are created. For instance, the graphic novel *Peyi an nou* and the children's book *Emil'Patt à Paris* focus on providing factual information about the Bureau in an accessible manner, and while they are not linear, chronological or historical accounts, they do give historical detail to explain to young (and older) audiences how the BUMIDOM has shaped French and Caribbean society. Other works which are less intentionally pedagogical also transmit histories and memories of migration, and reflect on the differences between the two, even if this is veiled behind fiction. The texts of life writing, for example, have more of a sociological than literary quality, no doubt a reflection of the fact that many of the authors are not established writers but ordinary people who have written about their own experiences of migration. This means that they contain a lot of factual detail about how the scheme operated. Films such as *Le Rêve français* and novels like *Là où les chiens aboient par la queue* paint a vivid and realistic picture of what it was like to migrate to mainland France in the mid-twentieth century through the story of different fictional characters. Furthermore, the songs I have analysed, produced both during the BUMIDOM era and today, also teach audiences about the specificities of migration through this scheme by including factual detail about the Bureau in their lyrics. Given that the BUMIDOM is such a little-known and misunderstood phenomenon, writers and filmmakers have not only had to represent and memorialise this very specific instance of migration, but also to teach it to different audiences in different ways, in order to eradicate the many misconceptions and misunderstandings about Caribbean migration.

Another unique feature about these representations is the vast array of media and genres used by cultural practitioners to transmit these histories and memories, and the fact that communities not habitually involved in creative practices (such as an older population) are creating work about the BUMIDOM. The Bureau features in cultural production more traditionally used by francophone practitioners to discuss migration, such as novels, films and life writing. Yet representations also go beyond these genres. In this book, I have examined how other, innovative forms – such as graphic novels and children's fiction, analysed in Chapter 5, and music, explored in Chapter 6 – combine text, image and sound to transmit memories of migration and to convert these memories into pedagogy. Artists are engaging with the BUMIDOM and its legacies in other innovative media which lie beyond the scope of this book. It would thus be productive to expand the current study to investigate how contemporary representations of the BUMIDOM, both on the islands and on the mainland, have moved beyond traditional print media. Theatre is a growing field for these representations. Françoise Do's monologue *Aliénations* [Alienations], first performed in Fort-de-France in 2017 in collaboration with the Martinican theatre Tropiques Atrium – Scène nationale, tells of a young woman's discovery of her mother's story of migration through the BUMIDOM. Moreover, Maroussia Pourpoint performed *Hommage(s) à la Martinique* [Homage(s) to Martinique] at the Hall de la Chanson in Paris on 25 and 26 June 2022. This performance was a tribute to Pourpoint's grandmother who migrated to France and highlights the sacrifices she made and the obstacles she had to overcome. In 2024, Fabienne Kanor published *La Grande Chambre* [The Big Chambre], a play which explores migration from the Caribbean to France alongside displacement during the transatlantic trafficking of enslaved Africans and the contemporary migration of Sub-Saharan Africans to France. Photography is another genre which emphasises the impacts of the migration scheme on individuals and communities. In 2022, the photographer, rapper and content producer Cédrick-Isham Calvados curated a photography collection entitled 'Moun An Ba La' [People from Over There], paying tribute to the Guadeloupean community who have settled in the Parisian region, including those who came over via the BUMIDOM (Calvados 2022). Other notable photography projects include Cédrine Scheidig's 'La Troisième Île' (2022) [The Third Island] and Roxane Mbanga's photographic and artistic work.[10] Furthermore, documentary films have provided a counter-memory to the discourses of migration proffered by the French state, and films have focused both on the Antillean case – such as Antoine Léonard-Maestrati's *L'Avenir est ailleurs* and Jackie Bastide's

BUMIDOM: des Français venus d'outre-mer – and the Reunionese situation, such as Erika Etangsalé's *Lèv la tèt dann fenwar*. These cultural works engage with the BUMIDOM and its legacies through different media and for different audiences, but what they have in common is their desire to honour the memories of those who left the Caribbean to make a new life in mainland France.

***

The BUMIDOM remains in living memory for many Caribbean communities, both in Martinique and Guadeloupe and in mainland France. It has had a long-lasting impact on the demographic composition of the mainland, as many people who arrived through the BUMIDOM have made France their permanent home. Antillean communities have been formed in large cities in the Hexagon, with Antillean restaurants, food shops and music marking the Antillean presence. The BUMIDOM has also impacted the Caribbean islands. It took young, working-class people away from the islands in the 1960s and 70s, and while many have returned after their retirement to be closer to their families in their old age, others have stayed away. The BUMIDOM changed lives for better or for worse, and so it is unsurprising that it continues to play a fundamental role in the Caribbean imagination. *BUMIDOM (1963–1982) and its Afterlives* has sought to shed light on this little-known historical event and reveal how people on both sides of the Atlantic are trying to keep their individual, familial and collective memories of this organised migration alive.

Notes

1. The exhibition was first held at 60 AdaDa art gallery in Saint-Denis from 31 October to 22 November 2020. I worked with the curators to adapt and translate the exhibition for an anglophone audience. 'Leaving for the Metropole: An Odyssey of the Working Class' was held at the Kuumba Imani Millennium Centre in Liverpool from 12 to 23 June 2023.
2. The event, held on 14 December 2023, featured debates with academics Sylvain Pattieu and Janoé Vulbeau, journalist Véronique Larose and actress Firmine Richard. The short documentary *BUMIDOM: une migration réussie?* was also screened, and guests had the opportunity to participate in discussions about the BUMIDOM and its legacy (Ledain 2023).

3. The new permanent exhibition at the Musée national de l'histoire de l'immigration opened on 17 June 2023. The exhibition is structured chronologically around key dates in France's history of immigration. There is a small section on the BUMIDOM in the section about 1962. It features two migration dossiers taken from the Archives nationales and a small information panel about the 'Enfants de la Creuse', as well as original panels from the graphic novel and a clip from the documentary.
4. It was reported in newspaper articles and historical accounts from the period that the *Empire Windrush* brought 492 passengers from Jamaica, and that number has since become mythologised. However, as Matthew Mead explains, the passenger logs show that 1,027 people travelled on the ship in total, including 531 Jamaicans (2009, 144). As part of the seventy-fifth anniversary celebrations, the *Empire Windrush* passenger list was on display at the National Archives in London in June 2023, and these lists provide important details about who was on the ship and for what purpose.
5. See Hakim Adi, *African and Caribbean People in Britain: A History* (2022) for a detailed history of the Black presence in Britain.
6. The Caribbean community has celebrated Windrush Day since 1988 when Sam King OBE and Arthur Torrington organised an event at Lambeth Town Hall, London, to celebrate the 40th anniversary of the arrival of the *Empire Windrush*. King and Torrington formed The Windrush Foundation in 1995 (The Windrush Foundation 2020). Patrick Vernon is working with Maritime Archaeology Sea Trust to raise £2 million to recover the anchors of the *Empire Windrush* from the Mediterranean Sea and create a new national monument (Patrick Vernon 2022).
7. A documentary programme which follows the process of creating these portraits was broadcast on National Windrush Day.
8. The compensation scheme has been criticised for being too slow and bureaucratic. It has also been denounced by Human Rights Watch for being run by the Home Office, the very institution that caused so much hardship (Nagesh 2023).
9. For instance, the Illegal Migration Act 2023 seeks to stop people arriving in the country irregularly. Those who do so will have their asylum claim deemed 'inadmissible'. They could be detained and sent back to their own country or removed to a 'safe third country', such as Rwanda, following the passing of the Rwanda Bill in April 2024. The Conservative UK government also announced changes to student visas to reduce net migration – from 2024, most international students will not be able to bring family members with them.
10. Roxane Mbanga is a Guadeloupean-Cameroonian-French photographer, performer and artist based in Amsterdam. She is currently working on a project on the BUMIDOM (Mbanga 2023).

Bibliography

Primary Sources

Barny, Jean-Claude, dir. 2016. *Le Gang des Antillais*. Paris: Les Films d'ici. DVD.

Bulle, Estelle-Sarah. 2018. *Là où les chiens aboient par la queue*. Paris: Liana Levi; 2022. *Where Dogs Bark with Their Tails: A Novel*. Translated by Julia Grawemeyer. New York: Farrar, Straus and Giroux.

Condé, Maryse. 1997. *Desirada*. Paris: Robert Laffont; 2000. *Desirada: A Novel*. Translated by Richard Philcox. New York: Soho Press.

Curier, Charlise. 2019. *Mon aventure avec le BUMIDOM*. Gourbeyre, Guadeloupe: Éditions Nestor.

Danchet, Marie-Louise. 2018. *Emil'Patt à Paris*. Gourbeyre, Guadeloupe: Éditions Nestor, 2018.

Dangreville-Bellemare, Lucienne. 2014. *Paroles de ma vie: de Fort-de-France Martinique à Saint-Denis (Seine Saint-Denis)*. Paris: Edilivre.

Ega, Françoise. 1978. *Lettres à une noire*. Paris: Éditions L'Harmattan.

Faure, Christian, dir. 2018. *Le Rêve français*. Paris: Eloa Prod. DVD.

Godard, Alex. 2014. *Maman-Dlo*. Paris: Albin Michel Jeunesse.

Kanor, Fabienne. 2004. *D'eaux douces*. Paris: Éditions Gallimard.

Légitimus, Pascal, dir. 2001. *Antilles-sur-Seine*. Paris: C.P.Z Productions/ Marie Galante Productions/TFI Vidéo. DVD.

Manicom, Jacqueline. 1972. *Mon examen de blanc*. Paris: Éditions Presses de la Cité.

Oublié, Jessica, and Marie-Ange Rousseau. 2017. *Peyi an nou*. Paris: Éditions Steinkis.

Zabulon, Michèle. 2017. *Parcours de vie d'une puéricultrice antillaise*. Orthez, France: Publishroom.

Discography

Admette, Michel. 1970. *Folklore de la Réunion*. Disques Festival, OM 2356 M.

BUMIDOM. 2019. *Histoire d'un expatrié*. Vibes Music.

Cosaque, Éric. 1987. *Erick Cosaque – X7 Nouvelle Dimension*. Yola Production, GP 1413.
Delgres. 2018. *Mo Jodi*. PIAS, 57160D.
——. 2021. *4.00am*. PIAS, PIA 04483.
——. 2024. *Promis Le Ciel*. PIAS, DISCO2302CD.
Kalme La Fournaise. 2014. *Bataille mi bataille*.
——. 2020. *Cahier de vie*. Agence Lyrics.
Kassav'. 1987. *Vini Pou*. Epic, EPC 460619 1.
——. 1989. *Majestik Zouk*. CBS, CBS 465494 1.
Konket, Guy. 1968. *Vélo. Lékol-la*. Aux Ondes.
La Perfecta. 1978. *L'Inoubliable*. HDebs Productions, HFD 3004-2.
Lechat, Jacky. 1979. *Joyeux Noël*. Disques Royal, DR 770061.
Loyson, Robert. 2007. *Nostalgies caraïbes*. Disques Célini, 5524.2.
Saint-Eloi, Patrick. 1982. *Misik Ce Lan-mou*. 2M Production, 2M 009.
Soft. 2006. *Kadans a péyi-là*. Aztec Musique, CM 3282.
——. 2007. *Partout étranger*. Section Zouk Records, CM 2197.
Super Combo. 1975. *Super Combo Mait'a Mannioc*. Disque Debs, HDD 569.
Voltage '8'. 1978. *Cosaque 78*. Capriccio, 37.020.

Archival Sources

Pierrefitte-sur-Seine, Archives nationales de France:

BDPA. Statut du migrant réunionnais, 1952. 19940380/6, Box 1, Folder 4.
——. Rapport d'Activités de Migration, 1960–1961, 27 March 1961. 19940380/6, Box 1, Folder 2.
BUMIDOM. Booklet Simandres: centre de préformation, 1968a. 19940380/7, Box 1, Folder 1.
——. Rapport no. 5 Centre d'adaptation et de formation de Crouy-sur-Ourcq, 1968b. 19820104/3, Box 1, Folder 7.
——. Requêtes Martinique, 1974. 199403880/22, Box 1, Folder 1.
——. Intervention pour une amélioration qualitative de la migration en provenance des Antilles, 1 March 1975a. 19840442/7, Box 1, Folder 3.
——. Requêtes Martinique, 1975b. 199403880/22, Box 1, Folder 3.
——. Évolution et bilan de la politique de migration dans les départements et dans les territoires d'outre-mer, 28 November 1978. 19840442/7, Box 1, Folder 2.
——. Eléments d'information: activité du BUMIDOM, 1981. 19840442/7, Box 1, Folder 1.
——. Communiqué de presse sur les voyages vacances. 4 June 1982. 19940380/63, Box 1, Folder 1.
CASODOM. Correspondence, 5 December 1969. 19940380/35, Box 1, Folder 1.

——. Rapport, 1978. 19940380/6, Box 1, Folder 7.
Collective Petition, 4 November 1973. 19840442/7, Box 1, Folder 3.
Gérard, Maurice. Correspondence, 1 October 1979. 19940380/1, Box 1, Folder 1.
Union générale des travailleurs réunionnais en France. L'Emigration originaire des DOM, March 1974. 19840442/7, Box 1, Folder 3.
Valence, Georges. 'L'Emigration des Antillais et des Guyanais en France.' *Le Progrès*, 2 February 1974. 19840442/7, Box 1, Folder 3.
Vié, Émile. Correspondence to Director of CASODOM, 15 May 1974. 19940380/35, Box 1, Folder 1.

Archives départementales de la Guadeloupe

BUMIDOM. Lettres migrantes, 1968. 1027 W36, Box 1, Folder 10.

Archives territoriales de la Martinique

Beausoley, Line. Correspondence, 13 October 1976. 1149 W47, Box 1, Folder 4.

Secondary Sources

Achille, Étienne, Charles Forsdick and Lydie Moudileno. 'Introduction: Postcolonializing *lieux de mémoire*'. In *Postcolonial Realms of Memory: Sites and Symbols in Modern France*, edited by Étienne Achille, Charles Forsdick and Lydie Moudileno, 1–19. Liverpool: Liverpool University Press.
Adi, Hakim. 2022. *African and Caribbean People in Britain: A History*. London: Penguin.
Ahmed, Maaheen, and Benoît Crucifix. 2018. 'Introduction: Untaming Comics Memory.' In *Comics Memory: Archives and Styles*, edited by Maaheen Ahmed and Benoît Crucifix, 1–12. Cham, Switzerland: Palgrave Macmillan.
Ali-Benali, Zineb, and Françoise Simasotchi-Bronès. 2009. 'Le Rire créole: entretien avec Maryse Condé.' *Littérature* 154, no. 2: 13–23.
Allen, Ray. 2019. *Jump Up!: Caribbean Carnival Music in New York City*. Oxford: Oxford University Press.
Allen, Rose Mary. 2012. 'Music in Diasporic Context: The Case of Curaçao and Intra-Caribbean Migration.' *Black Music Research Journal* 32, no. 2: 51–65.
Altman, Janet Gurkin. 1982. *Epistolarity: Approaches to a Form*. Columbus, OH: Ohio State University Press.
Ampigny, Marie-Line. 1992. 'Le Père de Kassav' se raconte.' *France Antilles Magazine*, 11–19 December 1992: 60–1.

Amrith, Megha, and Nina Sahraoui. 2018. 'Introduction.' In *Gender, Work and Migration: Agency in Gendered Labour Settings*, edited by Megha Amrith and Nina Sahraoui, 1–10. London and New York: Routledge.
Anselin, Alain. 1979. *L'Émigration antillaise en France: du Bantoustan au ghetto*. Paris: Éditions Anthropos.
Arnaud, Sylvie, and Fabienne Kanor. 2020. 'Fabienne Kanor.' *Mouvement*, 13 March 2020. https://www.mouvement.net/fabienne-kanor [accessed 6 May 2024].
Ash, Gwynne Ellen. 2012. 'Talking about Terrible Things: The Craft of Allegory in Children's Literature.' *Journal of Children's Literature* 38, no. 2: 90–1.
Ashcroft, Richard T., and Mark Bevir. 2018. 'Multiculturalism in Contemporary Britain: Policy, Law and Theory.' *Critical Review of International, Social and Political Philosophy* 21, no. 1: 1–21.
Assmann, Aleida. 2006. 'Memory, Individual and Collective.' In *The Oxford Handbook of Contextual Political Analysis*, edited by Robert E. Goodin and Charles Tilly, 210–24. Oxford: Oxford University Press.
——. 2008. 'Transformations between History and Memory.' *Social Research* 75, no. 1: 49–72.
Atger, Stéphanie, and Ericka Bareigts. 2020. 'Rapport d'information fait au nom de la délégation aux outre-mer sur le grand âge dans les outre-mer.' *Assemblée nationale*, 6 February 2020. https://www.assemblee-nationale.fr/dyn/15/rapports/om/l15b2662_rapport-information [accessed 21 March 2021].
Attarian, Hourig. 2011. 'Narrating Displacement: The Pedagogy of Exile.' In *Memory and Pedagogy*, edited by Claudia Mitchell, Teresa Strong-Wilson, Kathleen Pithouse and Susann Allnutt, 145–60. London: Routledge.
Baetens, Jan, and Hugo Frey. 2014. *The Graphic Novel: An Introduction*. Cambridge: Cambridge University Press.
Bagoé-Dubosq, Clarisse. 2009. *Buisson joyeux*. Matoury, French Guiana: Ibis Rouge Éditions.
Baily, John, and Michael Collyer. 2006. 'Introduction: Music and Migration.' *Journal of Ethnic and Migration Studies* 32, no. 2: 167–82.
Banfield-Nwachi, Mabel. 2023. 'Royal Mail Issues Stamps to Mark 75th Anniversary of Windrush Arrival.' *The Guardian*, 15 June 2023. https://www.theguardian.com/business/2023/jun/15/royal-mail-issues-stamps-to-mark-75th-anniversary-of-windrush-arrival [accessed 16 June 2023].
Barabantseva, Elena, and Claire Sutherland. 2011. 'Diaspora and Citizenship: Introduction.' *Nationalism and Ethnic Politics* 17, no. 1: 1–13.
Barny, Jean-Claude, dir. 2005. *Nèg maron*. Paris: Kasso Productions. DVD.
——. 2007. *Tropiques amers*. Paris: Lizland Films. DVD.
——. 2015. *Rose et le soldat*. Paris: Lizland Films. DVD.
——. 2020. *Fanon*. Baie-Mahault, Guadeloupe: Canal+ Antilles. DVD.
Bastide, Jackie, dir. 2010. *BUMIDOM, des Français venus d'outre-mer*. Paris: Temps Noir Productions and France 2. DVD.

BBC Media Centre. 2023. 'BBC Arts Announces Windrush: Portraits of a Generation with His Majesty The King, on BBC Two and BBC iPlayer.' *BBC*, 6 June 2023. https://www.bbc.co.uk/mediacentre/2023/bbc-arts-windrush-portraits-of-a-generation-with-his-majesty-the-king [accessed 8 June 2023].

Beaud, Stéphane, and Gérard Noiriel. 2021. *Race et sciences sociales. Essai sur les usages publics d'une catégorie*. Marseille: Agone.

Berger, James. 2007. 'Which Prosthetic? Mass Media, Narrative, Empathy, and Progressive Politics.' *Rethinking History* 11, no. 4: 597–612.

Bernis, Thérèse, and Catherine Vigor. 1997. *Parise, Souvenirs encombrants de la Guadeloupe: récit*. Paris: Éditions Ramsay.

Béroard, Jocelyn. 2013. 'Kassav' a toujours du punch.' *Le Parisien*, 6 June 2013. https://www.leparisien.fr/culture-loisirs/kassav-a-toujours-du-punch-06-06-2013-2870951.php [accessed 22 May 2023].

——. 2022. *Loin de l'amer*. Paris: Le Cherche Midi.

Berrian, Brenda, 2000. *Awakening Spaces: French Caribbean Popular Songs, Music, and Culture*. Chicago: University of Chicago Press.

Bidet, Jennifer. 2023. 'Reformer et réformer les familles: la politique de regroupement familial du BUMIDOM'. Paper presented at The BUMIDOM in Interdisciplinary Perspectives Conference, University of Liverpool, 22 June 2023.

Bidnall, Amanda. 2017. *The West Indian Generation: Remaking British Culture in London, 1945–1965*. Liverpool: Liverpool University Press.

Blanco, Stéphane, and Samuel Figuière. 2018. *Nengue: l'histoire oubliée des esclaves des Guyanes*. Paris: Éditions Steinkis.

Boittin, Jennifer. 2010. *Colonial Metropolis: The Urban Grounds of Anti-Imperialism and Feminism in Interwar Paris*. Lincoln, NA, and London: University of Nebraska Press.

Bond, Lucy, Stef Craps and Pieter Vermeulen. 2016. 'Introduction: Memory on the Move.' In *Memory Unbound: Tracing the Dynamics of Memory Studies*, edited by Lucy Bond, Stef Craps and Pieter Vermeulen, 1–26. New York and Berlin: Berghahn Books.

Bongrand, Luc, dir. 2012. *Les Larmes de la Rivière Piment*. Paris: France Mexique cinéma. DVD.

Bonilla, Yarimar. 2015. *Non-Sovereign Futures: French Caribbean Politics in the Wake of Disenchantment*. Chicago: University of Chicago Press.

Bonnet, Véronique. 2017. 'La littérature de la Caraïbe pour la jeunesse: des histoires à part ou l'histoire à part entière?' *Amnis* 16: 1–10.

Boscher, Marie, and Estelle-Sarah Bulle. 2019. 'Estelle-Sarah Bulle, portrait d'une autrice entre deux périphéries.' *La 1ère*, 17 March 2019. https://la1ere.francetvinfo.fr/estelle-sarah-bulle-portrait-autrice-entre-deux-peripheries-690364.html [accessed 8 December 2021].

Boum Make, Jennifer. 2020. 'Éthique et esthétique de l'intermédialité: études des stratégies de rapprochement pour l'émergence des mémoires du BUMIDOM dans *Peyi an nou* de Jessica Oublié et Marie-Ange Rousseau.' *Nouvelles études francophones* 35, no. 1: 117–37.

Boura, Smaragdi. 2006. 'Imagining Homeland: Identity and Repertories of a Greek Labour-Immigrant Musician in Germany.' *Forum: Qualitative Social Research* 7, no. 3: 1–11.

Bourdier, Maxime. 2021. 'Mort de Jacob Desvarieux, leader de Kassav' et père du Zouk.' *Huffington Post*, 31 July 2021. https://www.huffingtonpost.fr/culture/article/mort-de-jacob-desvarieux-leader-de-kassav-et-pere-du-zouk_184340.html [accessed 22 May 2023].

Brissac, Nicole. 2007. 'Nature idyllique, nature sauvage dans les faits d'écriture.' In *Les Risques majeurs aux Antilles: approche culturelle et prévention sociale*, edited by Paulette Jno-Baptiste and Alain Yacou, 35–55. Paris: Karthala.

Britton, Celia. 2008. *The Sense of Community in French Caribbean Fiction*. Liverpool: Liverpool University Press.

Brondy, Baptiste. 2022. 'Interview Delgres.' Radio Lomax, 26 March 2022. https://www.youtube.com/watch?v=KGk-dDM5AfA [accessed 31 May 2023].

Bulle, Estelle-Sarah. 2019. '*Là où les chiens aboient par la queue*: le premier roman d'Estelle-Sarah Bulle.' *La Grande librairie*, 14 March 2019. https://www.youtube.com/watch?v=v6ytI8E7aaw [accessed 8 December 2021].

Burgoyne, Robert. 2003. 'Memory, History and Digital Imagery in Contemporary Film.' In *Memory and Popular Film*, edited by Paul Grainge, 220–36. Manchester: Manchester University Press.

Burton, Richard D. E. 1995. 'Introduction: The French West Indies à l'heure de l'Europe: An Overview.' In *French and West Indian: Martinique, Guadeloupe and French Guiana Today*, edited by Richard D. E. Burton and Fred Reno, 1–19. Charlottesville, VA: University Press of Virginia.

Byron, Margaret, and Stephanie Condon. 2008. *Migration in Comparative Perspective: Caribbean Communities in Britain and France*. Abingdon and New York: Routledge.

Camal, Jérôme. 2019. *Creolized Aurality: Guadeloupean Gwoka and Postcolonial Politics*. Chicago and London: University of Chicago Press.

Carlsten, Jennie M., and Fearghal McGarry. 2015. 'Introduction.' In *Film, History and Memory*, edited by Jennie M. Carlsten and Fearghal McGarry, 1–17. Basingstoke: Palgrave Macmillan.

Castles, Stephen. 2000. 'International Migration at the Beginning of the Twenty-First Century: Global Trends and Issues.' *International Social Science Journal* 52, no. 165: 151–62.

Célestine, Audrey. 2011. 'French Caribbean Organizations and the "Black Question" in France.' *African and Black Diaspora: An International Journal* 4, no. 2: 131–44.

Célestine, Audrey, and Sarah Fila-Bakabadio. 2017. 'Introduction.' *African and Black Diaspora: An International Journal* 10, no. 1: 1–11.

Césaire, Aimé. 1975. 'Départements d'outre-mer.' Assemblée nationale, 13 November 1975: https://archives.assemblee-nationale.fr/5/cri/1975-1976-ordinaire1/058.pdf [accessed 1 October 2023].

Cham, Mbye. 1995. 'Shape and Shaping of Caribbean Cinema.' In *Cinemas of the Black Diaspora: Diversity, Dependence, and Oppositionality*, edited by Michael T. Martin, 241–65. Detroit, MI: Wayne State University Press.

Chamoiseau, Patrick. 1990. *Antan d'enfance*. Paris: Éditions Gallimard; 1999. *Childhood*. Translated by Carol Volk. London: Granta Books.

——. 2008. *Chronique des sept misères*. Paris: Éditions Gallimard; 1999. *Chronicle of the Seven Sorrows*. Translated by Linda Coverdale. Lincoln, NA: University of Nebraska Press.

Chapman, Adam. 2005. 'Breath and Bamboo: Diasporic Lao Identity and the Lao Mouth-Organ.' *Journal of Intercultural Studies* 26, no. 1–2: 5–20.

Chazeau, Jean-Marie. 2018. '*Le Rêve français*: le BUMIDOM en prime time.' *La 1ère*, 13 March 2018. https://la1ere.francetvinfo.fr/reve-francais-bumidom-prime-time-568297.html [accessed 18 May 2022].

Childers, Kristen Stromberg. 2016. *Seeking Imperialism's Embrace: National Identity, Decolonization, and Assimilation in the French Caribbean*. Oxford: Oxford University Press.

Chivallon, Christine. 2011. *The Black Diaspora of the Americas: Experiences and Theories out of the Caribbean*. Translated by Antoinette Titus-Tidjani Alou. Kingston, Jamaica: Ian Randle Publishers.

Chute, Hillary. 2016. *Disaster Drawn: Visual Witness, Comics, and Documentary Form*. Cambridge, MA: The Belknap Press of Harvard University Press.

Chute, Hillary, and Marianne DeKoven. 2006. 'Introduction: Graphic Narrative.' *MFS Modern Fiction Studies* 52, no. 4: 767–82.

Ciriez, Frédéric, and Romain Lamy. 2020. *Frantz Fanon*. Paris: La Découverte.

Clinton, Jane. 2024. 'Yvette Cooper promises Labour would "turn the page" on Windrush scandal.' *The Guardian*, 22 June 2024. https://www.theguardian.com/uk-news/article/2024/jun/22/yvette-cooper-promises-labour-would-turn-the-page-on-windrush-scandal [accessed 6 September 2024].

Cohen, Muriel. 2017. 'Post-colonial Algerian Immigration: Putting Down Roots in the Face of Exclusion.' Translated by Emma Mandley. *Le Mouvement social* 258, no. 1: 29–48.

Cohen, Paul. 2022. '"Zouk is the Only Medicine We Need": Kassav' and the Cultural Politics of Music in the French Caribbean.' *French Historical Studies* 45, no. 2: 319–53.

Condé, Maryse. 1997. *Pays mêlé: nouvelles*. Paris: Éditions Laffont.

——. 1999. *Le Cœur à rire et à pleurer: contes vrais de mon enfance*. Paris: Robert Laffont; 2001. *Tales from the Heart: True Stories from My Childhood*. Translated by Richard Philcox. New York: Soho Press.

——. 2001. *Rêves amers*. Paris: Bayard jeunesse.

——. 2012. *La Vie sans fards*. Paris: Éditions JC Lattès.

——. 2018. '*Le Rêve français* par Maryse Condé.' *Téléobs*, 21 March 2018. https://teleobs.nouvelobs.com/actualites/20180321.OBS3988/le-reve-francais-par-maryse-conde.html [accessed 7 June 2022].

Condon, Stephanie. 2020. 'Entre stratégies individuelles et stratégies de l'État: le genre de l'émigration antillaise dans les années 1960.' *Clio: Femmes, Genre, Histoire* 51: 119–41.

Confiant, Raphaël. 1993. *Ravines du devant-jour*. Paris: Éditions Gallimard.

——. 1994. *Mamzelle libellule*. Paris: Le Serpent à plumes; 2000. *Mamzelle Dragonfly*. Translated by Linda Coverdale. Lincoln, NA: University of Nebraska Press.

——. 2000. *Le Cahier de romances*. Paris: Éditions Gallimard.

Connerton, Paul. 1989. *How Societies Remember*. Cambridge: Cambridge University Press.

——. 2008. 'Seven Types of Forgetting.' *Memory Studies* 1, no. 1: 59–71.

Constant, Fred. 1987. 'La Politique française de l'immigration antillaise de 1946 à 1987.' *Revue européenne des migrations internationales* 3, no. 3: 9–30.

Constant, Fred, and Justin Daniel, eds. 1997. *1946–1996: Cinquante ans de départementalisation d'outre-mer*. Paris: Éditions L'Harmattan.

Coombes, Sam. 2019. 'Glissant and Diaspora Studies.' *Journal of Postcolonial Writing* 55, no. 6: 769–81.

Couti, Jacqueline. 2021. *Sex, Sea, and Self: Sexuality and Nationalism in French Caribbean Discourses, 1924–1948*. Liverpool: Liverpool University Press.

Crenshaw, Kimberlé. 1989. 'Demarginalizing the Intersection of Race and Sex: A Black Feminist Critique of Antidiscrimination Doctrine, Feminist Theory and Antiracist Politics.' *University of Chicago Legal Forum* 1: 139–67.

Crownshaw, Richard. 2016. 'Cultural Memory Studies in the Epoch of the Anthropocene.' In *Memory Unbound: Tracing the Dynamics of Memory Studies*, edited by Lucy Bond, Stef Craps and Pieter Vermeulen, 242–57. New York and Berlin: Berghahn Books.

Cutter, Martha J., and Cathy J. Schlund-Vials. 2018. 'Redrawing the Historical Past: History, Memory and Multiethnic Graphic Novels.' In Martha J. Cutter and Cathy J. Schlund-Vials (eds), *Redrawing the Historical Past: History, Memory and Multiethnic Graphic Novels*, 1–17. Athens, GA: University of Georgia Press.

Da Silva, Diane. 2008. 'Soft, un groupe de valeur(s).' *RFI Musique*, 4 February 2008. https://musique.rfi.fr/musique-antillaise/20080204-soft-groupe-valeurs [accessed 30 May 2023].

Dabitch, Christophe. 2009. 'Reportage et bande dessinée.' *Hermès, La Revue* 54, no. 2: 91–8.

Danaë, Pascal. 2020. '#Ma parole: Pascal Danaë.' *La 1ère*, 10 May 2020. https://la1ere.francetvinfo.fr/pascal-danae-j-ai-pris-en-pleine-tete-l-absurdite-et-l-atrocite-du-systeme-esclavagiste-maparole-1280688.html [accessed 23 May 2023].

——. 2021. 'Interview canapé: Delgres.' *109 Montluçon*, 7 October 2021. https://www.youtube.com/watch?v=I5TI4Bx0Qgw [accessed 31 May 2023].

Danchet, Marie-Louise. 2012. *Mawy*. Gourbeyre, Guadeloupe: Éditions Nestor, 2012.

——. 2013. *Ida, la Créole*. Gourbeyre, Guadeloupe: Éditions Nestor.

——. 2014. *Aux portes de la sagesse*. Gourbeyre, Guadeloupe: Éditions Nestor.

——. 2022. *Tikòk, le maître coq, Tikòk, majo savann*. Baie-Mahault, Guadeloupe: Nèg Mawon.

Daoudi, Bouziane. 2007. 'Soft, plus dur qu'il n'y paraît.' *La Libération*, 24 November 2007. https://www.liberation.fr/culture/2007/11/24/soft-plus-dur-qu-il-n-y-parait_106999/ [accessed 23 May 2023].

Décimus, Pierre-Édouard. 2023. *Kassav' – Love and Ka-dance*. Pointe-à-Pitre, Guadeloupe: Éditions Jasor.

Demasy, Rose-Hélène. 2001. 'La Métamorphose thériomorphe dans le conte antillais.' *Revue d'histoire littéraire de la France* 101, no. 2: 293–301.

DeNora, Tia. 2000. *Music in Everyday Life*. Cambridge: Cambridge University Press.

La Dépêche. 2018. '*Le Rêve français*: un pan méconnu de l'histoire des DOM se dévoile sur France 2.' *La Dépêche*, 20 March 2018. https://www.ladepeche.fr/article/2018/03/20/2763380-reve-francais-pan-meconnu-histoire-dom-devoile-france-2-2.html [accessed 7 June 2022].

Deshayes, Fred. 2020. 'I Am Karibbean: Fred Deshayes.' *I Am Karibbean*, 9 December 2022. https://www.youtube.com/watch?v=78eqLrfxYL4 [accessed 23 May 2023].

Diallo, Rokhaya, and Grace Ly. 2021. *Kiffe ta race: explorer les questions raciales sans tabou*. Paris: Éditions First.

Diarrassouba, Adiaratou, and Jean-Claude Barny. 2017. 'Entretien – Jean-Claude Barny ("Le Gang des Antillais"): "Chiwetel Ejiofor pour jouer Fanon, pourquoi pas?"' *L'Afro*, 6 July 2017. https://lafrolesite.wordpress.com/2017/07/06/entretien-jean-claude-barny-le-gang-des-antillais-chiwetel-ejiofor-pour-jouer-fanon-pourquoi-pas/ [accessed 1 June 2022].

Dicale, Betrand. 2019. 'Eric Cosaque, enfant et maître du gwo ka.' *Chinal Ka 1973–1995*. Heavenly Sweetness, HS200VL.

Do, Françoise, dir. 2017. *Aliénation(s)*. Fort-de-France: Tropiques Atrium Scène Nationale.

Do Canto, Violante. 1961. *Le Dépotoir: le journal d'une favelada*. Paris: Éditions Stock; 1962. *Child of the Dark: The Diary of Carolina Maria de Jesus*. Translated by David St Clair. New York: Mentor/Penguin.

Dobie, Madeleine. 2004. 'Invisible Exodus: The Cultural Effacement of Antillean Migration.' *Diaspora: A Journal of Transnational Studies* 13, no. 2/3: 149–83.

Donegani, Jean-Marie. 2004. 'Music and Politics: The Language of Music – Between Objective Expression and Subjective Reality.' *Raisons politiques* 14, no. 2: 5–19.

Donnell, Alison. 2019. 'Looking Back, Looking Forward: Revisiting the Windrush Myth.' In *The Cambridge History of Black and Asian British Writing*, edited by Susheila Nasta and Mark U. Stein, 195–211. Cambridge: Cambridge University Press.

Donnelly, Laura. 2017. 'Producing Space and Locality through Cultural Displays: A Creole Case Study.' *Space and Culture* 20, no. 1: 81–93.

Druelle, Aline. 2024. 'Retour en Outre-Mer: le "passeport pour le retour" se met en place.' *RCI*, 25 January 2024. https://rci.fm/deuxiles/infos/Societe/Retour-en-Outre-Mer-le-passeport-pour-le-retour-se-met-en-place [accessed 17 April 2024].

Edwards, Natalie, and Chris Hogarth. 2008. 'Introduction: Gender and Displacement: "Home" in Contemporary Francophone Women's Autobiography.' In *Gender and Displacement: 'Home' in Contemporary Francophone Women's Autobiography*, edited by Natalie Edwards and Chris Hogarth, 1–14. Newcastle: Cambridge Scholars Publishing, 2008).

Ega, Françoise. 1966. *Le Temps des madras: récit de la Martinique*. Paris: Éditions maritimes et d'outre-mer.

——. 2000. *L'Alizé ne soufflait plus (Antan Robè)*. Paris: Éditions L'Harmattan.

——. 2021. *Cartas a uma negra*. Translated by Vinícius Carneiro and Mathilde Moaty. São Paolo: Todavia.

Eguienta, Nora, and Sylvain Pattieu. 2023. 'The Immigrants of BUMIDOM and Their Resistance to Employment Assignments.' Translated by S. C. Kaplan. *Journal of Women's History* 35, no. 3: 103–24.

Elbadawi, Soeuf. 2001. '*Antilles-sur-Seine* de Pascal Légitimus.' *Africine.org*. 1 January 2001. http://www.africine.org/index.php/critique/antilles-sur-seine/1703 [accessed 31 May 2022].

Erll, Astrid. 2011a. *Memory in Culture*. Translated by Sara B. Young. Basingstoke: Palgrave Macmillan.

——. 2011b. 'Travelling Memory.' *Parallax* 17, no. 4: 4–18.

Erll, Astrid, and Ann Rigney. 2009. 'Introduction: Cultural Memory and its Dynamics.' In *Mediation, Remediation, and the Dynamics of Cultural Memory*, edited by Astrid Erll and Ann Rigney, 1–11. Berlin: De Gruyter, 2009.

Etangsalé, Erika, dir. 2021. *Lèv la tèt dann fenwar*. Paris: We Film, Les Films du Haut d'un Arbre, Le Fresnoy Studio National des Arts Contemporains. DVD.

Étienne, Guy. 2023. 'Le Successeur de Jacob Desvarieux s'appelle Karim Verger. . . un guitariste "d'une efficacité époustouflante."' *La 1ère*, 17 May 2023. https://la1ere.francetvinfo.fr/martinique/le-successeur-de-jacob-desvarieux-s-appelle-karim-verger-un-guitariste-d-une-efficacite-epoustouflante-1396534.html [accessed 6 June 2023].

Faist, Thomas. 2010. 'Diaspora and Transnationalism: What Kind of Dance Partners?' In *Diaspora and Transnationalism: Concepts, Theories and Methods*, edited by Rainer Bauböck and Thomas Faist, 9–14. Amsterdam: Amsterdam University Press.

Faner, Philippe. 1988. 'Le Souffle de Maméga.' *Echos de la ville*, 17 November 1988: 3–4.

Fanon, Frantz. 1952. *Peau noire, masques blancs*. Paris: Éditions du Seuil; 1967. *Black Skin, White Masks*. Translated by Charles L. Markmann. New York: Grove Press.

Feld, Steven. 1996. 'Waterfalls of Song: An Acoustemology of Place Resounding in Bosavi, Papua New Guinea.' In *Senses of Place*, edited by Steven Feld and Keith Basso, 91–136. Guinea: School of American Research Press.

Ferly, Jacques, dir. 1971. *Chronique d'un retour*. Paris: Institut de la formation cinématographique. DVD.

Fernandez, Rafaella Andréa. 2013. 'La Vie autobiographiée comme imperfection ou (hyper)fection de soi.' *Passages de Paris* 8: 139–52.

Fine, Ellen. 1988. 'The Absent Memory: The Act of Writing in Post-Holocaust French Literature.' In *Writing and the Holocaust*, edited by Berel Lang, 41–57. New York: Holmes and Meier.

Flannigan-Saint-Aubin, Arthur. 1992. 'Reading and Writing the Body of the Négresse in Françoise Ega's *Lettres à une Noire*.' *Callaloo* 15, no. 1: 49–65.

Foix, Alain. 2005. *Ta Mémoire, petit monde*. Paris: Éditions Gallimard.

Forsdick, Charles. 2019. '*Bande Dessinée* and the Penal Imaginary: Graphic Constructions of the Carceral Archipelago.' *European Comic Art* 12, no. 2: 1–16.

France Antilles Martinique. 2013. '27 artistes et deux ministres fêtent Konket à Paris.' 30 September 2013. https://www.martinique.franceantilles.fr/divers/27-artistes-et-deux-ministres-fetent-konket-a-paris-318903.php [accessed 18 May 2023].

Fressoz, Françoise, and Cédric Pietralunga. 2020. 'Après le déconfinement, L'Elysée craint un vent de révolte: "Il ne faut pas perdre la jeunesse."' *Le Monde*, 11 June 2020. https://www.lemonde.fr/politique/article/2020/06/10/il-ne-faut-pas-perdre-la-jeunesse-l-elysee-craint-un-vent-de-revolte_6042430_823448.html [accessed 24 January 2023].

Fridman, Oril. 2022. *Memory Activism and Digital Practices After Conflict: Unwanted Memories*. Amsterdam: Amsterdam University Press.

Fulton, Dawn. 2003. '"Romans de Nous": The First Person Plural and Collective Identity in Martinique.' *The French Review* 76, no. 6: 1104–14.

——. 2005. 'A Clear-Sighted Witness: Trauma and Memory in Maryse Condé's *Desirada.*' *Studies in 20th and 21st Century Literature* 29, no. 1: 47–62.

Gardner, Jared. 2012. *Projections: Comics and the History of Twenty-First-Century Storytelling*. Stanford, CA: Stanford University Press.

Genette, Gérard. 1991. 'Introduction to the Paratext.' Translated by Marie Maclean, *New Literary History* 22, no. 2: 261–72.

——. 1997. *Paratexts: Thresholds of Interpretation*. Translated by Jane E. Lewin. Cambridge: Cambridge University Press.

Gentleman, Amelia, and Rajeev Syal. 2023. 'Windrush Inquiry Head Disappointed as Braverman drops "Crucial" Measures.' *The Guardian*, 27 January 2023. https://www.theguardian.com/uk-news/2023/jan/26/windrush-inquiry-head-wendy-williams-disappointed-suella-braverman-drops-crucial-measures [accessed 13 June 2023].

Genvrin, Emmanuel. 2016. *Rock Sakay*. Paris: Éditions Gallimard.

Germain, Félix. 2010. 'Jezebels and Victims: Antillean Women in Postwar France, 1946–1974.' *French Historical Studies* 33, no. 3: 475–95.

——. 2016. *Decolonizing the Republic: African and Caribbean Migrants in Postwar Paris, 1946–1974*. East Lansing, MI: Michigan State University Press.

Gilbert Faraux, Victor. 2020. *Et ce fut l'opportunité d'un exil*. Paris: Éditions du Panthéon.

Gilroy, Paul. 1993. *The Black Atlantic: Modernity and Double Consciousness*. London: Verso.

Giraud, Alexandre, and Jessica Oublié. 2018. 'Jessica Oublié remporte le prix du livre politique France Culture.' *RCI Guadeloupe*, 23 April 2018. https://www.rci.fm/guadeloupe/infos/Culture/Jessica-Oublie-remporte-le-prix-du-livre-politique-France-Culture [accessed 15 December 2022].

Glissant, Édouard. 1956. *Le Soleil de la conscience*. Paris: Gallimard; 2020. *Sun of Consciousness*. Translated by Nathanaël. New York: Nightboat Books.

——. 1981. *Le Discours antillais*. Paris: Éditions Seuil; 1989. *Caribbean Discourse*. Translated by J. Michael Dash. Charlottesville, VA: University Press of Virginia.

——. 1990. *La Poétique de la relation*. Paris: Éditions Gallimard; 1997. *Poetics of Relation*. Translated by Betsy Wing. Ann Arbor, MI: University of Michigan Press.

Glissant, Gabriel, dir. 1972. *Le Pion*. Paris: Institut des hautes études cinématographiques. DVD.

Grams, Diane M. 2013. 'Freedom and Cultural Consciousness: Black Working-Class Parades in Post-Katrina New Orleans.' *Journal of Urban Affairs* 35, no. 5: 501–29.

Grayson, Hannah, and Nina Parish. 2024. 'Introduction: Responses to a Call for Action: New Directions and Directives in the French-Speaking World.' *Modern and Contemporary France* 32, no. 1: 1–7.

Gros-Dubois, Constant, dir. 1979. *Ô Madiana*. Paris: Madiana Productions. DVD.

Grosfoguel, Ramón, Margarita Cervantes-Rodríguez and Eric Mielants. 2009. 'Introduction: Caribbean Migrations to Western Europe and the United States.' In *Caribbean Migration to Western Europe and the United States: Essays on Incorporation, Identity, and Citizenship*, edited by Margarita Cervantes-Rodríguez, Ramón Grosfoguel and Eric Mielants, 1–17. Philadelphia, PA: Temple University Press.

Groupe d'action de la communauté antillo-Guyanaise. 1971. *Enquête sur un organisme au-dessus de tout soupçon*. Paris: Éditions Norman Bethune.

Guilbault, Jocelyne, with Gage Averill, Édouard Benoit and Gregory Rabess. 1993. *Zouk: World Music in the West Indies*. Chicago and London: The University of Chicago Press.

Gutman, Yifat. 2017. *Memory Activism: Reimagining the Past for the Future in Israel-Palestine*. Nashville, TS: Vanderbilt University Press.

Hackl, Andreas. 2022. 'Good Immigrants, Permitted Outsiders: Conditional Inclusion and Citizenship in Comparison.' *Ethnic and Racial Studies* 45, no. 6: 989–1010.

Haddad, Marine. 2018. 'L'Effet d'une politique d'État sur les migrations DOM-métropole. Les enseignements des recensements de 1962 à 1999.' *Population* 73, no. 2: 191–224.

Haecker, Dorothy. 1985. 'A Theory of Historical Truth.' *Philosophical Topics* 13, no. 2: 267–75.

Haigh, Sam. 2000. *Mapping a Tradition: Francophone Women's Writing from Guadeloupe*. London: MHRA.

——. 2007. '"Une histoire sérieuse de nègres"? Humour and the Refiguring of the Republic in Pascal Légitimus's *Antilles-sur-Seine*.' *Francophone Postcolonial Studies* 5, no. 1: 45–71.

Halbwachs, Maurice. 1925. *Les Cadres sociaux de la mémoire*. Paris: Félix Alcan; 1992. *On Collective Memory*, translated by Lewis A. Coser. Chicago and London: The University of Chicago Press.

Hardwick, Louise. 2013. *Childhood, Autobiography and the Francophone Caribbean*. Liverpool: Liverpool University Press.

——. 2014. 'Creolizing the Caribbean "Coolie": A Biopolitical Reading of Indian Indentured Labourers and the Ethnoclass Hierarchy.' *International Journal of Francophone Studies* 17, no. 3–4: 397–419.

——. 2015. 'Youth Dispossession, Volcanoes and Diaspora: Recent Developments in Francophone Caribbean Film.' *Caribbean Quarterly* 61, no. 2–3: 42–54.

——. 2018. *Joseph Zobel: Négritude and the Novel*. Liverpool: Liverpool University Press.

Herbeck, Jason, and Fabienne Kanor. 2013. 'Entretien avec Fabienne Kanor.' *The French Review* 86, no. 5: 964–76.

Hirsch, Marianne. 1997. *Family Frames: Photography, Narrative, and Postmemory*. Cambridge, MA, and London: Harvard University Press.

——. 2012. *The Generation of Postmemory: Writing and Visual Culture after the Holocaust*. New York: Columbia University Press.

Hitchcott, Nicki. 2021. 'Seeing the Genocide against the Tutsi through Someone Else's Eyes: Prosthetic Memory and *Hotel Rwanda*.' *Memory Studies* 14, no. 5: 935–48.

Hobbs, Mia Martin. 2021. '(Un)Naming: Ethics, Agency, and Anonymity in Oral Histories with Veteran-Narrators.' *The Oral History Review* 48, no. 1: 59–82.

Hondo, Med, dir. 1979. *West Indies ou les nègres marrons de la liberté*. Paris: Les Films Soleil Ô, DVD.

hooks, bell. 1986. 'Sisterhood: Political Solidarity between Women.' *Feminist Review* 23: 125–38.

Hoskins, Andrew, ed. 2018. *Digital Memory Studies: Media Pasts in Transition*. New York and Abingdon: Routledge.

Humbert Wozniak, Lucile. 2019. 'Une autre culture antillaise existe ici: entretien avec Alain Agat, scénariste, réalisateur de documentaires et écrivain.' *Hommes & migrations* 1325: 191–5.

Hungerford, Amy. 2003. *The Holocaust of Texts: Genocide, Literature, and Personification*. Chicago and London: The University of Chicago Press.

Hutton, Margaret-Anne. 2022. 'Putting Metaphor Centre-Stage: A Case Study of Alison Landsberg's "Prosthetic Memory."' *Memory Studies* 15, no. 1: 230–42.

Jahn, Jennifer. 2008. 'Enslaved Minds: The Complexity of Living in Ex-île for Martinican Women.' *Postcolonial Slavery: An Overview of Colonialism's Legacy*, edited by Charlotte Baker and Jennifer Jahn, 145–65. Newcastle: Cambridge Scholars Publishing.

Jocksan, Alfred. 2023. 'Le BUMIDOM fête ses 60 ans en débats à Saint-Denis.' *France Antilles Guadeloupe*, 20 March 2023. https://www.guadeloupe.franceantilles.fr/actualite/culture/le-bumidom-fete-ses-60-ans-et-en-debat-a-saint-denis-93-928680.php [accessed 7 June 2023].

Joseph-Gabriel, Annette K. 2020. *Reimagining Liberation: How Black Women Transformed Citizenship in the French Empire*. Urbana, IL: University of Illinois Press.

Kaes, Anton. 1990. 'History and Film: Public Memory in the Age of Electronic Dissemination.' *History and Memory* 2, no. 1: 111–29.

Kalouaz, Ahmed. 2016. *Enfants de l'exil: de l'île de la Réunion à la Creuse*. Paris: Oskar.

Kanapa, Jérôme, dir. 1978. *En l'autre bord*. Paris: Dimage, Société française de production. DVD.

Kanor, Fabienne. 2014. *Faire l'aventure*. Paris: Éditions Lattès.

——. 2024. *La Grande Chambre*. Le Lamentin, Martinique: Caraïbéditions.

Kanor, Fabienne, and Emmanuelle Bidou, dir. 2008. *Jambé dlo: une histoire antillaise*. Paris: Mat Films. DVD.

Keaton, Trica. 2023. *#You Know You're Black in France When . . . The Fact of Everyday Antiblackness*. Cambridge, MA: The MIT Press.

Knauer, Lisa Maya. 2008. 'The Politics of Afrocuban Cultural Expression in New York City.' *Journal of Ethnic and Migration Studies* 34, no. 8: 1257–81.

Knoepflmacher, U. C., and Mitzi Myers. 1997. '"Cross-writing" and the Reconceptualization of Children's Literary Studies.' *Children's Literature* 25: vii–xvii.

Krims, Adam. 2002. 'Foreword: Francophone Hip-Hop as a Colonial Urban Geography.' In *Black, Blanc, Beur: Rap Music and Hip-Hop Culture in the Francophone World*, edited by Alain-Philippe Durand, vii–x. Lanham, MD: Scarecrow Press.

Lachasse, Jérôme, and Pascal Légitimus. 2016. 'Pascal Légitimus: "J'ai envie de choses beaucoup plus corrosives."' *BFM TV*, 14 September 2016. https://www.bfmtv.com/people/pascal-legitimus-j-ai-envie-de-choses-beaucoup-plus-corrosives_AN-201609140061.html [accessed 1 June 2022].

Lacrosil, Michèle. 1960. *Sapotille et le serin d'argile*. Paris: Éditions Gallimard.

Ladal, Olivier, and Cyril Bordy, dir. 2013. *Guy Konket: La Résonance d'un maître Ka*. Baie-Mahault, Guadeloupe: Extérieur Jour and Guadeloupe. DVD.

LADOM. 2022. 'LADOM: le service public de la mobilité, rapport d'activité 2022.' https://ladom.fr/wp-content/uploads/2023/07/RAPPORT-D-ACTIVITE-LADOM-2022-PLANCHES_BD.pdf [accessed 3 October 2023].

Laguerre, Michel. 1998. *Diasporic Citizenship: Haitian Americans in Transnational America*. New York: St Martin's Press.

——. 2017. *The Postdiaspora Condition: Crossborder Social Protection, Transnational Schooling, and Extraterritorial Human Security*. Cham, Switzerland: Palgrave Macmillan.

Landsberg, Alison. 2004. *Prosthetic Memory: The Transformation of American Remembrance in the Age of Mass Culture*. New York: Columbia University Press.

Laouchez, Roland. 1975. *Confessions d'une prostituée antillaise à Paris*. Paris: Le Naïf.

Larrier, Renée. 2006. *Autofiction and Advocacy in the Francophone Caribbean*. Gainesville, FL: University Press of Florida.

Lavaine, Bertrand. 2018. 'Aux Antilles, Soft veut redonner le cap.' *RFI Musique*, 2 January 2018. https://musique.rfi.fr/musique-antillaise/20180102-soft-ti-gwadloupeyen [accessed 23 May 2023].

Ledain, Nicolas. 2023. 'Les 60 ans du BUMIDOM commémorés à l'Assemblée nationale.' *RCI*, 15 December 2023. https://rci.fm/deuxiles/infos/Societe/Les-60-ans-du-Bumidom-commemores-lAssemblee-nationale [accessed 25 April 2024].

Ledoux, Sébastien. 2013. '"Devoir de mémoire": The Post-colonial Path of a Postnational Memory in France.' *National Identities* 15, no. 3: 239–56.

Lejeune, Philippe. 1975. *Le Pacte autobiographique*. Paris: Éditions Seuil.

Levitt, Peggy. 2001. *The Transnational Villagers*. Berkeley, CA; Los Angeles, CA, and London: University of California Press.

Levy, Claire. 2002. 'Who is the "Other" in the Balkans? Local Ethnic Music as a Different Source of Identities in Bulgaria.' *Critical Studies: Music Popular Culture Identities* 19: 199–212.

Levy, Daniel, and Natan Sznaider. 2005. *The Holocaust and Memory in the Global Age*. Translated by Assenka Oksiloff. Philadelphia, PA: Temple University Press.

Lewis, Hannah. 2010. 'Community Moments: Integration and Transnationalism at "Refugee" Parties and Events.' *Journal of Refugee Studies* 23, no. 4: 571–88.

Lewis, Jonathan, and Antonia Wimbush. 2021. 'Introduction: Postcolonial Realms of Memory in the Francophone World.' *Francosphères* 10, no. 1: 1–7.

Lidskog, Rolf. 2016. 'The Role of Music in Ethnic Identity Formation in Diaspora: A Research Review.' *International Social Science Journal* 66: 23–38.

Lie, John. 1995. 'From International Migration to Transnational Diaspora.' *Contemporary Sociology* 24, no. 4: 303–6.

Lim, Jie-Hyun, and Eve Rosenhaft. 2021. 'Introduction: Mnemonic Solidarity – Global Interventions.' In *Mnemonic Solidarity, Entangled Memories in the Global South*, edited by Jie-Hyun Lim and Eve Rosenhaft, 1–14. New York: Palgrave Macmillan.

Liu, Qiang and David Turner. 2018. 'Identity and National Identity.' *Educational Philosophy and Theory* 50, no. 12: 1080–8.

Maestrati, Antoine-Léonard, dir. 2007. *L'Avenir est ailleurs*. La Garenne-Colombes: Cinéma Public Films. DVD.

Malignac, Georges. 1967. 'La Situation démographique des quatre départements d'outre-mer: Martinique, Guadeloupe, Réunion, Guyane.' *Economie et Statistique* 22, no. 11: 103–45.

Manicom, Jacqueline. 1974. *La Graine: journal d'une sage-femme*. Paris: Presses de la Cité.

Manuel, Peter. 1995. 'Introduction: The Caribbean Crucible.' In *Caribbean Currents: Caribbean Music from Rumba to Reggae*, edited by Peter Manuel, Kenneth Bilby, and Michael Largey, 1–6. London: Latin America Bureau.

Marchal, Quentin. 2021. 'Paulette Nardal, militante de la cause noire, naissait il y a 150 ans.' *RTL Culture*, 12 October 2021. https://www.rtl.fr/culture/culture-generale/paulette-nardal-militante-de-la-cause-noire-naissait-il-y-a-125-ans-7900084698 [accessed 26 October 2021].

Marie, Claude-Valentin. 2021. 'Mutations sociodémographiques et migrations: Les Nouvelles Configurations des sociétés ultramarines.' Migrations dans les départements et régions d'outre-mer Colloquium, Musée national de l'histoire de l'immigration, 17 September 2021.

Marivat, Gladys. 2016. 'Loïc Léry, le braqueur du gang des Antillais devenu aide-soignant.' *Le Monde*, 6 December 2016. <https://www.lemonde.fr/afrique/article/2016/12/06/loic-lery-le-braqueur-du-gang-des-antillais-devenu-aide-soignant_5044389_3212.html> [accessed 18 May 2022].

Marmande, Francis. 2012. 'Décès de Guy Konkèt, musicien guadeloupéen, l'âme du gwoka.' *Le Monde*, 29 May 2012. https://www.lemonde.fr/disparitions/article/2012/05/29/deces-de-guy-konket-musicien-guadeloupeen-l-ame-du-gwoka_1708934_3382.html [accessed 18 May 2023].

Martiniello, Marco, and Jean-Michel Lafleur. 2008. 'Ethnic Minorities' Cultural and Artistic Practices as Forms of Political Expression: A Review of the Literature and a Theoretical Discussion on Music.' *Journal of Ethnic and Migration Studies* 34, no. 8: 1191–215.

Maximin, Daniel. 2004. *Tu, c'est l'enfance*. Paris: Éditions Gallimard.

Mazouz, Sarah. 2020. *Race*. Paris: Anamosa.

Mbembe, Achille. 'The Power of the Archive and its Limits.' In *Refiguring the Archive*, edited by Carolyn Hamilton, Verne Harris, Jane Taylor, Michèle Pickover, Graeme Reid and Razia Saleh. 19–26. Dordrecht, Boston, MA, and London: Kluwer Academic Publishers.

McCusker, Maeve. 2004. 'Troubler l'ordre de l'oubli: Memory and Forgetting in French Caribbean Autobiography of the 1990s.' *Forum for Modern Language Studies* 40, no. 4: 438–50.

——. 2010. 'Mastering the Word: Appropriations of the Conte Créole in Antillean Theory.' In *The Conte: Oral and Written Dynamics*, edited by Janice Carruthers and Maeve McCusker, 153–71. Bern, Switzerland: Peter Lang.

Mead, Matthew. 2009. '*Empire Windrush*: The Cultural Memory of an Imaginary Arrival.' *Journal of Postcolonial Writing* 45, no. 2: 137–49.

Meehan, Kevin. 2006. 'Romance and Revolution: Reading Women's Narratives of Caribbean Decolonization.' *Tulsa Studies in Women's Literature* 25, no. 2: 291–306.

Mehta, Brinda. 2009. *Notions of Identity, Diaspora and Gender in Caribbean Women's Writing*. New York: Palgrave Macmillan.

Michel, Sabine. 2021. 'Inédit: Le Film documentaire *Erick Cosaque, "Lespwi Sanvann"*, ce vendredi soir, sur Guadeloupe La 1ère.' *La 1ère*, 1 October 2021. https://la1ere.francetvinfo.fr/guadeloupe/inedit-le-film-documentaire-erick-cosaque-lespwi-sanvann-ce-vendredi-soir-sur-guadeloupe-la-1ere-1118119.html [accessed 18 May 2023].

Mickenberg, Julia L., and Lynne Vallone. 2011. 'Introduction.' In *The Oxford Handbook of Children's Literature*, edited by Julia L. Mickenberg and Lynne Vallone, 3–22. Oxford: Oxford University Press.

Milia-Marie-Luce, Monique. 1997. 'Histoire d'une politique d'émigration organisée pour les départements d'outre-mer.' *Pouvoirs dans la Caraïbe*: 141–56.

——. 2007. 'La Grande migration des Antillais en France ou les années BUMIDOM.' In *Dynamiques migratoires de la Caraïbe*, edited by André Calmont and Cédric Audebert, 93–103. Paris: Éditions Karthala.

Mitchell, Claudia, Teresa Strong-Wilson, Kathleen Pithouse and Susann Allnutt. 2011. 'Introducing Memory and Pedagogy.' In *Memory and Pedagogy*, edited by Claudia Mitchell, Teresa Strong-Wilson, Kathleen Pithouse and Susann Allnutt, 1–13. London: Routledge.

Mohanty, Chandra Talpade. 1997. 'Women Workers and Capitalist Scripts: Ideologies of Domination, Common Interests, and the Politics of Solidarity.' In *Feminist Genealogies, Colonial Legacies, Democratic Futures*, edited by M. Jacqui Alexander and Chandra Talpade Mohanty, 3–29. New York: Routledge.

Le Monde and AFP. 2018. 'L'Assemblée supprime de la Constitution le mot "race" et interdit la "distinction de sexe."' *Le Monde*, 12 July 2018. https://www.lemonde.fr/politique/article/2018/07/12/l-assemblee-supprime-dans-la-constitution-le-mot-race-et-interdit-la-distinction-de-sexe_5330615_823448.html [accessed 25 January 2023].

Moudileno, Lydie. 2003. 'Le Rire de la grand-mère: insolence et sérénité dans *Désirada* [*sic*] de Maryse Condé.' *The French Review* 76, no. 6: 1151–60.

Moutoussamy, Laure. 2004. *Une étoile en dérive*. French Guyana: Ibis Rouge Éditions.

Munro, Martin. 2010. *Different Drummers: Rhythm and Race in the Americas*. Berkeley, CA: University of California Press.

Murdoch, H Adlai. 2002. 'Writing India in the West Indies: Indo-Caribbean Inscriptions in Trinidad and Guadeloupe.' *The CLR James Journal* 9, no. 1: 116–45.

——. 2008. 'Introduction: Departmentalization's Continuing Conundrum: Locating the DOM-ROM between "Home" and "Away."' *International Journal of Francophone Studies* 11, no. 1–2: 15–32.

——. 2012. *Creolizing the Metropole: Migrant Caribbean Identities in Literature and Film*. Bloomington, IN: Indiana University Press.

——. 2020. 'BUMIDOM.' In *Postcolonial Realms of Memory: Sites and Symbols in Modern France*, edited by Étienne Achille, Charles Forsdick and Lydie Moudileno, 244–54. Liverpool: Liverpool University Press.

——. 2021. 'Zouk and the Articulation of French Caribbean Culture: History, Identity, Creolization, and Relation in Kassav's "Medley Gwoka" and "Kavalié o Dam" (Live).' *Research in African Literatures* 52, no. 3: 187–222.

Murphy, David. 2015. 'The Emergence of a Black France, 1985–2015: History, Race and Identity.' *Nottingham French Studies* 54, no. 3: 238–52.

Mustakeem, Sowande M. 2016. *Slavery at Sea: Terror, Sex, and Sickness in the Middle Passage*. Champaign, IL: University of Illinois Press.

Nabizadeh, Golnar. 2019. *Representation and Memory in Graphic Novels*. London: Routledge.

Nagesh, Ashitha. 2023. 'Windrush Victims Being Failed by Compensation Scheme – Report.' *BBC News*, 17 April 2023. https://www.bbc.co.uk/news/uk-65264683 [accessed 13 June 2023].

Ndiaye, Pap. 2008. *La Condition noire*. Paris: Calmann-Lévy.

Niang, Mame-Fatou. 2020. 'Des particularités françaises de la négrophobie.' In *Racismes de France*, edited by Olivier Le Cour Grandmaison and Omar Slaouti, 151–69. Paris: La Découverte.

Nichols, Bill. 2017. *Introduction to Documentary*, 3rd edn. Bloomington, IN: Indiana University Press.

Niven, Bill. 2017. '*Generation War* and Post-Didactic Memory: The Nazi Past in Contemporary Germany.' In *Remembering the Second World War*, edited by Patrick Finney, 30–45. London: Routledge.

Nora, Pierre, ed. 1984–1992. *Les Lieux de mémoire*. Paris: Éditions Gallimard.

——. 1989. 'Between Memory and History: *Les Lieux de Mémoire*.' Translated by Marc Roudebush. *Representations* 26: 7–24.

Noxolo, Patricia. 2020. 'I Am Becoming My Mother: (Post)Diaspora, Local Entanglements and Entangled Locals.' *African and Black Diaspora: An International Journal* 13, no. 2: 134–46.

O'Donoghue, Samuel. 2018. 'Postmemory as Trauma? Some Theoretical Problems and their Consequences for Contemporary Literary Criticism.' *Passés Futurs* 3. https://www.politika.io/en/notice/postmemory-as-trauma-some-theoretical-problems-and-their-consequences-for-contemporary [accessed 20 January 2023].

Oostindie, Gert, and Inge Klinkers. 2003. *Decolonising the Caribbean: Dutch Policies in a Comparative Perspective*. Amsterdam: Amsterdam University Press.

Oublié, Jessica. 2021. 'Born in the Feminine Caribbean in the Post-BUMIDOM Migration: Legacies and Counter-legacies.' In *Memorializing and Decolonizing Practices in the Francophone Caribbean and Other Spaces*, edited by Stéphanie Melyon-Reinette, 117–38. Newcastle: Cambridge Scholars Publishing.

——. 2022. 'Jessica Oublié: "Le BUMIDOM laisse exsangue la Martinique et la Guadeloupe de leur jeunesse": #MaParole.' *La 1ère*, 18 January 2022. https://la1ere.francetvinfo.fr/jessica-oublie-le-bumidom-laisse-exsangue-la-martinique-et-la-guadeloupe-de-leur-jeunesse-maparole-1203772.html [accessed 20 December 2022].

Oublié, Jessica, Nicola Gobbi, Kathrine Avraam and Vinciane Lebrun. 2020. *Tropiques Toxiques: le scandale du chlordécone*. Paris: Les Escales.

Pairaudeau, Natasha. 2016. *Mobile Citizens: French Indians in Indochina, 1858–1954*. Copenhagen: NIAS Press.

Palmiste, Claire. 2012. 'Génocide par substitution: usages et cadre théorique.' In *Les outre-mers francais: actualités et études, vol. 1*, edited by Frédéric Angleviel, 153–78. Paris: Éditions L'Harmattan.

Pareles, Jon. 2021. 'Jacob Desvarieux, Guitarist Who Forged Zouk Style, Dies at 65.' *New York Times*, 8 August 2021. https://www.nytimes.com/2021/08/08/arts/music/jacob-desvarieux-dead.html [accessed 24 May 2023].

Paris, Myriam. 2020. '"Contre tous les pouvoirs": Le Militantisme intersectionnel de féministes réunionnaises émigrées en France (années 1960–1970).' *Revue d'histoire* 146, no. 2: 95–108.

Patel, Ian Sanjay. 2021. *We're Here Because You were There: Immigration and the End of Empire*. London: Verso.

Pattieu, Sylvain. 2016. 'Un traitement spécifique des migrations d'outre-mer: le BUMIDOM (1963–1982) et ses ambiguïtés.' *Politix* 116, no. 4: 81–113.

——. 2017. 'The BUMIDOM in Paris and its Suburbs: Contradictions in a State Migration Policy, 1960s–1970s.' *African and Black Diaspora: An International Journal* 10, no. 1: 12–24.

——. 2018. 'Migrants citoyens, migrants vacanciers: les voyages-vacances du BUMIDOM, 1965–1980.' *Genèses* 111, no. 2: 70–91.

Peach, Ceri. 1991. 'The Caribbean in Europe: Contrasting Patterns of Migration and Settlement in Britain, France and the Netherlands.' Research Paper in Ethnic Relations No. 15, Centre for Research in Ethnic Relations University of Warwick: 1–34.

Perina, Mickaella. 2006. 'Ongoing Diaspora: The Case of the French Caribbean.' *Revue européenne des migrations internationales* 22, no.1: 1–22.

Perry, Kennetta Hammond. 2015. *London is the Place for Me: Black Britons, Citizenship and the Politics of Race*. Oxford: Oxford University Press.

Pias. 2021. 'Proudly Presenting Delgres.' *Pias.com*, 11 February 2021. https://www.pias.com/proudly-presenting-delgres/ [accessed 31 May 2023].

Piantoni, Frédéric. 2009. 'La question migratoire en Guyane française: histoire, société et territoires.' *Hommes et migrations* 1278: 198–216.

Pidéri-Joncart, Marlène. 2024. *Mary-Yvonne et les autres*. Cayenne, French Guiana: Mahury Éditions.

Pineau, Gisèle. 1992. *Un papillon dans la cité*. Paris: Éditions Sépia.

——. 1996. *L'Exil selon Julia*. Paris: Éditions Stock; 2003. *Exile according to Julia*, translated by Betty Wilson. Charlottesville, VA, and London: University of Virginia Press.

——. 1999. *Caraïbes sur Seine*. Paris: Dapper jeunesse.

——. 2008. *Morne Câpresse*. Paris: Éditions Gallimard.

Plantinga, Carl. 2021. 'Collective Memory and the Rhetorical Power of the Historical Fiction Film.' *Global Storytelling: Journal of Digital and Moving Images* 1, no. 1: 113–32.

Pluskota, Marion. 2020. 'Freedom of Movement, Access to the Urban Centres, and Abolition of Slavery in the French Caribbean.' *International Review of Social History* 65: 93–115.

Ponchelet, David. 'Soirée spéciale BUMIDOM ce soir sur le réseau Outre-mer, en direct sur la1ere.fr.' *La 1ère*, 19 December 2013. https://la1ere.francetvinfo.fr/2013/12/19/soiree-speciale-bumidom-ce-soir-sur-le-reseau-outre-mer-en-direct-sur-la1erefr-95411.html [accessed 4 October 2023].

Post, Jennifer. 2017. 'Introduction: Redesigning and Redefining Ethnomusicology.' In *Ethnomusicology: A Contemporary Reader, Volume 2*, edited by Jennifer Post, 1–14. New York: Routledge.

Pourpoint, Maroussia, dir. 2022. *Hommage(s) à la Martinique*. Paris: Hall de la Chanson.

Pujar, Kelly. 2018. '*Peyi an nou* remporte le prix étudiant de la BD politique France Culture.' *La 1ère*, 9 April 2018. https://la1ere.francetvinfo.fr/peyi-an-nou-remporte-prix-etudiant-bd-politique-france-culture-577201.html [accessed 19 December 2022].

Pulimeno, Manuela, Prisco Piscitelli and Salvatore Colazzo. 2020. 'Children's Literature to Promote Students' Global Development and Wellbeing.' *Health Promotion Perspectives* 10, no. 1: 13–23.

Quijano, Aníbal. 2000. 'Coloniality of Power, Eurocentrism, and Latin America.' *Nepantla* 1, no. 3: 533–80.

Raczymow, Henri. 1994. 'Memory Shot Through with Holes.' Translated by Alan Astro, *Yale French Studies* 85: 98–105.

Radford, Daniel. 1993. *Le Maître-pièce*. Paris: Éditions du Rocher.

Rea, Annabel. 1997. 'Les Femmes au travail dans *Lettres à une noire*.' In *Elles écrivent des Antilles (Haïti, Guadeloupe, Martinique)*, edited by Suzanne Rinne and Joëlle Vitiello, 297–306. Paris: Éditions L'Harmattan.

Reading, Anna. 2011. 'Memory and Digital Media: Six Dynamics of the Globital Memory Field.' In *On Media Memory: Collective Memory in a New Media Age*, edited by Motti Neiger, Oren Meyers, and Eyal Zandberg, 241–52. Basingstoke: Palgrave Macmillan.

Red Pepper. 2023. 'Justice for Nahel.' *Red Pepper*, 18 July 2023. https://www.redpepper.org.uk/justice-for-nahel-france-police-killing-open-letter/ [accessed 8 September 2023].

Rey, Nicolas. 2015. *An Dot Soley: regards noirs sur la ville lumière*. Paris: Éditions Syllepse.

Rigney, Ann. 2010. 'The Dynamics of Remembrance: Texts between Monumentality and Morphing.' *A Companion to Cultural Memory Studies*, edited by Astrid Erll and Ansgar Nünning, 345–53. Berlin: De Gruyter.

Rosello, Mireille. 1996. *Infiltrating Culture: Power and Identity in Contemporary Women's Writing*. Manchester and New York: Manchester University Press.

Ross, Kristin. 1995. *Fast Cars, Clean Bodies: Decolonization and the Reordering of French Culture*. Cambridge, MA, and London: The MIT Press.

Rothberg, Michael. 2009. *Multidirectional Memory: Remembering the Holocaust in the Age of Decolonization*. Stanford, CA: Stanford University Press.

Rothberg, Michael, Debarati Sanyal and Max Silverman. 2010. 'Editors' Note: *Nœuds de mémoire*: Multidirectional Memory in Postwar French and Francophone Culture.' *Yale French Studies* 118, no. 19: 1–2.

Saada, Emmanuelle. 2007. *Les Enfants de la colonie: les métis de l'Empire français entre sujétion et citoyenneté*. Paris: Éditions La Découverte.

Said, Edward W. 1993. *Culture and Imperialism*. London: Vintage Books.

Saint-Just, Sophie. 2016. 'Écologies du déracinement féminin antillais: conflits, émigration et folie dans *Fichues racines*.' In *Racines et déracinements au grand écran: trajectoires migratoires dans le cinéma français du XXIème siècle*, edited by Marianne Bessy and Carole Salmont, 170–91. Leiden and Boston, MA: Brill.

Samyde, Jean-Claude. 2023. 'Le Retour au pays: un choix éclairé et soutenu par des associations des Antilles-Guyane et de la Réunion.' *La 1ère*, 17 July 2013. https://la1ere.francetvinfo.fr/le-retour-au-pays-un-choix-eclaire-et-soutenu-par-des-associations-des-antilles-guyane-et-de-la-reunion-1414394.html [accessed 5 September 2023].

Sankara, Edgard. 2011. *Postcolonial Francophone Autobiographies: From Africa to the Antilles*. Charlottesville, VA: University of Virginia Press.

Schwerdtner, Karin. 2005. 'Wandering, Women and Writing: Maryse Condé's *Desirada*.' *Dalhousie French Studies* 73: 129–37.

Semley, Lorelle. 2017. *To be Free and French: Citizenship in France's Atlantic Empire*. Cambridge: Cambridge University Press.

Service politique. 2022. 'L'Historien Pap Ndiaye, nouveau ministre de l'éducation nationale et de la jeunesse, ciblé par l'extrême droite.' *Le Monde*, 20 May 2022. https://www.lemonde.fr/politique/article/2022/05/20/l-historien-pap-ndiaye-nomme-ministre-de-l-education-nationale-et-de-la-jeunesse_6127014_823448.html [accessed 25 January 2023].

Sharpley-Whiting, Tracy Denean. 2015. *Bricktop's Paris: African American Women between the Two World Wars*. Albany, NY: The State University of New York Press.

——. 2022. *Negritude Women*. Minneapolis, MN, and London: University of Minnesota Press.

Shelemay, Kay Kaufman. 2006. 'Music, Memory and History: In Memory of Stuart Feder.' *Ethnomusicology Forum* 15, no. 1: 17–37.

Siar, Claudy. 2016. 'Entretien avec Jean-Claude Barny, réalisateur du film *Le Gang des Antillais*.' *RFI*, 30 November 2016. https://www.rfi.fr/fr/emission/20161201-entretien-jean-claude-barny-realisateur-film-le-gang-antillais-2 [accessed 7 June 2022].

Sibeud, Emmanuelle, Sylvain Pattieu and Tyler Stovall. 2022. 'Introduction: A Historical Mosaic.' In *The Black Populations of France: Histories from*

Metropole to Colony, edited by Emmanuelle Sibeud, Sylvain Pattieu and Tyler Stovall, 1–10. Lincoln, NA: University of Nebraska Press.

Silverman, Max. 2013. *Palimpsestic Memory: The Holocaust and Colonialism in French and Francophone Fiction and Film*. New York and Oxford: Berghahn Books.

Simon, Roger I., Sharon Rosenberg and Claudia Eppert. 2000. 'Introduction: Between Hope and Despair: Pedagogy and the Remembrance of Historical Trauma.' In *Between Hope and Despair: The Pedagogical Encounter of Historical Remembrance*, edited by Roger I. Simon, Sharon Rosenberg and Claudia Eppert, 1–8. Lanham, MD: Lexington Books.

Slaouti, Omar, and Olivier Le Cour Grandmaison. 2020. 'Introduction: La France, raciste?' In *Racismes de France*, edited by Olivier Le Cour Grandmaison and Omar Slaouti, 9–21. Paris: La Découverte.

Small, Christopher. 1998. *Musicking: The Meanings of Performing and Listening*. Middletown, CT: Wesleyan University Press.

Smith, Anthony D. 2010. *Nationalism: Theory, Ideology, History*, 2nd edn. Cambridge: Polity Press.

Sotès, Vianney, and Barbara Olivier-Zandronis. 2020. *La Martinique, l'île des aînés*. Remire-Montjoly, French Guiana: Bérénice Médias Corp.

Soumahoro, Maboula. 2020. *Le Triangle et l'Hexagone: réflexions sur une identité noire*. Paris: La Découverte; 2021. *Black is the Journey, Africana the Name*. Translated by Kaiama L. Glover. Cambridge: Polity Press.

Spencer, Aisha Takiyah. 2020. '"Let Every Child Run Wild": Cultural Identity and the Role of the Child in Caribbean Children's and Young Adult Fiction.' In *Caribbean Literature in Transition: 1970–2020*, edited by Ronald Cummings and Alison Donnell, 164–80. Cambridge: Cambridge University Press.

Stewart, Ian M. 2022. 'Interview with Delgres band leader Pascal Danaë: A Historical Nod.' *VPM*, 1 April 2022. https://www.vpm.org/listen/2022-04-01/interview-with-delgres-band-leader-pascal-danae-a-historical-nod [accessed 23 May 2023].

Stovall, Tyler. 2009. 'No Green Pastures: The African Americanization of France.' In *Black Europe and the African Diaspora*, edited by Darlene Clark Hine, Trica Danielle Keaton and Stephen Small, 180–98. Champaign, IL: University of Illinois Press.

——. 2015. *Transnational France: The Modern History of a Universal Nation*. Boulder, CO: Westview Press.

Suaudeau, Julien. 2020. 'La nostalgie amnésique de "la France d'avant" est un séparatisme de la majorité.' *Slate.fr*, 11 December 2020. http://www.slate.fr/story/198032/nostalgie-amnesique-cetait-mieux-avant-trente-glorieuses-colonialisme-histoire-france [accessed 28 October 2021].

Suaudeau, Julien, and Mame-Fatou Niang. 2022. *Universalisme*. Paris: Anamosa.

Taombé, Olivette, dir. 2017. *De la Sakay à la Carapa*. Paris: Laterit Productions. DVD.

Taylor, Diana. 2003. *The Archive and the Repertoire: Performing Cultural Memory in the Americas*. Durham, NC: Duke University Press.

Tehem. 2020. *Piments Zoizos: les enfants oubliés de la Réunion*. Paris: Éditions Steinkis.

Trouillot, Michel-Rolph. 1995. *Silencing the Past: Power and the Production of History*. Boston, MA: Beacon Press.

Turim, Maureen. 1989. *Flashbacks in Film: Memory and History*. London: Routledge.

Turino, Thomas. 2008. *Music as Social Life: The Politics of Participation*. Chicago and London: The University of Chicago Press.

Valeurs actuelles. 2020. '"Génocide par substitution": une vidéo sur le déconfinement d'une école en Guadeloupe suscite des commentaires anti-blancs.' *Valeurs actuelles*, 14 May 2020. https://www.valeursactuelles.com/societe/genocide-par-substitution-une-video-sur-le-deconfinement-dune-ecole-en-guadeloupe-suscite-des-commentaires-anti-blancs/ [accessed 3 November 2021].

van Alphen, Ernst. 2006. 'Second-Generation Testimony, Transmission of Trauma, and Postmemory.' *Poetics Today* 27, no. 2: 473–88.

Vergès, Françoise. 2017. *Le Ventre des femmes: capitalisme, racialisation, féminisme*. Paris: Albin Michel; 2020. *The Wombs of Women: Race, Capital, Feminism*. Translated by Kaiama L. Glover. Durham, NC: Duke University Press.

Vernon, Patrick. 2022. 'Monument for Windrush Generation.' *Patrickvernon.org.uk*, 20 June. https://patrickvernon.org.uk/campaigns/monument-for-windrush-generation/ [accessed 16 June 2023].

Vertovec, Steven. 2005. 'The Political Importance of Diasporas.' Working Paper Number 13, Centre on Migration, Policy and Society, University of Oxford: 1–11.

Volle, Hortense. 2021. '*4am*: l'heure du combattant Delgrès.' *Pan African Music*, 27 April 2021. https://pan-african-music.com/4-am-delgres/ [accessed 30 May 2023].

Wilson, Betty. 1987. 'Sexual, Racial, and National Politics: Jacqueline Manicom's *Mon examen de blanc*.' *Journal of West Indian Literature* 1, no. 2: 50–7.

Wimbush, Antonia. 2018. 'Depicting French Caribbean Migration through *Bande Dessinée*.' *International Journal of Francophone Studies* 21, no. 1/2: 9–29.

——. 2021. *Autofiction: A Female Francophone Aesthetic of Exile*. Liverpool: Liverpool University Press.

——. 2022. 'The Windrush and the BUMIDOM: The Memorialization of Caribbean Migration.' *Memory Studies* 16, no. 5: 1–15.

——. 2023. 'An Oral History of the BUMIDOM.' *Nottingham French Studies* 62, no. 3: 282–96.

——. 2024. 'Reading the BUMIDOM along the Archival Grain.' *Bulletin of Francophone Postcolonial Studies* 14, no. 1: 2–14.

Wood, Nancy. 1999. *Vectors of Memory: Legacies of Trauma in Postwar Europe*. Oxford: Berg.
Wood, Sarah. 2015. 'Tensions of Development and Negotiations of Identity at the Periphery of France: Guyane Française since 1946.' PhD thesis, University of Manchester.
Zancarini-Fournel, Michelle. 2019. 'Contraception and Abortion in the French Antilles (Guadeloupe and Martinique, 1964–1975).' Translated by Regan Kramer. *Clio. Women, Gender, History* 50, no. 2: 87–108.
Zobel, Joseph. 1950. *La Rue Cases-Nègres*. Éditions Jean Froissart; 1980. *Black Shack Alley*. Translated by Keith Q. Warner. Boulder, CO: Lynne Rienner Publishers.
——. 1953. *La Fête à Paris*. Paris: La Table ronde.
——. 1979. *Quand la neige aura fondu*. Paris: Éditions caribéennes.

Online Sources

Alex Godard personal website: https://www.alexgodard.com/ [accessed 21 December 2022].
Cédrick-Isham Calvados personal website: https://cedrickisham.com/moun-an-ba-la-projet-en-cours/ [accessed 16 June 2023].
Charlise Curier. 2019b. 'Charlise Curier présente *Mon aventure avec le Bumidom*.' *Max Darlis MY TV Côte Caraïbe*, 6 June 2019, https://www.youtube.com/watch?v=NZeaLCrE7hw [accessed 11 October 2023].
——. 2022. Radio Horizon AP, 27 October 2022, https://www.facebook.com/100063589421867/videos/632569615242825 [accessed 12 January 2023].
Comité Mam'Ega vivre ensemble: https://vivreensemble.org/ [accessed 8 October 2023].
Delgres website: https://www.delgresmusic.com/lyrics2 [accessed 31 May 2023].
'Génération Bumidom chanté par les artistes réunionnais', 2013: https://www.dailymotion.com/video/x18o0d6 [accessed 28 April 2023].
Gov.uk, '2023 Windrush Day Grant Scheme: Projects to be Funded': https://www.gov.uk/guidance/2023-windrush-day-grant-scheme-projects-to-be-funded [accessed 8 June 2023].
I-Profs Portal: https://www.i-profs.fr/litt-c3-Maman_Dlo.php [accessed 22 December 2022].
Kalme La Fournaise social media: https://www.instagram.com/kalme974/?hl=en; https://soundcloud.com/kalme974 [accessed 24 May 2023].
LADOM website: https://ladom.fr/ [accessed 27 April 2024].
Michèle Zabulon Facebook page: https://www.facebook.com/zabulonmichele/ [accessed 23 June 2021].
Peyi an nou website: https://peyiannou.wordpress.com/ [accessed 15 September 2023].

Roxane Mbanga personal website: https://nataal.com/roxane-mbanga-home [accessed 1 September 2023].

Soft song lyrics: https://greatsong.net/TRADUCTION-SOFT,DOUDOU-O-ON-KAT-POSTAL,103841608.html [accessed 30 May 2023].

The Windrush Foundation: https://windrushfoundation.com/about-us/ [accessed 16 June 2023].

Index

EU Authorised Representative:
Easy Access System Europe Mustamäe tee 50, 10621 Tallinn, Estonia
gpsr.requests@easproject.com

Printed and bound by CPI Group (UK) Ltd, Croydon, CR0 4YY
29/09/2026
02224981-0014